REDESIGNING SOCIAL INQUIRY

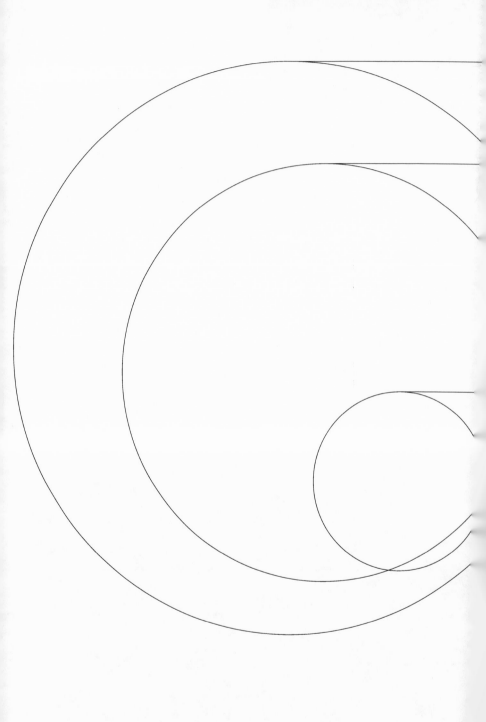

CHARLES C. RAGIN

Redesigning Social Inquiry
Fuzzy Sets and Beyond

University of Chicago Press: Chicago and London

CHARLES C. RAGIN is professor of sociology and political science at the University of Arizona, Tucson, positions he has held since 2001. Prior to that, Ragin was professor of sociology at Northwestern University (1981–2001) and Indiana University (1975–1981). He has also taught at the University of Oslo. Ragin has written several books, including *Fuzzy-Set Social Science* (University of Chicago Press, 2000), *Constructing Social Research: The Unity and Diversity of Method* (Pine Forge, 1994), and *The Comparative Method: Moving beyond Qualitative and Quantitative Strategies* (University of California Press, 1987), and he has edited or coedited several more. Ragin has also published more than one hundred articles.

The University of Chicago Press, Chicago 60637
The University of Chicago Press, Ltd., London
© 2008 by The University of Chicago
All rights reserved. Published 2008
Printed in the United States of America

16 15 14 13 12 11 10   2 3 4 5

ISBN-13: 978-0-226-70273-5 (cloth)
ISBN-13: 978-0-226-70275-9 (paper)
ISBN-10: 0-226-70273-1 (cloth)
ISBN-10:0-226-70275-8 (paper)

Ragin, Charles C.
  Redesigning social inquiry : fuzzy sets and beyond /
Charles C. Ragin.
    p. cm.
  Includes bibliographical references and index.
  ISBN-13: 978-0-226-70273-5 (cloth : alk. paper)
  ISBN-13: 978-0-226-70275-9 (pbk. : alk. paper)
  ISBN-10: 0-226-70273-1 (cloth : alk. paper)
  ISBN-10: 0-226-70275-8 (pbk. : alk. paper) 1. Social
sciences—Research—Methodology. 2. Fuzz sets. I. Title.
  H62.R235 2008
  300.72—dc22

                                    2008009112

∞ The paper used in this publication meets the minimum
requirements of the American National Standard for Information
Sciences—Permanence of Paper for Printed Library
Materials, ANSI Z39.48–1992.

CONTENTS

ACKNOWLEDGMENTS

It is impossible to list all the people who have contributed over the past several years to the ideas that I present in this book. I am sure I will miss many, including some who have been very influential. Perhaps my greatest debt is to unidentified questioners at talks and workshops where I have presented this material. I hope that my response, presented in the pages that follow, is finally adequate.

I owe a deep debt to my colleagues, local and long distance, who have commented on various versions of the ideas presented in this book. I thank Edwin Amenta, Howard Becker, Henry Brady, Ron Breiger, David Byrne, David Collier, Barry Cooper, Gary Goertz, Lane Kenworthy, Bruce Kogut, Jim Mahoney, Michael Minkenberg, Lars Mjøset, Benoit Rihoux, Carsten Schneider, Svend-Erik Skaaning, Steve Vaisey, Claudius Wagemann, and the readers for the University of Chicago Press. Special thanks also go to Sean Davey, who implemented my ideas in easy-to-use software and swatted logic bugs that almost got away, and to Sarah Strand, who helped with the bibliography and the index. I also thank Doug Mitchell and his colleagues at the University of Chicago Press for their steadfast support and encouragement.

A variety of institutions and organizations also have supported this work. Direct and indirect support came from the National Science Foundation, the University of Oslo, and various units of the University of Arizona, including the Udall Center for Studies in Public Policy, the Social and Behavioral Sciences Research Institute, and the departments of Sociology and Political Science. This project was initiated while I was a fellow at the Center for Advanced Study in the Behavioral Sciences in Stanford, California.

I also thank my wife, Mary Driscoll, and dedicate this book to her. Not only did she make room for this book in our life together but she also helped me struggle with the ideas, from the day it was launched to the day it was complete.

INTRODUCTION

First, a word about this book's title, *Redesigning Social Inquiry:* while I sometimes have ambitions of truly redesigning social inquiry, it is a huge task that will require the work of many thoughtful scholars over several decades. In this book, my goal is to provide some possible leads for this important undertaking. Of course, there are those who would say that social inquiry does not need to be redesigned; it simply needs to be properly executed. The usual argument is that there is a well-developed and well-known template for conducting social research and that the problem is that too few researchers adhere to it. According to this view, the proper template is provided by large-N quantitative research, with its well-defined and seemingly limitless populations and its focus on calculating the net effects of "independent" variables in properly specified linear models. It is this template for conducting research that is at issue in this book. But the problem is not that it is a bad template. It is a wonderful, well-articulated template. The problem is that it is too often promoted as the best template or even the *only* template (e.g., by King, Keohane, and Verba 1994), when in fact there are powerful and productive alternatives. This book promotes a new alternative, one based on the analysis of set relations.

While critical of the conventional quantitative template, *Redesigning Social Inquiry* is not a critique of Gary King, Robert Keohane, and Sidney Verba's *Designing Social Inquiry* (1994). Henry Brady and David Collier's *Rethinking Social Inquiry* (2004) offers a thorough analysis and critique, from the perspective of both statistical theory and qualitative research. Instead, my book charts a middle path between quantitative and qualitative social research. This middle path is not a compromise between qualitative and quantitative methods, nor is it an attempt to reshape one in the image of the other. Rather, my goal in this book is to advance an approach that transcends some of the limitations of conventional quantitative and qualitative research by extending and elaborating set-theoretic principles of social research (Ragin 1987, 2000).

The unifying theme of this book is that the analysis of set relations is critically important to social research. Even though qualitative researchers rarely speak in these terms, qualitative analysis is fundamentally about set relations. Consider this simple example: if all (or almost all) of the anorectic teenage girls I interview have highly critical mothers (that is, the anorectic girls constitute a *consistent subset* of the girls with highly critical mothers), then I will no doubt consider this connection when it comes to explaining the causes and contexts of anorexia. This attention to *consistent* connections (e.g., causally relevant commonalities that are more or less uniformly present in a given set of cases) is characteristic of qualitative inquiry. It is the cornerstone of the technique commonly known as analytic induction (Lindesmith 1947). However, its set-theoretic nature is not widely recognized, even though this aspect has far-reaching implications for any attempt to bridge qualitative and quantitative approaches. Compounding the problem of the unrecognized importance of the analysis of set relations is the simple fact that many social scientists do not see any difference between studying set relations and studying statistical associations. If they have given it any thought at all, they think of set relations as the cross-tabulation of nominal-scale variables and thus see the study of set relations as a rudimentary form of quantitative analysis. One aim of this book is to put to rest these and other fundamental misunderstandings about the use of sets in social research.

It is also important to recognize that because almost all social science theory is verbal in nature, it, too, is fundamentally about sets and set relations.[1] If I assert that a close connection exists between democracy

---

1. The fact that qualitative analysis and social science theory are both set theoretic in nature partially explains the natural affinity between qualitative research and

and development and that, consequently, the developed countries are all democracies, in essence I am arguing that the set of developed countries constitutes a subset of the set of democracies. The fact that there are less-developed countries that are also democracies (thus providing evidence that other paths can be taken to democracy) does not undermine this claim in any direct way. After all, the argument addresses the developed countries, asserting, in effect, that development is sufficient for democracy. The set-theoretic nature of almost all social science theory is not acknowledged by most social scientists today. They are locked into the notion that set-theoretic arguments must be reformulated as symmetric correlational arguments before they can be "tested." In fact, empirical evidence can give strong support to a set-theoretic argument (e.g., showing that the developed countries are indeed almost uniformly democratic), despite a relatively modest correlation (e.g., attenuated by other paths to democracy present in the subset of less-developed countries). Should a weak or only modest correlation cast doubt on the set-theoretic claim? A central argument of this book is that set-theoretic arguments—the bread and butter of social science theory—should be evaluated on their own terms, that is, as (asymmetric) set relations and not as (symmetric) correlational arguments.

Social scientists generally avoid set-theoretic analysis because it appears to require the use of nominal-scale variables and seemingly primitive forms of analysis (e.g., simple cross-tabulation). Since the advent of fuzzy sets (Zadeh 1965), however, the use of these scales and forms of analysis is no longer necessary. With fuzzy sets, it is possible to use set-theoretic reasoning (i.e., the type of reasoning that is central to both qualitative research and social science theory) and allow for fine gradations in degree of membership (e.g., degree of membership in the set of democratic countries). The resulting analysis is not correlational, but instead retains all the power and analytic rigor that comes from working with sets and operations on sets (e.g., subsets, supersets, intersection, union, negation, use of De Morgan's Law, truth tables,

---

theory development, especially concept formation and elaboration. See also Eckstein (1975).

and so on). This book demonstrates how to join set theory, qualitative and quantitative analysis, and fidelity to theoretical discourse in the effort to redesign social inquiry.

King, Keohane, and Verba's Middle Path

This book's vision of a middle path that transcends, rather than compromises, is very different from that presented in *Designing Social Inquiry* (King, Keohane, and Verba 1994). King, Keohane, and Verba's vision of the middle path is straightforward. Unlike some, such as Lieberson (1992, 1998), who criticizes small-N research, they accept the scientific validity and utility of qualitative research, acknowledging its many strengths. Their core recommendation is that qualitative researchers conduct their research in ways that enhance its compatibility with quantitative research. For example, King, Keohane, and Verba criticize the common qualitative strategy of looking for shared causal conditions across multiple instances of the same outcome (e.g., the causally relevant conditions shared by countries that make a successful transition from authoritarianism to democracy). From the viewpoint of variable-oriented research, this strategy is flawed because (1) neither the outcome nor the shared causal conditions *vary* across cases and (2) it commits the error of "selecting on the dependent variable," a practice that is universally discouraged in textbooks on quantitative methods.[2] King, Keohane, and Verba's implicit argument is that if qualitative researchers would abandon this and other unscientific practice, then reconciling the results of qualitative research with the findings of quantitative research would be easier to do.

Of course, this misguided recommendation ("Never select on the dependent variable!") is only one among the many suggestions offered by King, Keohane, and Verba (1994). Their recommendations are gen-

---

2. As I demonstrate in *Fuzzy-Set Social Science* (Ragin 2000) and elsewhere (e.g., Ragin 1997), not only is "selecting on the dependent variable" a useful strategy, especially when researchers are interested in studying necessary conditions (Clément 2004), but it is also an essential step in the constitution of theoretically defined (as opposed to "given") populations. See also Mahoney and Goertz (2004).

erally thoughtful, and most are quite useful. However, their advice assumes the priority and preeminence of quantitative research, and their vision of the middle path is that it is an extension of the core principles of quantitative research to qualitative research. While ambitious, this view is limited.

Its first shortcoming is that it assumes that valid general knowledge follows directly from proper application of quantitative methods. In essence, King, Keohane, and Verba assert that social science already has a good technology for generating general knowledge and that the task at hand is to remake qualitative methods so that they are more consistent with the template of quantitative research. The problem with this view is that it leaves unquestioned the assumption that the quantitative template is the best (the only?) way to produce useful and valid general knowledge. Most social scientists concede that more than one route may be taken to general knowledge.

The second problem with their vision of the middle path is that it is at odds with everyday logic and experience. The most common route to general knowledge, especially to that of social phenomena, is through accumulated knowledge of specific instances or cases. In everyday experience we build knowledge of the general from knowledge of the specific. For example, we learn about the temperaments of our colleagues from our repeated interactions with them. Sometimes we test what we have learned, as when we predict what a colleague will say or do in an upcoming meeting, but our "tests" rest on a firm foundation of knowledge of specific instances. In this light, the middle path between qualitative and quantitative research should consist of methods for building general knowledge from case-oriented knowledge— from understandings of specific cases in specific contexts (Ragin 2003a, 2004b). That is, it should articulate the different contexts and conditions that enable or disable specific empirical connections and outcomes. It should not consist of methods that supplant case-oriented knowledge with an altogether different form of knowledge, for example, one that is organized around the attempt to isolate the net effects of independent variables—a central goal of conventional quantitative analysis.

Third, and finally, the middle path that King, Keohane, and Verba (1994) chart is essentially one that is a restricted or compromised version of existing qualitative methods. They argue, in effect, that some qualitative practices are more productive than others and that researchers should utilize only the most productive practices (i.e., those that offer the greatest "analytic leverage"). Thus, the bridge they build from qualitative research to quantitative research establishes a link to only a relatively narrow subset of existing qualitative methods. By contrast, the alternate vision I offer seeks a path that is not a compromise between quantitative and qualitative, but one that transcends many of their respective limitations. In short, my goal is to propose a real alternative to conventional practices.

Four Oppositions

Four basic oppositions organize the chapters that follow: set-theoretic versus correlational connections, calibration versus measurement, configurations of conditions versus "independent" variables, and the analysis of causal complexity versus the analysis of net effects. These four oppositions all contrast set-theoretic analysis with conventional quantitative analysis.

I focus explicitly on this contrast for several reasons. The first is that the template of conventional quantitative analysis is well articulated, and it is clearly the dominant way of conducting social research, especially in the United States today. Because it is so well articulated, the contrasts with set-theoretic analysis are both broad and sharply defined. Second, the distinctiveness of the analysis of set relations is most apparent when contrasted with conventional quantitative research. Consider, for example, the fact that the cornerstone of conventional quantitative research, the correlation coefficient, is almost completely irrelevant to set theoretic analysis. Third, and somewhat paradoxically, the contrast with conventional quantitative research is important because many social scientists believe that conventional quantitative analysis subsumes the analysis of set relations. For example, they see a direct correspondence between set-theoretic analysis and the conventional analysis of cross-tabulations. While it is certainly possible to examine crisp (i.e., Boolean) sets using tables, set-theoretic analysis essentially "deconstructs" the conventional cross-tabulation. Fourth, I wish to demonstrate through the contrast with conventional quantitative analysis that the analysis of set relations is not restricted to small- or medium-N research. In both *The Comparative Method* (Ragin 1987) and *Fuzzy-Set Social Science* (Ragin 2000), I emphasize small- and medium-N research, a territory largely ignored by conventional quantitative methods. In part, my goal in these two books was to fill this void and demonstrate that systematic cross-case analysis does not require large samples of cases.[3] However, it became clear to me that the set-theoretic methods I had developed for small- and medium-N research could be productively extended to large-N research. This book offers that extension, articulated through the four major contrasts.

Set-theoretic versus correlational connections. In part I (chapters 1–3), I present important background material for understanding the distinctiveness of the analysis of set relations in social research. A key contrast is the difference between the correlation (and most other measures of association), which is symmetrical by design, and the set relation, which is fundamentally asymmetrical. This distinction is important because set-theoretic analysis, like qualitative research more generally, focuses on uniformities and near uniformities, not on general patterns of association. As chapter 1 demonstrates, it is possible to deconstruct a single symmetrical analysis (a 2×2 cross-tabulation) into two asymmetric set-theoretic analyses, one focusing on sufficiency, the other on necessity. The key is to understand that the disaggregated subset relations provide important information about how social phenomena are connected and that this information is obscured in correlations. I extend these arguments to fuzzy sets in chapter 2 and

---

3. While it is true that almost any method that relies on probability theory abhors a small or even moderate number of cases, social scientists should not turn away from the challenge of making sense of five to fifty cases, especially when they have the opportunity to gain in-depth knowledge of these cases. See also Berg-Schlosser (2002).

then show how to fashion quantitative measures of the consistency and empirical importance of set-theoretic connections in chapter 3. These simple descriptive measures provide essential tools for refining both crisp-set and fuzzy-set analysis.

Calibration versus measurement. Part II (chapters 4 and 5) addresses the important issue of the calibration of measures. In sharp contrast with the physical sciences, calibration is virtually unknown in the social sciences. Instead, measures are simply required to vary in ways that reflect relevant underlying concepts. This lack of concern for calibration is reinforced by the use of the correlation coefficient as the bedrock of conventional quantitative analysis, for correlational analysis requires only that measures vary around an inductively derived, sample-specific mean. The actual metric of the measures used in conventional quantitative research is too often ignored, as is the substantive interpretation of specific scores or ranges of scores. By contrast, it is impossible to conduct meaningful fuzzy set–theoretic analysis without attending to issues of calibration. All fuzzy sets must be calibrated, which means that scores must be interpreted according to external standards. For example, what income qualifies a person for full membership in the set with "high income" parents? This is not a numerical value that can be induced directly from a frequency distribution; it must be based instead on external standards or guidelines that have face validity. Chapter 4 addresses the long-standing neglect of calibration in empirical social science and argues that the key to "bringing calibration in" is through the use of fuzzy sets. Chapter 5 presents two methods for calibrating interval and ratio scales as fuzzy sets. I demonstrate how researchers can use their theoretical and substantive knowledge to transform their precise but uncalibrated interval- and ratio-scale measures into well-calibrated fuzzy sets.

Configurations of conditions versus "independent" variables. Part III (chapters 6 and 7) develops the contrast between a core focus of conventional quantitative methods—treating each independent variable in a given analysis as analytically distinct and separate—and a core focus of set-theoretic methods—studying cases as configurations of causes and conditions. The key difference between the two is captured by the idea of a causal "recipe"—a specific combination of causally relevant ingredients linked to an outcome. In set-theoretic work, the idea of a causal recipe is straightforward, for the notion of combined causes is directly captured by the principle of set intersection. With fuzzy sets, assessing the degree to which cases have membership in a given causal recipe is a simple matter; it is shown by their degree of membership in the intersection of the fuzzy-set causal conditions that comprise the recipe. By contrast, one of the main strengths of conventional quantitative methods such as regression analysis is their ability to parse explained variation in a dependent variable—to divide it among analytically separate independent variables. To examine combinations of conditions with conventional quantitative methods, it is necessary to use multiplicative interaction terms, which are not only cumbersome and difficult to interpret but also tend to be highly collinear with each other and their component variables. Chapter 6 elaborates basic principles regarding the study of cases as configurations of conditions, with a special focus on the idea of causal recipes. Chapter 7 deepens the approach by showing how to use truth tables to synthesize the results of fuzzy-set analyses of the logically possible configurations of a given set of causal conditions.

The analysis of causal complexity versus the analysis of net effects. In part IV (chapters 8–11) I offer a set-theoretic approach to the analysis of causal complexity, based in part on an examination of the role of counterfactual analysis in social research.[4] A thorough examination of causal complexity entails consideration of all logically possible combinations of causal conditions. However, naturally occurring social data are severely limited in their diversity and typically present only a minority of the relevant empirical combinations. It follows that researchers must engage *counterfactual cases* in some way, either directly, using thought experiments, or indirectly, via assumptions about the nature of causation (e.g., the assumption of additivity

---

4. A counterfactual case is a substantively relevant combination of causal conditions that nevertheless does not exist empirically. Counterfactual analysis involves evaluating the outcome that such a case would exhibit if, in fact, it existed.

in conventional quantitative research). Chapter 8 presents a set-theoretic approach to counterfactual analysis, using truth tables to elaborate the idea of limited diversity. Viewed through this lens, it is clear that counterfactual analysis is almost always an issue in non-experimental social research, regardless of the number of cases examined. I emphasize the theory and knowledge dependence of all social research and criticize conventional quantitative researchers for ignoring both the need for explicit counterfactual analysis and its knowledge-dependent nature. Chapter 9 presents the distinction between "easy" and "difficult" counterfactuals and shows how the incorporation of easy counterfactuals (a process that is implicit in much case-oriented research) can be formalized using set-theoretic methods. Bridging my discussion of counterfactual analysis (chapters 8 and 9) and my empirical demonstration (chapter 11) is an examination in chapter 10 of the limitations of what I call *net effects thinking,* the analytic metatheory that dominates the social sciences today. Chapter 11 concludes the book by providing a demonstration, using a large-N data set known as the *Bell Curve* data (Herrnstein and Murray 1994). I present a fuzzy-set analysis of the combinations of individual-level characteristics linked to poverty and contrast these results with a conventional, net-effects analysis of the same data.

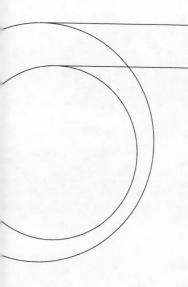

PART I

Set-Theoretic versus
Correlational Connections

1: Set Relations in Social Research
Basics Concepts

When quantitative social scientists think *sets,* they usually do not get very far. They think, "OK, nominal-scale variables. I can transform them into dummy variables and use them in linear models." Or perhaps they think, "Hmmm, I've got subpopulations." Qualitative researchers are not much different. They think, "OK, typologies of cases. I can construct (and deconstruct) those." Missing in both views is recognition of the importance of the *analysis of set relations* in social research. Consider that almost all social science theory is verbal and, as such, is formulated in terms of sets and set relations. When a theory states, for example, that "small farmers are risk averse," the claim is set theoretic: small farmers constitute a rough subset of risk-averse individuals. Such statements are usually transformed by social scientists into hypotheses about correlations between variables, which are then evaluated using standard correlational techniques (e.g., multiple regression analysis). This chapter argues that theory formulated in terms of set relations should be evaluated on its own terms, that is, as statements about set relations, not about correlations. In the process, it offers a general overview of set relations in social research.

The Nature of Set Relations

The simplest and most basic set relation is the subset, which is easiest to grasp when it involves nested categories. Dogs are a subset of the set of mammals; Protestants are a subset of the set of Christians, who in turn are a subset of the set of monotheists. These subset relations are straightforward and easy to accept as valid because they are definitional in nature: dogs have all the characteristics of mammals; the set of Christians is partially constituted by the set of Protestants. These examples also involve conventional, *crisp* sets and thus they are easy to grasp and simple to represent using Venn diagrams. The circle representing the set of dogs, for example, is entirely contained within a larger circle representing the set of mammals. (Of course, many observers would argue that the set of Protestants is not crisp, but instead is a truly *fuzzy* set. I address the question of fuzzy sets in chapter 2.)

More important than these simple, definitional subsets are subset relations that describe social phenomena that are connected causally or in some other integral manner. When researchers argue, for example, that "religious fundamentalists are politically conservative," they are stating, in effect, that they believe that religious fundamentalists form a rough subset of the set of political conservatives, and may even go so far as to argue that their fundamentalism is the cause of their conservatism. Likewise, a researcher who argues that having a strong "civil society" is a necessary or essential part of being a "developed country" implies that the developed countries constitute a consistent subset of those with strong civil societies. In this example, the connection is *constitutive,* as opposed to causal.

When set relations reflect integral social or causal connections and are not merely definitional in nature, they require explication—that is, they are theory and knowledge dependent. Assume, for example, that among third-wave democracies, all those that adopted parliamentary governments soon failed. Thus, third-wave democracies with parliamentary governments form a subset of failed third-wave democracies. Were the failures just bad luck, a coincidence? Or did a causal or some other kind of integral connection exist between third-wave democracies adopting a parliamentary form of government and their subsequent failure? The set-theoretic connection in this example is not definitional; it must be explicated in some way. This type of set relation, the kind that is central to almost all social science theorizing, is the main focus of this chapter and this book.

Set-Theoretic Connections Are Asymmetrical

An important aspect of set-theoretic connections, as opposed to correlational connections, is that they are *asymmetrical*. For example, the fact that there are many political conservatives who are not religious fundamentalists does not in any way challenge the claim that religious fundamentalists are politically conservative. In another example, if my theory states that the developed countries are democratic, in essence I am stating that the set of developed countries is a subset of the set of democratic countries. The fact that there are less-developed countries that are also democracies does not undermine my set-theoretic claim. Of course, such cases *do* undermine the correlation between development and democracy—that is, they would count against my argument if it had been formulated symmetrically. The fully symmetric version would be, "the developed countries are democratic, and the less developed countries are not democratic." However, this reformulation of the argument extends it in ways that may not be warranted or intended. As originally stated, the argument is asymmetric, as are set-theoretic formulations in general.

Set-theoretic arguments are often erroneously reformulated as correlational hypotheses. This mistake is, in fact, one of the most common in all of contemporary social science. For example, a theory may claim that because of the many external vagaries faced by newly formed democracies, third-wave democracies adopting parliamentary governments are unlikely to endure. After reading this argument, the conventional social scientist would try to test it by examining the correlation between "parliamentary government" and "failure" using data on third-wave democracies. Suppose, again, that the set-theoretic evidence supports the theory; that is, third-wave democracies adopting parliamentary governments are a subset of failed third-wave democracies. Despite this clear connection, the correlation between "parliamentary form" and "failure" still might be relatively weak, due to the fact that there are many other paths to failure and thus there are instances of failed democracies with presidential or other forms of nonparliamentary government. The set-theoretic claim that "third-wave democracies with parliamentary governments fail" is not refuted by these cases. However, these nonparliamentary paths to failure seriously undermine the correlation between "parliamentary form" and "failure."

Consider the "democratic peace" argument that democracies do not go to war against each other. This statement is essentially a claim that country dyads in which both parties are democratic constitute a perfect (or near-perfect) subset of nonwarring country dyads. Of course, the rate of warring may be very low both in the set of democratic dyads and in the set of dyads in which at least one of the parties is not a democracy. The point of the argument is not the *difference* between these two rates but that the rate of warring is *zero or close to zero* in the set of democratic dyads. The fact that democratic dyads constitute a near-perfect subset of nonwarring dyads signals that this arrangement (international relations between democracies) may be *sufficient* for peaceful coexistence. Of course, many other paths may be taken to peaceful coexistence, and the correlation between "democratic dyad" and "nonwarring" may be weak because of these many alternate paths.

The key difference between correlational and set-theoretic connections is illustrated in tables 1.1 and 1.2. Table 1.1 shows a pattern of results consistent with the existence of a correlational connection between parliamentary government and failure among third-wave democracies. The first column shows the tendency for nonparliamentary governments to survive; the second column shows the tendency for the parliamentary governments to fail. While very satisfying from a correlational viewpoint, this table would be unsatisfying to a researcher interested in set-theoretic connections, for there are no connections in the table that could be described as explicit or consistent. Table 1.2, however, would be of great interest to this researcher because it shows a consistent connection between parliamentary form and failure—all sixteen cases with this governmental form failed, as shown in the second column of this table. While significant to the researcher interested in set-theoretic connections, this table would disappoint the

Table 1.1: A correlational connection

	Presidential form	Parliamentary form
Third-wave democracy failed	7	11
Third-wave democracy survived	17	5

Table 1.2: A set-theoretic connection

	Presidential form	Parliamentary form
Third-wave democracy failed	15	16
Third-wave democracy survived	9	0

researcher interested in correlational connections, for the correlation between form of government and survival versus failure is relatively weak.

To summarize, set relations in social research (1) involve causal or other integral connections linking social phenomena (i.e., are not merely definitional), (2) are theory and knowledge dependent (i.e., require explication), (3) are central to social science theorizing (because theory is primarily verbal in nature, and verbal statements are often set theoretic), (4) are asymmetric (and thus should not be reformulated as correlational arguments), and (5) can be very strong despite relatively modest correlations (as illustrated in tables 1.1 and 1.2).

Two Important Types of Set-Theoretic Relations

Case-oriented researchers—and qualitative researchers more generally—are centrally concerned with the analysis of set relations, which is evident in their efforts to identify *explicit* connections (Ragin and Rihoux 2004). They rarely see their work in set-theoretic or formal terms, however, so I sometimes refer to them as *implicit* Booleans. For example, case-oriented researchers often seek to identify *commonalities* across a set of cases, usually while focusing on a relatively small number of purposefully selected cases (e.g., Vaughan 1986). Why look for commonalties? They are suggestive of important empirical connections. For example, suppose all (or almost all) of the anorectic teenage girls in my study say that they get a sense of accomplishment from their food and body practices. A light bulb goes on in my head, and I explore the connection further. These kinds of commonalities are, in fact, set-theoretic relations. Consider another example: an examination of social revolutions indicates that some form of prior state breakdown occurred in every case (Skocpol 1979). The evidence indicates that a set-theoretic relation exists between state breakdown and social revolution. In this instance, it might be reasonable to speculate that the set of social revolutions is a subset of the set of state breakdowns and that an important causal link exists between the two.

Two general analytic strategies involve searching for commonalities. The first strategy is to examine cases sharing a given outcome (e.g., consolidated third-wave democracies) and attempt to identify their shared causal conditions (e.g., the possibility that they share the presidential form of government).[1] The second strategy is to examine cases sharing a specific causal condition or, more commonly, a specific combination of causal conditions, and assess whether these cases exhibit the same outcome (e.g., do the countries that combine party fractionalization, a weak executive, and a low level of economic development all suffer democratic breakdown?). Both strategies are set theoretic in nature. The first is an examination of whether instances of a specific outcome constitute a subset of instances of a cause. The second is an examination of whether instances of a specific causal condition or combination of causal conditions constitute a subset of instances of an outcome. These two strategies are illustrated with Venn diagrams in figure 1.1.

Both strategies are methods for establishing *explicit* connections. If it is found, for example, that all (or nearly all) consolidated third-wave democracies have presidential systems, then an explicit connection

---

1. The term *causal condition* is used generically here and elsewhere in this book to refer to an aspect of a case that is relevant in some way to the researcher's account or explanation of some outcome.

A. Identify causal conditions shared by instances of an outcome

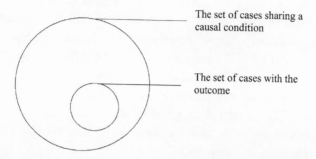

The set of cases sharing a causal condition

The set of cases with the outcome

B. Assess whether cases with the same causal conditions share the same outcome

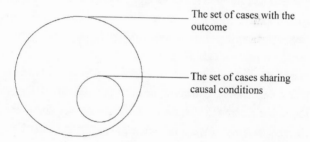

The set of cases with the outcome

The set of cases sharing causal conditions

Figure 1.1 Venn diagram representing two different kinds of case-oriented research

has been established between presidentialism and consolidation.[2] Likewise, if it is found that all (or nearly all) third-wave democracies that share a low level of economic development, party fractionalization, and a weak executive failed as democracies, then an explicit connection has been established between this combination of conditions and democratic breakdown. As previously noted, establishing explicit

2. Neither of these two strategies expects or depends on demonstrations of *perfect* set-theoretic relations. For example, if *almost all* (as opposed to *all*) instances of democratic consolidation involved presidential systems, then the researcher would no doubt accept this as evidence of an integral connection between presidentialism and democratic consolidation. Specific procedures for probabilistic assessment of set-theoretic patterns using benchmarks are presented in Ragin (2000).

connections is not the same as establishing correlations. For example, assume that the survival rate for third-wave democracies with presidential systems is 60 percent, while the survival rate for third-wave democracies with parliamentary systems is 35 percent. Clearly, a correlation exists between these two aspects conceived as variables (presidential versus parliamentary system, survival versus failure). However, the evidence does not come close to approximating a set-theoretic relation. Thus, in this instance evidence would show a correlational connection, but not an explicit connection between presidential systems and democratic survival.

As explained in Ragin (2000), the first analytic strategy—identifying causal conditions shared by cases with the same outcome—is appropriate for the assessment of necessary conditions. The second strategy—examining cases with the same causal conditions to see if they also share the same outcome—is suitable for the assessment of sufficient conditions, especially sufficient *combinations* of conditions. Establishing conditions that are necessary or sufficient is a long-standing interest of many researchers, especially those working at the macrosocial or macropolitical level (see, e.g., Goertz and Starr 2002). However, it is important to point out that the use of set-theoretic methods to establish explicit connections does not necessarily entail the use of the concepts or the language of necessity and sufficiency, or any other language of causation. A researcher might observe, for example, that instances of democratic breakdown are all former colonies without drawing any causal connection from this observation. In a simpler example, colleagues might "act out" only in faculty meetings, but that does not mean that analysts must therefore interpret faculty meetings as a necessary condition for acting out. Demonstrating explicit connections is central to social science, whether or not there is interest in necessary or sufficient causation or any other kind of causation.

How Correlational Methods Sometimes Miss Connections

The mismatch between correlational methods and the study of explicit connections is clearly visible in the simplest form of variable-

Table 1.3: Conventional cross-tabulation of presence/absence of an outcome against presence/absence of a causal condition

	Causal condition absent	Causal condition present
Outcome present	cell 1: cases here undermine researcher's argument	cell 2: cases here support researcher's argument
Outcome absent	cell 3: cases here support researcher's argument	cell 4: cases here undermine researcher's argument

oriented analysis, the 2 × 2 cross-tabulation of the presence/absence of an outcome against the presence/absence of a hypothesized cause, as illustrated in table 1.3. The correlation focuses simultaneously and equivalently on the degree to which instances of the cause produce instances of the outcome (the number of cases in cell 2 relative to the sum of cases in cells 2 and 4) *and* on the degree to which instances of the absence of the cause are linked to the absence of the outcome (the number of cases in cell 3 relative to the sum of cases in cells 1 and 3).[3] (Alternatively, it could be stated that the correlation focuses simultaneously and equivalently on the degree to which instances of the outcome are linked to instances of the cause and on the degree to which instances of the absence of the outcome are linked to instances of the absence of the cause.) The central point is that the correlation is an omnibus statistic that rewards researchers for producing an abundance of cases in either cells 2 or 3 and penalizes them for depositing cases in either cell 1 or 4. Thus, it is a good tool for studying general cross-case *tendencies*.

A researcher who is interested in explicit connections, however, is interested in only specific components of the information that is pooled and conflated in a correlation. For example, researchers interested in causal conditions shared by instances of an outcome would focus on cells 1 and 2 of table 1.3. Their goal would be to identify relevant causal conditions that deposit as few cases as possible (ideally none) in cell 1. Likewise, researchers interested in whether cases that

---

3. I use the term *correlation* generically here to refer to the examination of the strength of the association between two variables, and not as a specific reference to Pearson's r or the calculations used to produce Pearson's r.

are similar with respect to causal conditions experience the same outcome would focus on cells 2 and 4. Their goal would be to identify relevant combinations of causal conditions that deposit as few cases as possible (ideally none) in cell 4. It is clear from these examples that the correlation has two major shortcomings when viewed from the perspective of explicit connections: (1) it attends only to relative differences (e.g., relative survival rates for presidential versus parliamentary systems), and (2) it conflates different kinds of causal assessment. Notice further that a cell that is very important in correlational analysis, cell 3—where neither the cause nor the outcome is present—is not directly relevant to the assessment of either of the two types of explicit connections.

Thus, the study of explicit connections involves a *decomposition* of the most basic unit of variable-oriented analysis—the correlation. This decomposition makes it possible to employ qualitative research strategies that, I have argued, are fundamentally set theoretic in nature: (1) studying cases with the same outcome and in order to identify their causally relevant features and (2) studying cases with the same combination of causally relevant conditions in order to see if they exhibit the same outcome.

It is important to point out that the correlation is not simply a bivariate statistic. It is the cornerstone of most forms of conventional variable-oriented social research, including some of the most sophisticated forms of quantitative analysis available today. A matrix of bivariate correlations, along with the means and standard deviations of the variables included in the correlation matrix, is all that is needed to compute complex regression analyses, factor analyses, and even structural equation models. In essence, these varied techniques offer diverse ways of representing the bivariate correlations in a matrix and the various partial relations (e.g., the net effect of an independent variable in a multiple regression) that can be constructed using formulas based on three or more bivariate correlations. Because they rely on the bivariate correlation as the cornerstone of empirical analysis, these sophisticated quantitative techniques eschew the study of explicit connections, as described here. This underlying, fundamental shortcoming of the correlation is at the root of the rejection of correlational methods by many scholars who conduct qualitative and case-oriented research.

Qualitative Comparative Analysis and Explicit Connections

In contrast to correlational techniques, qualitative comparative analysis (QCA) is grounded in set theory and thus is ideally suited for studying explicit connections, such as those sketched in figure 1.1. An especially useful feature of QCA is its capacity for analyzing complex causation, defined as a situation in which an outcome may follow from several different combinations of causal conditions, that is, from different causal "recipes." For example, a researcher may have good reason to suspect that there are several different recipes for the consolidation of third-wave democracies. By examining the fate of cases with different configurations of causally relevant conditions, it is possible, using QCA, to identify the decisive recipes and thereby unravel causal complexity.

The key tool for analyzing causal complexity using QCA is the truth table, a tool that allows structured, focused comparisons (George 1979). Truth tables list the logically possible combinations of causal conditions and the empirical outcome associated with each configuration.[4] Thus, they directly implement the second type of explicit connection described above. For example, based on theoretical and substantive knowledge, a scholar might argue that a key recipe for democratic consolidation involves the following combination of conditions: a presidential form of government, a strong executive, a low level of party fractionalization, and a noncommunist past. Table 1.4 illustrates the truth table operationalizing this argument. With

---

4. It is important to point out that the procedures described here are not dependent on the use of dichotomies. Truth tables can be built from fuzzy sets (with set membership scores ranging from 0 to 1) without dichotomizing the fuzzy scores. These procedures take full advantage of the graded membership scores central to the fuzzy-set approach (see chapters 3 and 7 of this book and also Ragin 2000, 2004a; Rihoux and Ragin 2008).

Table 1.4: Hypothetical truth table showing causal conditions relevant to democratic consolidation

Presidential form	Strong executive	Low party fractionalization	Noncommunist	Consolidated
no	no	no	no	—
no	no	no	yes	no
no	no	yes	no	no
no	no	yes	yes	—
no	yes	no	no	no
no	yes	no	yes	no
no	yes	yes	no	—
no	yes	yes	yes	yes
yes	no	no	no	no
yes	no	no	yes	—
yes	no	yes	no	—
yes	no	yes	yes	—
yes	yes	no	no	yes
yes	yes	no	yes	yes
yes	yes	yes	no	—
yes	yes	yes	yes	yes

Note: The "—" entries indicate that there are no empirical cases with the combination of conditions listed in the row.

four causal conditions, sixteen combinations of conditions (causal configurations) are logically possible. In more complex analyses, the rows (representing combinations of causal conditions) may be quite numerous, for the number of causal combinations is an exponential function of the number of causal conditions (number of causal combinations = 2^k, where k is the number of causal conditions).

The use of truth tables to unravel causal complexity is described in detail elsewhere (e.g., Ragin 1987, 2000; De Meur and Rihoux 2002). The essential point is that the truth table elaborates and formalizes one of the key analytic strategies of comparative research—examining cases sharing specific combinations of causal conditions to see if they share the same outcome. Indeed, the main goal of truth table analysis is to identify explicit connections between combinations of causal conditions and outcomes. By listing the different logically possible combinations of conditions, it is possible to assess not only the sufficiency of a specific recipe (e.g., the recipe presented in the last row of table 1.4, with all four causal conditions present) but also the sufficiency of the other logically possible combinations of conditions that can be constructed from these causal conditions. For example, if the cases with all four conditions present experience democratic consolidation and the cases with three of four conditions present (and one absent) also experience consolidation, then the researcher can conclude that the causal condition that varies across these two combinations is irrelevant to the recipe. The key ingredients for the outcome are the remaining three conditions. Various techniques and procedures for logically simplifying patterns in truth tables, in addition to the simple one just described, are detailed in Ragin (1987, 2000), De Meur and Rihoux (2002), and Rihoux and Ragin (2008).

Often the move from a hypothesized recipe to a truth table stimulates a reformulation or an expansion of a recipe, based on an examination of relevant cases. For example, suppose the truth table revealed substantial inconsistency in the last row—that is, suppose some cases in the last row failed to consolidate, in addition to the several that did. This inconsistency in outcomes signals to the investigator that more in-depth study of cases is needed. By comparing the cases in this row failing to consolidate with those that did consolidate, it would be possible to elaborate the recipe. Suppose this comparison revealed that the cases that failed to consolidate all had severe elite divisions. This ingredient (absence of elite divisions) could then be added to the recipe, and the truth table could then be respecified with five causal conditions (and thus thirty-two rows).

The task of truth table refinement is demanding, for it requires in-depth knowledge of cases and many iterations between theory, cases, and truth table construction. In effect, the truth table disciplines the research process, providing a framework for comparing cases as configurations of similarities and differences while exploring patterns of consistency and inconsistency with respect to case outcomes.

Looking Ahead

The set-theoretic principles described here provide the foundation for the techniques of social inquiry presented in chapters that follow. One limitation of the set-theoretic principles described in this chapter is that they involve only crisp (Boolean) sets and thus may seem crude. Indeed, one reason that social scientists disdain set-theoretic analysis is the perception that it is restricted to nominal-scale variables. Chapter 2 addresses this limitation, showing that key set-theoretic principles can be applied as well to fuzzy sets, which scale degree of membership in sets to values ranging from 0.0 to 1.0.

Practical Appendix: Constructing Truth Tables

Using fuzzy-set qualitative comparative analysis (fsQCA) (Ragin, Drass, and Davey 2007), which can be downloaded from http://www.fsqca.com, it is a simple matter to construct a crisp truth table from dichotomous data. The assumption here is that the researcher has a simple data set composed of binary variables, coded 1 for "present" and 0 for "absent" (the construction of truth tables from fuzzy sets is addressed in chapter 7). The goals of crisp truth table construction are to (1) examine the distribution of cases across the logically possible combinations of a given set of dichotomous causal conditions and (2) examine the degree to which cases with each combination of causal conditions agree with respect to a given outcome.

1. Create the data set. This task can be accomplished using fsQCA, which includes procedures for inputting data directly and for importing data sets from other programs (e.g., comma-delimited files from Excel or tab-delimited files from SPSS). The imported files must have simple variables names (with no embedded spaces or punctuation) as the first line of the data set. Missing data should be entered as blanks.

2. Once the data set has been inputted or imported and appears in the data spreadsheet window, click *Analyze,* then *Crisp Sets,* and then *Truth Table Algorithm.* A dialogue box labeled *Select Variables* will open, which allows specification of the outcome and the causal condi-

tions. A box can also be checked for analyzing the negation (reverse) of the chosen outcome.

3. After specifying the outcome and the causal conditions, click *Run,* and fsQCA will generate the full truth table for the specified outcome using the specified causal conditions. A separate window with the truth table spreadsheet opens.

4. The first item of interest is the *number* column, which shows the distribution of cases across causal combinations. The truth table is first presented with the causal combinations sorted according to frequency, along with the cumulative percentage of cases (shown in the *number* column). The information in this column should be used to select any frequency threshold that might be used as a cut-off value. When the total number of cases in a study is small, the threshold should be at least one case, and truth table rows with no cases (*number* = 0) should be deleted. When the total number of cases is large, however, a higher threshold may be used, to allow for measurement and assignment error or to generate a "coarse grained" analysis. To delete rows, simply click on the first (top-most) row to be deleted, click *Edit,* and then click *Delete current row to last row.*

5. The second main item of interest is the set-theoretic consistency scores, shown in the *consistency* column. With crisp sets, this calculation is simply the proportion of cases in a given row that display the outcome in question. A score of 1.0 (or close to 1.0) indicates high consistency—that the cases in the row agree in displaying the outcome. A score of 0.0 (or close to 0.0) indicates that the cases in the row agree in *not* displaying the outcome. With crisp sets, consistency scores in the middle (0.30 to 0.70) indicate that the cases in a given row are strongly divided with respect to presence/absence of the outcome.

Consistency scores have two main uses. They can be used to code the outcome column in the truth table, which is done manually by entering 1s and 0s in the column labeled with the outcome name, or they can be used to guide further research. Suppose, for example, that several rows have consistency scores indicating that the cases are contradictory—that is, many display the outcome and many do not. By identifying these cases and studying them closely, it is often possible to specify a causal condition that can be added to the truth table in order to resolve contradictions. The researcher can then respecify the truth table, including this additional condition. Further details on the refinement and use of truth tables constructed from crisp sets can be found in Ragin (1987).

2: Fuzzy Sets and Fuzzy-Set Relations

Many of the phenomena that interest social scientists vary by level or degree. For example, while it is clear that some countries are democracies and some are not, many in-between cases can be found as well. These latter countries are not fully in the set of democracies, nor are they fully excluded from this set. The fact that so many of the things that interest social scientists do not fit neatly into crisp sets may seem to nullify all the good reasons sketched in chapter 1 for analyzing social phenomena in terms of set relations. Does it make sense, for example, to think about the developed countries as a subset of the democratic countries if both development and democracy are measured on fine-grained, interval scales? One reason social scientists are reluctant to study social phenomena in terms of set relations is that they think that the study of set relations is restricted to nominal-scale measures. Not only are such scales considered "primitive," but interval and ratio scales that have been recoded to nominal scales (and thus "downgraded") are almost always suspect. Has a researcher selected cut-points in a biased way, to favor a particular conclusion?

Fortunately, a well-developed mathematical system is available for addressing degree of membership in sets: fuzzy-set theory (Zadeh 1965). Fuzzy sets are especially powerful because they allow researchers to calibrate partial membership in sets using values in the interval between 0.0 (nonmembership) and 1.0 (full membership) without abandoning core set theoretic principles and operations (e.g., the subset relation). As explained in chapter 1, set relations are central to social science theory, yet the assessment of set relations is outside the scope of conventional correlational methods.

The Nature of Fuzzy Sets

Fuzzy sets are simultaneously qualitative and quantitative, for they incorporate both kinds of distinctions in the calibration of degree of set membership. Thus, fuzzy sets have many of the virtues of conventional interval- and ratio-scale variables, but at the same time they permit *qualitative* assessment. Consider an example: The United States might receive a membership score of 1.0 (full membership) in the set of developed countries but a score of only 0.9 (slightly less than full membership) in the set of democratic countries, especially in the wake of its performance in the 2000 presidential election. A membership score of 1.0 indicates full membership in a set; scores close to 1.0 (e.g., 0.8 or 0.9) indicate strong but not quite full membership in a set; scores less than 0.5 but greater than 0.0 (e.g., 0.2 or 0.3) indicate that objects are more "out" than "in" a set, but still weak members of the set; a score of 0.0 indicates full nonmembership in a set. The 0.5 score is also qualitatively anchored, for it indicates the point of maximum ambiguity (i.e., fuzziness) in the assessment of whether a case is more in or out of a set.

A fuzzy set can be seen as a continuous variable that has been *purposefully calibrated* to indicate degree of membership in a well-defined and specified set (see chapters 4 and 5). Such calibration is possible only through the use of theoretical and substantive knowledge, which is essential to the specification of the three qualitative breakpoints (full membership, full nonmembership, and maximum ambiguity). For example, cases in the lower ranges of a conventional continuous variable may all be fully out of the set in question, with fuzzy membership scores truncated to 0.0, while cases in the upper ranges of this same continuous variable may be all fully in the set, with fuzzy membership scores truncated to 1.0.

For illustration of the general idea of fuzzy sets, consider a simple three-value set that allows cases to be in the gray zone between in and out of a set. As shown in table 2.1, instead of using only two scores, 0.0 and 1.0, three-value logic adds a third value, 0.5, to identify objects that are neither fully in nor fully out of the set in question (compare

Table 2.1: Crisp versus fuzzy sets

Crisp set	Three-value fuzzy set	Four-value fuzzy set	Six-value fuzzy set	"Continuous" fuzzy set
1 = fully in	1 = fully in	1 = fully in	1 = fully in	1 = fully in
			0.8 = mostly but not fully in	
		0.67 = more in than out		Degree of membership is more "in" than "out": $0.5 < X_i < 1$
			0.6 = more or less in	
	0.5 = neither fully in nor fully out			0.5 = cross-over: neither in nor out
			0.4 = more or less out	(maximum ambiguity)
		0.33 = more out than in		Degree of membership is more "out" than "in": $0 < X_i < 0.5$
			0.2 = mostly but not fully out	
0 = fully out	0 = fully out	0 = fully out	0 = fully out	0 = fully out

columns 1 and 2 of table 2.1). This three-value set is a rudimentary fuzzy set. A more elegant but still simple fuzzy set uses four numerical values, as shown in column 3 of table 2.1. The four-value scheme uses the numerical values 0.1, 0.67, 0.33, and 0.0 to indicate "fully in," "more in than out," "more out than in," and "fully out," respectively. The four-value scheme is especially useful in situations where researchers have a substantial amount of information about cases, but the evidence is not systematic or strictly comparable from case to case. A more fine-grained fuzzy set uses six values, as shown in column 4 of table 2.1. Like the four-value fuzzy set, the six-value fuzzy set utilizes two qualitative states (fully out and fully in). The six-value fuzzy set inserts two intermediate levels between fully out and the crossover point ("mostly out" = 0.2 and "more or less out" = 0.4) and two inter-mediate levels between the crossover point and fully in ("more or less in" = 0.6 and "mostly in" = 0.8).

At first glance, the four-value and six-value fuzzy sets might seem equivalent to ordinal scales. In fact, they are fundamentally different from such scales. An ordinal scale is a mere ranking of categories, usu-ally without reference to such criteria as set membership. When con-structing ordinal scales, researchers do not peg categories to degree of membership in sets; rather, the categories are simply arrayed relative to each other, yielding a rank order. For example, a researcher might develop a six-level ordinal scheme of country wealth, using categories that range from destitute to super rich. It is unlikely that this scheme would translate automatically to a six-value fuzzy set, with the lowest rank set to 0.0, the next rank to 0.2, and so on (as in column 4 of ta-ble 2.1). Assume the relevant fuzzy set is the set of rich countries. The lowest two ranks of the ordinal variable might both translate to fully out of the set of rich countries (fuzzy score = 0.0). The next rank up might translate to 0.3 rather than 0.2. The top two ranks might trans-late to fully in (fuzzy score = 1.0), and so on. In short, the specific translation of ordinal ranks to fuzzy membership scores depends on the fit between the specific content of the ordinal categories and the researcher's conceptualization and labeling of the fuzzy set. This point underscores the fact that researchers must use substantive and theo-retical knowledge to calibrate membership in fuzzy sets. Calibration of degree of membership in sets should be purposeful and thoughtful, never mechanical.[1]

Finally, a continuous fuzzy set permits cases to take values any-where in the interval from 0.0 to 1.0, as shown in the last column of table 2.1. The continuous fuzzy set, like all fuzzy sets, utilizes the two qualitative states (fully out and fully in) and also uses the crossover point to distinguish cases that are more out from those that are more in. As an example of a continuous fuzzy set, consider membership in

---

1. Specific techniques of fuzzy-set calibration are discussed in detail in chapter 5.

the set of rich countries, based on gross national product (GNP) per capita. The translation of this variable to fuzzy membership scores is neither automatic nor mechanical. It would be a serious mistake, for instance, to score the poorest country 0, score the richest country 1, and then array all the other countries between 0 and 1, depending on their positions in the range of GNP per capita values. Likewise, it would be a serious mistake to base fuzzy membership scores on the rank order of GNP per capita values. Instead, the first task in this translation would be to specify three important qualitative anchors: the point on the GNP per capita distribution at which full membership is reached (i.e., definitely a rich country), the point at which full nonmembership is reached (i.e., definitely not a rich country), and the point of maximum ambiguity in considering whether a country is more in or more out of the set of rich countries (a membership score of 0.5, the crossover point). When specifying these qualitative anchors, the investigator should have an explicit rationale for each breakpoint.

Qualitative anchors make it possible to distinguish between relevant and irrelevant variation. Variation in GNP per capita among the unambiguously rich countries is *not* relevant to degree of membership in the set of rich countries, at least from the perspective of fuzzy sets. If a country is unambiguously rich, then it is accorded full membership. Similarly, variation in GNP per capita among the unambiguously not-rich countries is also *not* relevant to membership in the set of rich countries. Thus, in research using fuzzy sets, it is not enough simply to develop scales that show the positions of cases relative to each other (e.g., a conventional index of country wealth such as GNP per capita). It is also necessary to use substantive and theoretical knowledge to map the links between specific scores on continuous variables (e.g., an index of wealth) and specific fuzzy-set membership scores (e.g., full membership in the set of rich countries). It follows that when a researcher reconceptualizes and relabels a set (e.g., shifting the focus from the set of rich countries to the set of "middle income countries"), the membership scores change accordingly, even though the underlying index variable (e.g., GNP per capita) may be the same.

Using Fuzzy Sets: The Basics

When using fuzzy sets to assess set-theoretic relations, both the outcome and the causal conditions can be represented in terms of membership scores.[2] Consider, for example, the first five columns of table 2.2, which show a simple data matrix containing fuzzy membership scores. This data set, which is used in the examples that follow, addresses class voting in the advanced industrial democracies. In this example, the outcome of interest is the degree of membership in the set of countries with weak class voting (**W**). This fuzzy set was constructed from survey evidence, compiled by Paul Nieuwbeerta (1995), covering the post–World War II era. While levels of class voting have generally declined across the advanced industrial countries, the rank order of these countries with regard to levels of class voting has remained relatively stable over time. This analysis focuses on the conditions linked to persistently low levels of class voting. The causal conditions used in this example are (1) degree of membership in the set of countries with strong unions (**U**), (2) degree of membership in the set of countries with a high percentage of workers employed in manufacturing (**M**), (3) degree of membership in the set of highly affluent countries (**A**), and (4) degree of membership in the set of countries with substantial income inequality (**I**). Strong unions and manufacturing employment tend to strengthen class voting, while affluence and inequality tend to undermine it. All fuzzy sets used in this analysis are six-value sets and are based on general characterizations of these countries over the post–World War II period. While finer gradations are possible with these data (as in column 5 of table 2.1), the intent here is to demonstrate operations on fuzzy sets with a simple data set.[3]

---

2. Crisp-set causal conditions can be included along with fuzzy-set causal conditions in a fuzzy-set analysis.

3. The primary goal here is to illustrate fuzzy-set principles. Accordingly, this presentation does not focus on how these fuzzy sets were calibrated or even on the issue of which causal conditions might provide the best possible specification of the social structural circumstances linked to persistently low levels of class voting. Instead, the focus is on practical procedures.

Table 2.2: Fuzzy-set data on class voting in the advanced industrial societies

Country	Weak class voting (W)	Affluent (A)	Income inequality (I)	Manufacturing (M)	Strong unions (U)	~M	A~M	A+~M
Australia	0.6	0.8	0.6	0.4	0.6	0.6	0.6	0.8
Belgium	0.6	0.6	0.2	0.2	0.8	0.8	0.6	0.8
Denmark	0.2	0.6	0.4	0.2	0.8	0.8	0.6	0.8
France	0.8	0.6	0.8	0.2	0.2	0.8	0.6	0.8
Germany	0.6	0.6	0.8	0.4	0.4	0.6	0.6	0.6
Ireland	0.8	0.2	0.6	0.8	0.8	0.2	0.2	0.2
Italy	0.6	0.4	0.8	0.2	0.6	0.8	0.4	0.8
Netherlands	0.8	0.6	0.4	0.2	0.4	0.8	0.6	0.8
Norway	0.2	0.6	0.4	0.6	0.8	0.4	0.4	0.6
Sweden	0.0	0.8	0.4	0.8	1.0	0.2	0.2	0.8
United Kingdom	0.4	0.6	0.6	0.8	0.6	0.2	0.2	0.6
United States	1.0	1.0	0.8	0.4	0.2	0.6	0.6	1.0

Three common operations on fuzzy sets are set negation, set intersection (logical *and*), and set union (logical *or*). The discussion of these three operations provides important background knowledge for understanding how to work with fuzzy sets.

Negation. Like conventional crisp sets, fuzzy sets can be negated. With crisp sets, negation switches membership scores from 1.0 to 0.0 and from 0.0 to 1.0. The negation of the crisp set of democracies, for example, is the crisp set of not-democracies. This simple mathematical principle holds in fuzzy algebra as well, but the relevant numerical values are not restricted to the two Boolean values 0.0 and 1.0; rather, they extend to values between 0.0 and 1.0. To calculate the membership of a case in the negation of fuzzy set **M**, simply subtract its membership in set **M** from 1.0, as follows:

(membership in set ~**M**) = 1.0 – (membership in set **M**)

or

$$\sim\!\mathbf{M} = 1.0 - \mathbf{M}$$

where ~ signals negation. Thus, for example, the United States has a membership score of 0.4 in the set of countries with high manufacturing employment; therefore, it has a score of 0.6 in the set of cases with not-high manufacturing employment. For further illustration, examine the sixth data column of table 2.2, which shows the negated membership scores of set **M** (high manufacturing employment) for all twelve countries. The negated set is labeled ~**M**, for not-high manufacturing employment.

Logical and. Compound sets are formed when two or more sets are combined, an operation commonly known as *set intersection*. A researcher interested in the fate of class voting in relatively inhospitable settings might want to draw up a list of countries that combine not-high manufacturing employment (~**M**) with "highly affluent" (**A**). Conventionally, these countries would be identified using crisp sets by cross-tabulating the two dichotomies (not-high versus high manufacturing employment and highly affluent versus not-highly affluent) and seeing which countries are in the not-high manufacturing/highly affluent cell of this 2 × 2 table. This cell, in effect, would show the cases that exist in the intersection of the two crisp sets.

With fuzzy sets, logical *and* is accomplished by taking the minimum membership score of each case in the sets that are combined. For example, if a country's membership in the set of countries with not-high manufacturing employment is 0.6 and its membership in the set of highly affluent countries is 1.0, its membership in the set of countries that combine these two traits is the lesser of these two scores, 0.6. A score of 0.6 indicates that this case is still more in than out of the intersection. For further illustration of this principle, consider the seventh data column of table 2.2, which demonstrates the operation of logical *and*. This column shows the intersection of the ~**M** (not-high manufacturing) and **A** (highly affluent) sets, yielding membership in the set of countries that combine these two traits. The algebraic expression for this intersection is **A·~M**; the midlevel dot is used to indicate set intersection (combinations of aspects).

Logical or. Two or more sets also can be joined through logical *or*—the union of sets. For example, a researcher might be interested in countries that have *either* not-high manufacturing employment (~**M**) or high affluence (**A**), based on the conjecture that these two conditions might offer equivalent, substitutable bases for some outcome (e.g., weak class voting, **W**). When using fuzzy sets, logical *or* directs the researcher's attention to the *maximum* of each case's memberships in the component sets. That is, a case's membership in the set formed from the *union* of two or more fuzzy sets is the maximum value of its memberships in the component sets. Thus, if a country has a score of 0.2 in the set of affluent countries and a score of 0.8 in the set of not-high manufacturing countries, it has a score of 0.8 in the set of countries that have *either* of these two traits. For illustration of the use of logical *or*, consider the eighth data column of table 2.2. This column shows countries that have either a not-high percentage of workers in manufacturing (~**M**) or high affluence (**A**); the algebraic expression is ~**M** + **A**, where the addition sign is used to indicate logical *or*.

Fuzzy-Set Relations

Chapter 1 presents my rationale for studying set relations in social research. Set relations reflect the explicit connections that are central to social science theorizing. Theory is largely verbal in nature; thus, set relations are central to social theory, just as they are to verbal statements in general. One of the great strengths of fuzzy sets is that they make set theoretic analysis possible while retaining fine-gained empirical gradations. In short, it is possible to determine if one set is a subset of another (e.g., do the developed countries constitute a subset of the democratic countries?) *without* reverting to nominal-scale measurement (i.e., crisp sets).

With crisp sets, determining whether the cases sharing a specific combination of conditions share the same outcome, and thus constitute a subset of the cases with the outcome, is a simple matter. (Recall that this is one of the two important types of explicit connections described in chapter 1.) The researcher simply examines cases sharing the relevant combination of conditions and assesses whether they agree in displaying the outcome. This assessment can be seen as an evaluation of the second column of the cross-tabulation of the presence/absence of the outcome in question against the presence/absence of a given combination of causal conditions (see table 2.3). The subset relation is indicated when the cell corresponding to the presence of the causal combination and the absence of the outcome is empty and the cell corresponding to the presence of the causal combination and the presence of the outcome is populated with cases.[4]

Obviously, these procedures cannot be duplicated with fuzzy sets. There is no simple way to isolate the cases sharing a specific combination of causal conditions because each case's array of membership scores may be unique. Cases also have different degrees of membership in the outcome, complicating the assessment of whether they "agree" on the outcome. While these properties of fuzzy sets make

---

4. Of course, cell 4 may not be completely empty. In case-oriented research, however, the researcher should be able to explain the errant cases that may find their way into cell 4.

Table 2.3: Crisp-set assessment of the connection between a combination of causal conditions and an outcome (causal combination is a subset of the outcome)

	Causal combination absent	Causal combination present
Outcome present	cell 1: not directly relevant to the assessment	cell 2: cases here support researcher's argument that this is a connection
Outcome absent	cell 3: not directly relevant to the assessment	cell 4: should be empty or nearly empty; cases here undermine argument

it difficult to duplicate crisp-set procedures for assessing subset relationships, the fuzzy subset relation can be assessed using fuzzy algebra. With fuzzy sets, a subset relation is indicated when membership scores in one set (e.g., a causal condition or combination of causal conditions) are consistently less than or equal to their corresponding membership scores in another set (e.g., the outcome).

For illustration, consider the data listed in table 2.4 and plotted in figure 2.1. Table 2.4 shows membership scores in two fuzzy sets, the set of countries with weak class voting (W) and the set of countries lacking strong unions ($\sim U$), using data from table 2.2. Observe that the weak class voting membership scores are consistently greater than or equal to not-strong unions scores. This pattern is consistent with the fuzzy subset relation. If membership in the causal condition is high, then membership in the outcome also must be high. Note, however, that the reverse does not have to be true. That is, the fact that there are cases with relatively low membership in the causal condition but substantial membership in the outcome (e.g., Ireland and Belgium) is not problematic from the viewpoint of set theory because the expectation is that there may be several different ways to generate high membership in the outcome (i.e., there are causal pathways to weak class voting in addition to the one illustrated). Cases with low scores in the causal condition (or combination of conditions) but high scores in the outcome indicate the operation of alternate causal conditions or alternate combinations of causal conditions.

Table 2.4: Illustration of fuzzy subset relation (~U ≤ W)

Country	Weak class voting (W)	Not-strong unions (~U)
Australia	0.6	0.4
Belgium	0.6	0.2
Denmark	0.2	0.2
France	0.8	0.8
Germany	0.6	0.6
Ireland	0.8	0.2
Italy	0.6	0.4
Netherlands	0.8	0.6
Norway	0.2	0.2
Sweden	0	0
United Kingdom	0.4	0.4
United States	1	0.8

Figure 2.1 illustrates the fuzzy subset relation using the membership scores from table 2.4. The characteristic upper-left triangular plot indicates that the set plotted on the horizontal axis (not-strong unions, ~**U**) is a subset of the set plotted on the vertical axis (weak class voting, **W**). The points in the upper-left region of the plot are not "errors," as they would be regarded in a linear regression analysis. Rather, these points have strong membership in the outcome due to the operation of other causal conditions or other combinations of causal conditions. The vacant lower triangle in this plot of fuzzy sets corresponds to empty cell 4 of table 2.3, which uses crisp sets. Just as cases in cell 4 of table 2.3 would violate the crisp subset relation, cases in the lower-right triangle of figure 2.1 would violate the fuzzy subset relation.

Table 2.4 and figure 2.1 illustrate the fuzzy subset relation using a single causal condition. Note, however, that this same assessment could have been conducted using degree of membership in a *combination* of causal conditions. As noted previously, in order to compute a case's degree of membership in a combination of conditions, it is necessarily simply to use the lowest (minimum) membership score among the causal conditions, which follows from the application of fuzzy algebra's logical *and* operation. Degree of membership in a causal combination can then be used to assess the fuzzy subset relation by comparing scores in the causal combination (horizontal axis) with membership scores in the outcome (vertical axis). This examination establishes whether degree of membership in a combination of causal conditions is a fuzzy subset of degree of membership in the outcome, a pattern of results consistent with an argument of sufficient causation (Ragin 2000). An upper-left triangular plot, with degree of membership in the causal combination on the horizontal axis and degree of membership in the outcome on the vertical axis, signals the fuzzy subset relation. (See especially chapter 6 for an in-depth examination of the study of configurations of set memberships.)

Recall several of the main points about set relations in social research presented in chapter 1, namely (1) set relations often involve causal or other integral connections between social phenomena, (2) they are fundamentally asymmetric, and (3) they can be strong despite relatively weak correlations. Consider the statement, "Among the advanced industrial democracies, those lacking strong unions have weak

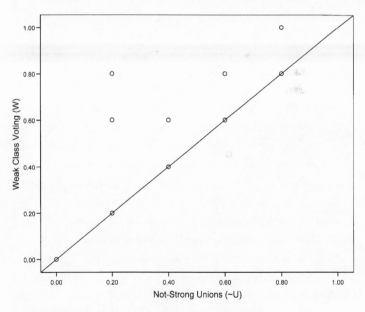

Figure 2.1 Plot of fuzzy sets showing subset relationship

class voting." The statement hypothesizes an explicit link from weak unions to weak class voting. Like many such statements, it lists the subset first (weak class voting) and claims, in essence, that the set of countries with weak unions constitutes a subset of the countries with weak class voting. The statement is fundamentally asymmetric. It does not claim that countries with *strong* unions are somehow barred or prevented from having weak class voting, and thus it leaves open the possibility that other obstacles to class voting may exist. Such evidence does not directly challenge the claim that there is a path through weak unions. Finally, from a set-theoretic viewpoint, the evidence presented is *perfectly* consistent with the set-theoretic claim: all cases are in the upper-left triangle of the plot. From a correlational viewpoint, however, the evidence is imperfect, as indicated in the scatter of the points (Pearson's $r = .766$).

Looking Ahead

Chapter 3 presents two simple descriptive measures for evaluating set theoretic connections, such as the one shown in figure 2.1. Specifically, chapter 3 demonstrates that it is possible to assess both the degree to which empirical evidence is consistent with the claim that a set-theoretic connection exists and the empirical importance or relevance of that connection.

Practical Appendix: Fuzzy-Set Relations

Fuzzy-set relations are easy to spot using simple XY plots of fuzzy membership scores. In general, triangular plots, with points consistently above or consistently below either diagonal of the plot, signal a fuzzy subset relation of some sort. Fuzzy-set qualitative comparative analysis (fsQCA) includes facilities for plotting fuzzy-set relations.

1. Create a data set with fuzzy membership scores. Fuzzy membership scores can be assigned, or they can be computed using the procedures detailed in chapters 4 and 5. Data can be entered directly into fsQCA or imported into fsQCA as comma-delimited files (e.g.,

from Excel) or tab-delimited files (e.g., from SPSS). Simple variable names should appear on the first line of the data set (see chapter 1, Practical Appendix).

2. Once the data set is visible in the data spreadsheet window of fsQCA, click *Graphs,* then *Fuzzy,* then *XY Plot.* Specify the fuzzy sets to be plotted on the X and Y axes by clicking the adjacent down arrows and then clicking the relevant variable names. It is also possible to negate fuzzy sets before plotting them; click the *Negate* box next to the variable name. Specify an optional *case Id variable* so that the case or cases that reside on specific points in the plot can be readily identified.

3. Click *Plot.* Examine the pattern. Click on any point in the plot, and its information will appear at the bottom of the plot.

4. The numbers shown in the boxes above the upper-left corner and below the lower-right corner of the plot are consistency and coverage scores, which are explained in chapter 3.

3: Evaluating Set Relations
Consistency and Coverage

This chapter presents simple descriptive measures for evaluating the strength of the empirical support for arguments specifying set-theoretic connections. To structure the presentation, I focus primarily on arguments stating that a specific cause or combination of causal conditions constitutes one of several possible paths to an outcome (see discussion of explicit connections in chapter 1). When this is true, cases displaying a specified causal combination should constitute a subset of the cases displaying the outcome, as illustrated in chapter 2. I present measures for assessing two distinct aspects of set-theoretic connections. Set-theoretic *consistency* gauges the degree to which the cases sharing a given combination of conditions (e.g., democratic dyad) agree in displaying the outcome in question (e.g., peaceful coexistence). That is, consistency indicates how closely a perfect subset relation is approximated. Set-theoretic *coverage,* by contrast, assesses the degree to which a cause or causal combination "accounts for" instances of an outcome. When there are several paths to the same outcome, the coverage of a given causal combination may be small. Thus, coverage gauges empirical relevance or importance.

These same measures can be used to evaluate situations where the researcher suspects that a causal condition is necessary (but not sufficient) for an outcome, that is, where instances of an outcome constitute a subset of instances of a cause. (This set relation is the other type of explicit connection discussed in chapter 1.) In this context, *consistency* assesses the degree to which instances of the outcome agree in displaying the causal condition thought to be necessary, while *cover-*

age assesses the relevance of the necessary condition—the degree to which instances of the condition are paired with instances of the outcome. This discussion of necessary conditions builds on the work of Goertz (2002, 2003), Goertz and Starr (2002), and Braumoeller and Goertz (2000).

These assessments of set relations are important in the analysis of explicit connections in the same way that assessments of significance and strength are important in the analysis of correlational connections. Consistency, like significance, signals whether an empirical connection merits the close attention of the investigator. If a hypothesized subset relation is not consistent, then the researcher's theory or conjecture is not supported. Coverage, like strength, indicates the empirical relevance or importance of a set-theoretic connection. As shown in this chapter, just as it is possible in correlational analysis to have a significant but weak correlation, it is possible in set-theoretic analysis to have a set relation that is highly consistent but low in coverage. I argue here and show in subsequent chapters that these set-theoretic measures provide vital tools for refining both crisp-set and fuzzy-set analysis in social research.

Set-Theoretic Consistency

Perfectly consistent set relations are relatively rare in social research. They usually require either small Ns or macrolevel data or both. Generally, social scientists are able to identify only rough subset relations because exceptions are almost always present (e.g., a war between two democratic countries). It is important, therefore, to develop useful descriptive measures of the degree to which a set relation has been approximated, that is, the degree to which the evidence is consistent with the argument that a set relation exists. First, the chapter addresses the evaluation of the consistency of crisp-set relations, where a very simple measure suffices, and then turns to fuzzy sets.

When conducting consistency evaluations, it is prudent to take the number of cases into account. Perfect consistency does not guarantee that a meaningful set-theoretic connection exists. Suppose, for example, that all three third-wave democracies that adopted parliamentary governments subsequently failed. The prudent conclusion would be that this connection, while interesting and perfectly consistent from a set-theoretic viewpoint, might well be happenstance (see also Dion 1998; Ragin 2000). Most social scientists would be more convinced of an explicit connection between parliamentary government and failure if the tally was, say, seventeen out of twenty, instead of three out of three. This example also underscores the fact that "close counts" in social science. While not 100 percent, a rate of 17 out of 20 (85 percent) is substantial enough to indicate, to a social scientist at least, that some sort of integral connection may exist that is worthy of further investigation.

This example suggests a straightforward measure of the consistency of set relations using crisp sets: the proportion of cases with a given cause or combination of causes that also display the outcome. With three out of three cases consistent, the proportion is 1.0; with seventeen out of twenty cases consistent, the proportion is 0.85. As explained in *Fuzzy-Set Social Science* (Ragin 2000), the N of cases can be taken into account by using benchmarks and an exact probability test. For example, with three cases, a proportion consistent of 1.0 is not significantly greater than a benchmark proportion of 0.65, using a significance level (alpha) of 0.05. However, a proportion of 0.85 with an N of 20 passes this test. In general, consistency scores should be as close to 1.0 (perfect consistency) as possible. When observed consistency scores are below 0.75, maintaining on substantive grounds that a set relation exists, even a very rough one, becomes increasingly difficult (see also Ragin 2004a).

The assessment of the consistency of *fuzzy-set* relations is more interesting and more challenging than that of the crisp-set case. An overview of the use of fuzzy sets in social research is presented in *Fuzzy-Set Social Science* (Ragin 2000; see also Smithson and Verkuilen 2006, and chapter 2 of this book). The key point for present purposes is that with fuzzy sets, cases can have varying degrees of membership in sets, with membership scores ranging from 0.0 to 1.0. For example, a country might have only partial membership in the set of democracies. The calibration of degree of membership in a fuzzy set involves both quantitative and qualitative assessment and must be grounded in theoretical and substantive knowledge (Ragin 2000; Smithson and Verkuilen 2006; see also chapters 4 and 5 of this book).

As explained in chapter 2, a fuzzy subset relation exists when the membership scores in one set are consistently less than or equal to their corresponding membership scores in another. For example, if degree of membership in "parliamentary form of government" is consistently less than or equal to degree of membership in "failure of democracy" across relevant third-wave democracies, then the former is a subset of the latter. Recall that with crisp sets, it does not matter that instances of failure exist that are not also instances of parliamentary government because there are (hypothetically) many ways to fail (see table 1.2). With fuzzy sets, the parallel situation occurs when cases display outcome membership scores that greatly exceed their membership scores in the causal condition. For example, a case might have a score of 0.90 in failure but a score of only 0.20 in parliamentary government. As in the crisp analysis, this case is not inconsistent with the set-theoretic argument because there may be several ways to fail, including paths for countries with weak membership in the set of countries with parliamentary governments. By contrast, a country with a membership score of 0.80 in parliamentary government but a membership of only 0.30 in failure clearly contradicts the set-theoretic claim.

The fuzzy subset relation has a triangular form when depicted as a plot of two fuzzy sets, as shown in figure 3.1. In this figure, the causal condition (X) is a subset of the outcome (Y); thus, all X_i values are less than or equal to their corresponding Y_i values, where i indicates reference to individual X or Y values or specific observations of X or Y. Note that cases in the upper-left corner of the plot do not contradict the idea that this cause may be sufficient but not necessary for the outcome, because these cases have high membership in the outcome due to the operation of causal conditions other than X (an argument of sufficiency without necessity permits multiple paths). Thus, when membership in X is low, a wide range of Y_i values is permissible. When membership in X is high, however, many more opportunities may be

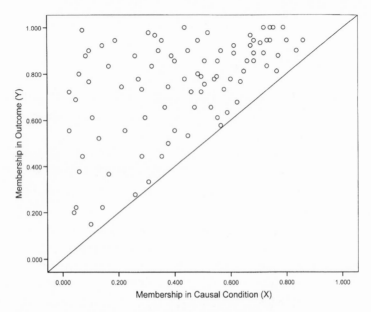

Figure 3.1 Fuzzy subset relation consistent with sufficiency

present to violate the subset relation, as the range of permissible Y_i values narrows. Of course, in a conventional correlational analysis, points in the upper-left corner would be considered errors, which in turn would undermine the correlation between **X** and **Y**.

In *Fuzzy-Set Social Science* (Ragin 2000), the definition of the consistency of a fuzzy-set relation is straightforward but simplistic. In the plot of membership in the outcome (**Y**) against membership in a causal condition or combination of causal conditions (**X**), *consistency* is defined as the proportion of cases on or above the main diagonal of the plot. If membership in **X** is consistently less than or equal to membership in **Y**, then all the cases will plot on or above the main diagonal, yielding a consistency score of 1.0 (or 100 percent consistent). In the "fuzzy inclusion" algorithm described in Ragin (2000), consistency scores are computed for different combinations of causal conditions, and these scores provide the basis for evaluating sufficiency (see Ragin, Drass, and Davey 2007; Ragin 2007). For example, if significantly greater than 80 percent of the cases plot on or above the main diagonal in the plot just described, then the investigator might claim that the cause or causal combination X is "almost always" sufficient for the outcome Y.

The procedures presented in *Fuzzy-Set Social Science* for the evaluation of the sufficiency of causal combinations are based on the simple categorization of cases as either consistent or inconsistent and the computation of the simple proportion of consistent cases. In short, the procedures closely follow the crisp-set template. One issue in the use of this procedure concerns the contrast between cases with strong versus weak membership in the causal condition or combination of causal conditions (X). Specifically, cases with strong and weak membership in the causal combination are weighted equally in the calculation, yet they differ substantially in their relevance to the set-theoretic claim and thus to the argument that X is sufficient for Y. For example, a case with a membership of only 0.25 in the set of cases with the causal combination (X) and a score of 0.0 in the outcome set (Y) is just as inconsistent as a case with a score of 1.0 in the causal combination and a score of 0.75 in the outcome. (A membership score of 0.25 indicates that a case is more out than in a set; 0.5 is the crossover point.) In fact, however, the second inconsistent case, with full membership in X, clearly has more bearing on the set-theoretic argument because it is a much better instance of the causal combination. It thus constitutes a more glaring inconsistency than the first case despite the equal gaps—the X_i values exceed the Y_i values by the same amount.

The same reasoning holds for consistent cases. A consistent case with two high membership scores (e.g., 0.9 in the causal combination and 1.0 in the outcome) is clearly more relevant to the set-theoretic argument than a consistent case with two low scores (e.g., 0.1 in the causal combination and 0.2 in the outcome) or a consistent case with a low score in the causal combination (say, 0.15) and a high score in the outcome (say, 0.8). Yet all are counted equally in the formula for consistency used in Ragin (2000) (the proportion of cases on or above the main diagonal in the fuzzy plot). Imagine trying to support an argument in an oral presentation to colleagues using in-depth evidence on a case with only weak membership in the relevant sets. The common-sense thinking that indicates that this presentation would be a waste of time is precisely formalized in fuzzy membership scores. Cases with strong membership in the causal condition provide the most relevant consistent cases and the most relevant inconsistent cases.

This commonsense idea is operationalized in the alternate measure of the consistency of fuzzy-set data with set-theoretic arguments recommended in this chapter. This alternate procedure, like the one proposed in Ragin (2000), differentiates between consistent and inconsistent cases using the diagonal of the plot. A case on or above the main diagonal is consistent because its membership in the causal condition is less than or equal to its membership in the outcome. A case below the main diagonal is inconsistent because its membership in the causal condition is greater than its membership in the outcome. However, rather than simply calculating the raw proportion of consistent cases, the alternate procedure uses fuzzy membership scores.

Consider, for example, the hypothetical fuzzy-set data on degree of membership in "strong left parties" and "generous welfare states" for twelve advanced industrial countries in table 3.1. Notice that the data in this table are perfectly consistent from a set-theoretic viewpoint; that is, all the membership scores in the causal condition are less than or equal to their corresponding membership scores in the outcome (see chapter 2). Based on this evidence, a researcher could claim that this causal condition (having strong left parties) is a subset of the outcome (having generous welfare states). Thus, having strong left parties could be interpreted (hypothetically, with these data) as a sufficient condition for having a generous welfare states. As previously noted, however, social science data are rarely this uniform. When cases are inconsistent with the subset relation, the researcher must assess the *degree* to which the empirical evidence is consistent with the set relation in question. For example, suppose the score for strong left parties in the first row of table 3.1 was 1.0 instead of 0.70. It would be inconsistent with the set relation because this value exceeds the corresponding outcome membership score, 0.90. While the set relation would no longer hold consistently across the cases listed in table 3.1, it would

Table 3.1: Illustration of a simple fuzzy-subset relation (hypothetical data for twelve countries)

Strong left parties	Generous welfare states
0.7	0.9
0.1	0.9
0.1	0.1
0.3	0.3
0.9	0.9
0.7	0.7
0.3	0.9
0.3	0.7
0.3	0.7
0.1	0.1
0.0	0.0
0.9	1.0

still be very close to perfectly consistent, with eleven out of the twelve cases consistent and only one near miss.

One straightforward measure of set-theoretic consistency using fuzzy membership scores is the sum of the *consistent* membership scores in a causal condition or combination of causal conditions divided by the sum of *all* the membership scores in a cause or causal combination (Ragin 2003b). In table 3.1, the value of this measure is 1.0 (4.7/4.7) because all the membership scores in column 1 are consistent. If the score for strong left parties in the first row of table 3.1 is changed to 1.0, however, consistency drops to 0.8 (4/5). The numerator is 1.0 fuzzy unit lower than the denominator because of the one inconsistent score of 1.0. The reduction of consistency to 0.8 (from perfect consistency, 1.0) is substantial because 1.0 (the value substituted for 0.70 in the first row) is a large membership score.

This consistency measure can be refined further so that it gives credit for near misses and penalties for causal membership scores that exceed their marks, the corresponding outcome membership scores, by wide margins.[1] This adjustment can be accomplished by adding to

---

1. The formula described here is the one implemented in the fuzzy-truth table algorithm of fsQCA (Ragin, Drass, and Davey 2007).

the numerator in the formula just sketched (the sum of the consistent scores divided by the sum of all membership scores in the cause or causal combination) the part of each *inconsistent* causal membership score that is consistent with the outcome. For example, if the score for strong left parties in the first row of table 3.1 is changed to 1.0, then most of its score is consistent, up to the value of the outcome membership score, 0.90. This portion is added to the numerator of the consistency measure. Using this more refined measure of consistency yields an overall consistency score of 0.98 (4.9/5). This adjusted consistency score is more compatible with the evidence. After all, only one of the scores is inconsistent, and it is a very near miss. Thus, a consistency score close to 1.0 should be expected.

Notice that the revised measure of consistency prescribes substantial penalties for *large* inconsistencies. Suppose again that the score for strong left parties in the first row of table 3.1 is 1.0, but this time assume that the corresponding value of the outcome, generous welfare states, is only 0.3. The consistent portion of the 1.0 membership score is 0.3, yielding an overall addition of only 0.3 to the numerator. The resulting consistency score in this instance would be 0.86 (4.3/5). This lower score reflects the fact that the one inconsistent score exceeds its target by a wide margin.

It is possible to formalize the calculation of fuzzy set–theoretic consistency as follows:

$$\text{Consistency } (X_i \leq Y_i) = \Sigma[\min(X_i, Y_i)]/\Sigma(X_i)$$

where min indicates the selection of the lower of the two values (see also Kosko 1993; Smithson and Verkuilen 2006). When the X_i values are all less than or equal to their corresponding Y_i values, the consistency score is 1.0; when there are only a few near misses, the score is slightly less than 1.0; when there are many inconsistent scores, with some X_i values greatly exceeding their corresponding Y_i values, consistency may drop below 0.5. Note that the same procedures for incorporating probabilistic criteria, mentioned above and discussed in detail in Ragin (2000), can be applied here. These probabilistic tests require a benchmark value (e.g., 0.75 consistency) and an alpha level (e.g., 0.05 significance). Finally, when the formula for the calculation of fuzzy set–theoretic consistency is applied to crisp-set data, it returns the simple proportion of consistent cases. Thus, the formula can be applied to crisp and fuzzy membership scores alike.

This same general formula also can be applied to the assessment of the consistency of a set relation indicating that a causal condition is a necessary condition for an outcome. An argument of causal necessity is supported when it can be demonstrated that instances of an outcome constitute a subset of instances of a causal condition. With fuzzy sets, the consistency of the necessary condition relationship depends on the degree to which it can be shown that membership in the outcome is consistently less than or equal to membership in the cause, $Y_i \leq X_i$. Figure 3.2 illustrates this fuzzy-set relation. In this figure, the outcome (Y) is a subset of the causal condition (X); thus, all Y_i values are less than or equal to their corresponding X_i values. Note that cases in the lower-right corner of the plot do not contradict necessity, for these are cases that have low membership in the outcome because they lack some other, unspecified causal condition. After all, the causal condition in this example is only necessary, not sufficient. Of course, in a conventional correlational analysis, cases in the lower-right corner would be considered errors, which in turn would undermine the correlation between X and Y. Note, however, that when membership in X is low, membership in Y also must be low. Thus, in the low range of X, many opportunities exist to violate the subset relation, with only a narrow range of permissible Y_i values.

Because the inequality signaling necessity ($Y_i \leq X_i$) is the reverse of the inequality that defines sufficiency ($X_i \leq Y_i$), a simple measure of the consistency of the subset relationship for a necessary condition is:

$$\text{Consistency } (Y_i \leq X_i) = \Sigma[\min(X_i, Y_i)]/\Sigma(Y_i)$$

When all Y_i values are less than or equal to their corresponding X_i values, this formula returns a value of 1.0. When many Y_i exceed their corresponding X_i values by wide margins, the computation returns a value less than 0.5.

Of course, it is important to remember that the interpretation of any set-theoretic relation as either necessary or sufficient must be built on a solid foundation of theoretical and substantive knowledge. Causal

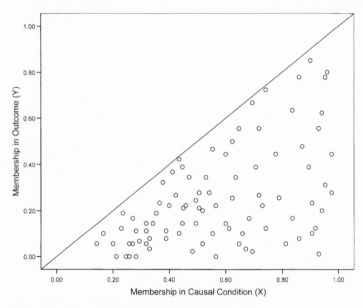

Figure 3.2 Fuzzy subset relation consistent with necessity

connections are not inherent in data. Set-theoretic consistency is only one piece of evidence in the array of support that must be brought to bear when a researcher makes a claim of either sufficiency or necessity or any other kind of causal or constitutive connection.

Set-Theoretic Coverage

When researchers allow for equifinality (Mackie 1965; George 1979; George and Bennett 2005) and causal complexity (Ragin 1987), a common finding is that a given outcome may result from several different combinations of conditions. These combinations are generally understood as alternate causal paths or "recipes" for the outcome. Usually, these alternate paths are treated as logically equivalent (i.e., as substitutable). However, it is common in crisp-set analyses to assess the proportion of cases following each path—that is, the number of cases following a specific path to the outcome divided by the total number of instances of the outcome. This simple proportion is a direct measure of set-theoretic coverage and is a straightforward indicator of the empirical importance of a causal combination. Clearly, a causal combination that covers or accounts for only a small proportion of the instances of an outcome is not as empirically important as one that covers a large proportion.[2]

Coverage is distinct from consistency, and the two sometimes work against each other because high consistency may yield low coverage. Complex set-theoretic arguments involving the intersection of many sets can achieve remarkable consistency but low coverage. For example, consider the adults in the United States who combine excellent school records, high achievement test scores, college-educated parents, high parental income, graduation from Ivy League universities, and so on. It would not be surprising to learn that 100 percent of these individuals are able to avoid poverty. Perfect set-theoretic consistency is unusual with individual-level data, but it is certainly not impossible. There are, however, relatively few individuals with this specific combination of highly favorable circumstances among the many who successfully avoid poverty. From a practical viewpoint, therefore, this high level of set-theoretic consistency is not compelling because the causal combination is so narrowly formulated that its coverage is trivial.

While there is often a trade-off between consistency and coverage, it is reasonable to calculate coverage *only after establishing that a set relation is consistent.* It is pointless to compute the coverage of a cause or combination of causes that is not a consistent subset of the outcome. Also, as will become clear in the discussion that follows, the same set-theoretic calculation has different meanings, depending on the context of the calculation. Thus, it is important to adhere to the protocol described here for the results of assessments of consistency and coverage

---

2. Note that coverage gauges only empirical importance, not theoretical importance. A sufficient relation may be quite "rare" from an empirical point of view (and thus exhibit low coverage), but it still could be centrally relevant to theory. For example, the sufficient relation might be proof that a path that was thought to be empirically impossible, at least from the perspective of theory, in fact is not.

to be meaningful: set-theoretic consistency must be established before coverage can be assessed.

For illustration of the general idea of coverage, consider table 3.2, which shows a hypothetical cross-tabulation of poverty status (in poverty versus not-in poverty) against educational achievement (high versus not-high), using crisp sets and individual-level data. This crude analysis using binary data supports the argument that individuals with high educational achievement are able to avoid poverty. This set-theoretic argument is supported by the high proportion of cases in the second column that are not in poverty (cell b divided by the sum of cells b and d yields a consistency score of 0.964). But how important is this path when it comes to avoiding poverty? The simplest way to answer this question is to calculate the proportion of the individuals not in poverty who have high educational achievement—that is, cell b divided by the sum of cells a and b, which is 0.326. This calculation shows that the path in question covers almost a third of the cases not in poverty, which is substantial.

For comparison purposes, consider table 3.3, which has the same total number of cases as table 3.2, but some of the cases have been shifted from cell b to cell a and from cell d to cell c. The proportion of cases consistent with the set-theoretic argument in table 3.3 is 0.967, about the same as in table 3.2 (0.964). Thus, from a set-theoretic point of view, the evidence is again highly consistent. But how important is this path, using the hypothetical frequencies presented in table 3.3? Its importance can be ascertained by computing the proportion of cases avoiding poverty that are covered by the set-theoretic argument, which is only 0.0325 (147/4,520). Thus, in table 3.3 the set-theoretic pattern is again highly consistent, but coverage is very low, indicating

Table 3.2: Cross-tabulation of poverty status and educational achievement: preliminary frequencies

	Low/average educational achievement	High educational achievement
Not-in poverty	a. 3,046	b. 1,474
In poverty	c. 625	d. 55

Table 3.3: Cross-tabulation of poverty status and educational achievement: altered frequencies

	Low/average educational achievement	High educational achievement
Not-in poverty	a. 4,373	b. 147
In poverty	c. 675	d. 5

(hypothetically) that having high educational achievement is not an important path to the outcome, avoiding poverty.

The procedures for calculating set-theoretic coverage using fuzzy sets parallel the computations for crisp sets presented above. Another way to understand the calculation of coverage using conventional crisp sets (cell b divided by the sum of cells a and b) is to visualize table 3.2 as a Venn diagram showing a subset relationship, as in figure 3.3. The basic idea behind the calculation of coverage is to assess the degree to which the subset (the set of cases with high educational achievement in this example) physically covers the larger set (the set of cases avoiding poverty). Thus, *coverage,* a gauge of empirical weight or importance, can be seen as the size of the overlap of the two sets relative to the size of the larger set (representing the outcome). The calculation of the size of the overlap of two fuzzy sets is given by their intersection:

$$\text{Overlap} = \Sigma[\min(X_i, Y_i)]$$

which is the same as the numerator in the calculation of fuzzy set–theoretic *consistency* described previously. With fuzzy sets, the size of the larger set (the relevant denominator) is given directly by the sum of the membership scores in that set, that is, the sum of the membership scores in the outcome, $\Sigma(Y_i)$. This calculation parallels the simple counting of the number of cases in a set (e.g., the number of cases not in poverty) using crisp sets. Thus, the measure of fuzzy-set coverage is simply the overlap expressed as a proportion of the sum of the membership scores in the outcome:

$$\text{Coverage } (X_i \leq Y_i) = \Sigma[\min(X_i, Y_i)]/\Sigma(Y_i)$$

In short, the formula for coverage of Y by X substitutes $\Sigma(Y_i)$ for $\Sigma(X_i)$ in the denominator of the formula for consistency.

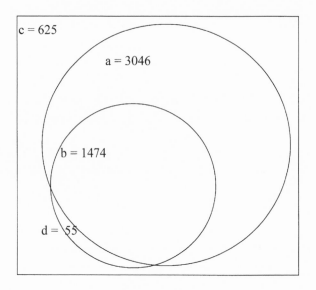

Area a =	Cases with low/average educational achievement, not in poverty
Area b =	Cases with high educational achievement, not in poverty
Area c =	Cases with low/average educational achievement, in poverty
Area d =	Cases with high educational achievement, in poverty

Figure 3.3 Venn diagram illustrating concept of coverage using hypothetical data (from table 3.2)

Observe that this formula is identical to the formula for the *consistency* of **Y** as a subset of **X** (i.e., $Y_i \leq X_i$), presented in the discussion of the assessment of the consistency of a necessary conditions relationship. Recall, however, that in the present context (assessing sufficiency), the coverage of **Y** by **X** (i.e., as in the equation above) is calculated *only after* it has been established that **X** is a consistent subset of **Y**. Thus, the purpose of the calculation in the context of sufficiency is to assess the magnitude of X relative to Y, given that most, if not all, X_i values are less than or equal to their corresponding Y_i values. In the necessary-conditions context, by contrast, the goal is to assess the consistency of Y as a subset of X. Thus, in that context the expectation is that most, if not all, Y_i values will be less than or equal to their corresponding X_i values—indicating a necessary-conditions relationship. Indeed, if this is not the case, then the result of the calculation will be a consistency score (for $Y_i \leq X_i$) that falls far short of perfect consistency (i.e., substantially less than 1.0), indicating that Y is *not* a consistent subset of X.[3] In short, context must be taken into account when conducting these assessments.

Figure 3.4 depicts the concept of coverage relevant to the fuzzy subset relation, with $X_i \leq Y_i$. As in figure 3.1, condition X is a subset of outcome Y. Points below the main diagonal constitute violations of consistency and thus undermine the argument that X is a subset of Y. However, there are only two such points, and the subset relationship is largely consistent. When calculating coverage, only the portion of the X_i score that is above the main diagonal is counted as consistent (and thus included as part of the overlap between X and Y). Most of the points in figure 3.4 are above the main diagonal and thus consistent with $X_i \leq Y_i$. When X_i values are small relative to their corresponding Y_i values, they are closer to the Y axis than they are to the main diagonal. While these points are consistent with the subset relation $X_i \leq Y_i$, they contribute relatively little to coverage, especially when the Y_i values are above 0.5. The dotted horizontal lines in the figure show the portions of the X_i values counted as consistent; these values are

---

3. It follows that it is possible to find a $\Sigma[\min(X_i,Y_i)]$ that is close to $\Sigma(Y_i)$—thus yielding a very high coverage score—only if the values of X_i are roughly equal to their corresponding Y_i values. This situation would correspond to a close *coincidence* of the two sets. Set coincidence is not the same as correlation, but rather is a special case of correlation. In a plot of two fuzzy sets, any straight line that is neither vertical nor horizontal yields a perfect correlation coefficient. However, perfect set coincidence occurs only when all the cases plot exactly on the main diagonal of the fuzzy plot. A simple measure of the degree to which the membership scores in two sets coincide is $\Sigma[\min(X_i,Y_i)]/\Sigma[\max(X_i,Y_i)]$, where max indicates using the larger of the two scores. See also Smithson and Verkuilen (2006), who contrast comorbidity, covariation, and co-occurrence.

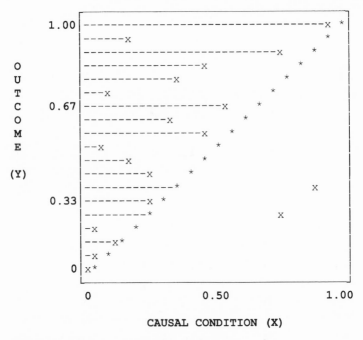

Figure 3.4 Illustration of the concept of coverage

added to the numerator of the formula for coverage. The denominator is the sum of the Y_i values. The gaps from the consistent X_i values to the main diagonal show the part of set **Y** that is *not* covered by set **X**.

The calculation of coverage also can be applied to the assessment of necessary conditions, where the outcome is a subset of the cause. Goertz (2003, 2006), building on Braumoeller and Goertz (2000), presents an approach to the assessment of necessary conditions that addresses some of the same issues discussed in this chapter. A key focus in his work is the distinction between trivial and nontrivial necessary conditions. A trivial necessary condition is one that is strongly present in most cases, whether or not these cases display the outcome. For example, "grievances" may be a necessary condition for the organization and activation of a social movement, but grievances are almost always present, and the absence of grievances rarely gets the chance to act in a constraining manner on social movement organization. Thus, the existence of grievances could be seen as an empirically trivial necessary condition. By contrast, an open and permissive political climate (i.e., the absence of government repression) could be seen as a nontrivial necessary condition, for social movements routinely encounter government repression. While the specific computational formula recommended in this chapter for assessing the relevance of necessary conditions differs in its details from the one suggested by Goertz (2003, 2006), the underlying goals are similar.[4]

A simple measure of the importance or relevance of **X** as a necessary condition for **Y** is given by the degree of coverage of **X** by **Y**:

$$\text{Coverage } (Y_i \leq X_i) = \Sigma[\min(X_i, Y_i)]/\Sigma(X_i)$$

When the coverage of **X** by **Y** is small, the constraining effect of **X** on **Y** is negligible. Conceptually, very low coverage corresponds to an empirically irrelevant or even meaningless necessary condition. For example, almost all heroine addicts in the United States are former milk drinkers, but it would be difficult to portray milk drinking as a relevant necessary condition (i.e., as a gateway substance) for heroine addiction because the set of former milk drinkers completely dwarfs the set of heroine addicts. By contrast, when the coverage of **X** by **Y** is substantial, then the constraining effect of **X** as a necessary condition may be great. For example, if a substantial proportion of people who associate with heroine addicts later become addicts and only a very small number of people become addicted to heroine without first associating with heroine addicts, then coverage is high and "associating with heroine addicts" may be considered a relevant necessary condition for heroine addiction.

The contrast between these two situations, high versus low relevance in the analysis of necessary conditions, is depicted in figure 3.5.

---

4. In Goertz's (2003, 2006) approach, membership scores are divided at the case level, and then these ratios are averaged. In effect, this procedure assigns cases equal importance in the computation of a given measure. In the approach advocated here, however, cases with low fuzzy membership scores are given less weight because they are weak instances of the phenomenon in question. This computational strategy makes the resulting measures more reflective of patterns observed in the best instances.

Figure 3.5(a) depicts a necessary condition that exerts some constraint on the outcome (coverage is nontrivial). Figure 3.5(b) depicts an empirically trivial necessary condition (very low set-theoretic coverage). Using fuzzy sets, the situation depicted in figure 3.5(b) would appear as a plot in which almost all cases have very strong membership in X (the causal condition) and thus would plot to the far right (see also Goertz 2003, 2006).

As with the assessment of the coverage of a sufficient condition, it is important to assess the relevance of a necessary condition (i.e., its constraining impact) *only after* establishing that the subset relation is consistent. That is, it must first be established that Y is a consistent subset

a. Empirically Relevant Necessary Condition

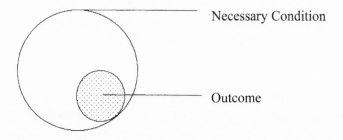

b. Empirically Irrelevant Necessary Condition

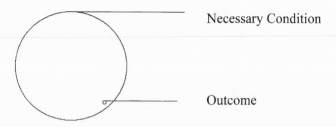

Figure 3.5 Venn diagram illustrating necessary conditions

Table 3.4: Protocol for assessing consistency and coverage

Procedure	Type of set-theoretic relation	
	Cause (X) is a subset of outcome (Y) (sufficiency)	*Outcome (Y) is a subset of cause (X) (necessity)*
Step 1	Assess consistency using $\Sigma[\min(X_i, Y_i)]/\Sigma(X_i)$	Assess consistency using $\Sigma[\min(X_i, Y_i)]/\Sigma(Y_i)$
Step 2	If consistent, assess coverage using $\Sigma[\min(X_i, Y_i)]/\Sigma(Y_i)$	If consistent, assess coverage using $\Sigma[\min(X_i, Y_i)]/\Sigma(X_i)$

of X before assessing the size of Y relative to size of X. Adherence to this protocol prevents confusion regarding the interpretation of what are essentially identical calculations: the calculation of the consistency of a sufficiency relationship is identical to the calculation of the coverage (relevance) of a necessity relationship, while the calculation of the coverage of a sufficiency relationship is identical to the calculation of the consistency of a necessity relationship. The protocol for assessing consistency and coverage for these two types of set-theoretic relations is summarized in table 3.4.

Partitioning Coverage

When more than one condition or combination of conditions is sufficient for an outcome (i.e., when there is equifinality), the assessment of the coverage of alternate causal combinations provides direct evidence of their relative empirical importance. Further, the assessments of "raw" coverage can be complemented with assessments of each combination's "unique" coverage, for it is possible to partition coverage in set-theoretic analysis in a manner that is analogous to the partitioning of explained variation in multiple regression. The discussion of the partitioning of coverage that is presented here assumes that the researcher has demonstrated that the relevant conditions or combinations of conditions are consistent subsets of the outcome.

For purposes of illustration, consider evidence from a fuzzy-set analysis of individual-level data. The data set is the National Longitudinal

Table 3.5: Calculation of coverage

Causal conditions	Sum of consistent scores	Sum of outcome scores	Coverage
T·I	307.387	1385.25	0.2219
C	548.559	1385.25	0.3960
T·I + C	607.709	1385.25	0.4387

Survey of Youth (better known as the *Bell Curve* data; see Herrnstein and Murray 1994). The sample is white males, interviewed as young adults. The outcome is the fuzzy set of cases not in poverty (~**P**, where **P** indicates degree of membership in the set of cases in poverty and ~ indicates negation). The three causal conditions are the fuzzy set of cases with high test scores (**T**), the fuzzy set of cases with high parental income (**I**), and the fuzzy set of cases with college education (**C**). (The calibration of these fuzzy sets is described in chapter 11.) Applying fuzzy-set qualitative comparative analysis (Ragin, Drass, and Davey 2007) to these data yields two recipes for avoiding poverty, namely, the combination of high test scores and high parental income (**T·I**) and college education (**C**) by itself.

The calculation of the raw coverage of these two recipes for the outcome, avoiding poverty (~**P**), is shown in table 3.5. The first row reports the coverage calculation for the combination of high test scores and high parental income (**T·I**). The sum of the overlap between **T·I** and the outcome is 307.387. The sum of the memberships in the outcome is 1385.25. Thus, this combination covers about 22.19 percent of the total membership in the outcome (307.387/1,385.25 = 0.2219). Using these same procedures, condition **C** covers about 39.6 percent of the total membership of the outcome (see row two of table 3.5). Thus, both combinations cover a substantial proportion of the outcome. However, the raw coverage of condition **C** (college education) is much greater.

For comparison purposes, table 3.5 also shows the coverage of the two combinations (**T·I** and **C**) conceived as alternate paths to the same outcome, using logical *or*. When causal combinations are joined by logical *or,* each case's score in the union is the maximum value of the two paths (i.e., the larger of the two scores, membership in **T·I** versus membership in **C**). In other words, when there is more than one path to an outcome, it is possible to calculate how close a case is to the outcome by finding its highest membership score among the possible paths. The degree of coverage of the outcome by this maximum score, in turn, can be calculated using the same procedures applied separately to the two components. This calculation is shown in the third row of table 3.5, which reports a coverage of 43.87 percent, greater than the coverage of either of the two components (compare row 3 of table 3.5 with the first two rows). However, the coverage of the two-path model (43.87 percent) is only modestly superior to the raw coverage of the best single path (path **C**, with 39.6 percent).

Table 3.5 provides all the information that is needed to partition coverage, following the procedure that is used to partition explained variation in multiple regression analysis. To assess an independent variable's separate or unique contribution to explained variation in a multiple regression involving several correlated predictor variables, researchers calculate the *decrease* in explained variation that occurs once the variable in question is removed from the fully specified multivariate equation. For example, to find the unique contribution of X_1 to explained variation in **Y**, it is necessary to compute the multiple regression equation with all relevant independent variables included and then to recompute the equation *excluding* X_1. The difference in explained variation between these two equations shows the unique contribution of X_1. These procedures ensure that the explained variation that X_1 shares with correlated independent variables is not credited to X_1. The goal of partitioning in fuzzy-set analysis, by contrast, is to assess the relative importance of different *combinations* of causally relevant conditions. Thus, the issue in set-theoretic analyses is not correlated independent variables because causal conditions are not viewed in isolation from one another, as they are in multiple regression analysis. Rather, partitioning coverage is important because some cases conform to more than one path. Using our example, there are surely many individuals who combine high test scores, high-income parents, *and* college education.

Table 3.6: Partitioning coverage

	Total coverage	Without term	Unique
Unique to T·I	0.4387	0.3960	0.0427
Unique to C	0.4387	0.2219	0.2168

Consider the crisp-set case. Suppose a researcher finds that two combinations of conditions generate outcome **Y: A·B** and **C·D**. The researcher calculates the coverage of these two paths and finds that the first embraces 25 percent of the instances of **Y** (coverage = 0.25), while the second embraces 30 percent (coverage = 0.3). However, when calculating their coverage as alternate paths (i.e., their union: **A·B + C·D**, where addition indicates logical *or*), the researcher finds that together they embrace only 35 percent of the instances of the outcome (coverage = 0.35). The reason that this quantity is substantially less than the sum of the two separate coverage scores (i.e., $0.35 < 0.25 + 0.3 = 0.55$) is because the two paths partially overlap. That is, there are cases that combine all four causal conditions (i.e., instances of **A·B·C·D**) and the coverage of these instances is counted twice when raw coverage is calculated separately for the two causal combinations.

Fortunately, it is a simple matter to partition total coverage (0.35 in this example) into its three components: uniquely due to **A·B**, uniquely due to **C·D**, and overlapping (i.e., due to the existence of cases of **A·B·C·D**). The unique coverage of each term can be calculated by subtraction, following the template provided by regression analysis. The unique coverage of path **A·B** is $0.35 - 0.3 = 0.05$; the unique coverage of path **C·D** is $0.35 - 0.25 = 0.10$; and the remainder of total coverage is due to the overlap between these two terms. In short, these simple calculations indicate that 20 percent of the instances of the outcome are **A·B·C·D**; 5 percent of the instances of the outcome are **A·B** without **C·D**; and 10 percent are **C·D** without **A·B**.

The calculation of the unique coverage of a combination of conditions in fuzzy-set analysis is exactly parallel, as shown in table 3.6, which uses the same individual-level data used in table 3.5. The coverage of the outcome (avoiding poverty) that is uniquely due to path **T·I** is the difference between the coverage of the two-path model (0.4387) and the coverage that is obtained once this path (**T·I**) is removed from the two-path model, which in this example is equivalent to the coverage of the other path (**C**) by itself. Thus, the unique coverage of path **T·I** is 0.0427, that is, 0.4387 (the combined coverage of the two paths) less 0.3960 (the single coverage of path **C**). Likewise, the coverage of the outcome that is uniquely due to path **C** is the difference between the coverage of the two-path model (0.4387) and the coverage of path **T·I** by itself (0.2219), or 0.2168. These calculations reveal that the unique coverage of path **C** is much greater than the unique coverage of path **T·I**. In fact, the coverage of **T·I** is almost entirely a subset of the coverage of **C**. (In other words, most of **T·I** is **T·I·C**.) Much of the coverage of the two-path model is overlapping. This proportion can be calculated by computing the difference between the coverage of the two-path model (0.4387) and the sum of the two unique portions (0.0427 + 0.2168 = 0.2595), which is 0.1792. Figure 3.6 illustrates these results using a Venn diagram.

When many different paths can lead to the same outcome, it is important to calculate both the raw and unique coverage of each causal

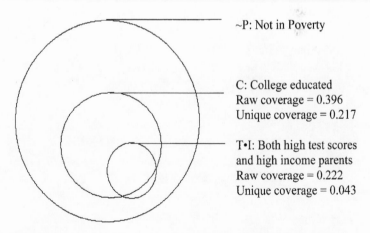

~P: Not in Poverty

C: College educated
Raw coverage = 0.396
Unique coverage = 0.217

T•I: Both high test scores
and high income parents
Raw coverage = 0.222
Unique coverage = 0.043

Figure 3.6 Venn diagram representing the partitioning of set-theoretic coverage using fuzzy sets

combination. These calculations often reveal that only a few high-coverage causal combinations exist, even in analyses that have many sufficient combinations. While it is useful to know all the different causal combinations linked to an outcome, it is also important to assess their relative empirical weight. Calculations of raw and unique coverage provide these assessments directly.

Looking Ahead

As will become clear in the chapters that follow, these measures of set-theoretic consistency and coverage have many uses. They can, for example, aid the construction of "crisp" truth tables from fuzzy-set data, which is the foundation of the "fuzzy truth table" algorithm described in chapter 7.

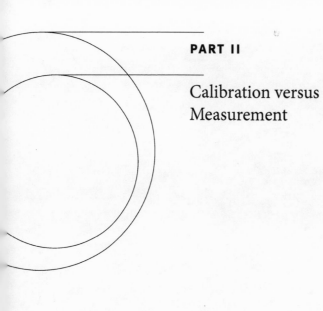

PART II

Calibration versus
Measurement

4: Why Calibrate?

Fuzzy sets are relatively new to social science. The first comprehensive introduction of fuzzy sets to the social sciences was offered by Michael Smithson in 1987. However, applications were few and far between until the basic principles of fuzzy-set analysis were elaborated through qualitative comparative analysis (QCA) (see Ragin 1987, 2000), an analytic system that is fundamentally set theoretic, as opposed to correlational, in both inspiration and design. The marriage of these two yields fuzzy-set QCA (fsQCA), a family of methods that offers social scientists an alternative to conventional quantitative methods, which are based almost exclusively on correlational reasoning.

The key to useful fuzzy-set analysis is well-constructed fuzzy sets, which in turn raise the issue of calibration. How does a researcher calibrate degree of membership in a set, for example, the set of Democrats? How should this set be defined? What constitutes full membership? What constitutes full nonmembership? What would a person with 0.75 membership in this set (more in than out, but not fully in) be like? How would this person differ from someone with 0.9 membership? The main message of this chapter is that fuzzy sets, unlike conventional variables, must be calibrated. Because they must be calibrated, they are superior in many respects to conventional measures, as they are used today in both quantitative and qualitative social science. In essence, I argue that fuzzy sets offer a middle path between quantitative and qualitative measurement. However, this middle path is not a compromise between these two; rather, it transcends many of the limitations of both.

What Is Calibration?

Calibration is a necessary and routine research practice in such fields as chemistry, astronomy, and physics (Pawson 1989, 135–37). In these and other natural sciences, researchers *calibrate* their measuring devices and the readings these instruments produce by adjusting them so that they match or conform to dependably known standards. These standards make measurements directly interpretable (Byrne 2002). A temperature of 20 °Celsius is interpretable because it is situated in between 0 degrees (water freezes) and 100 degrees (water boils). By contrast, the calibration of measures according to agreed upon standards is relatively rare in the social sciences.[1] Most social scientists are content to use uncalibrated measures, which simply show the positions of cases relative to each other. Uncalibrated measures, however, are clearly inferior to calibrated measures. With an uncalibrated measure of temperature, for example, it is possible to know that one object has a higher temperature than another or even that it has a higher temperature than average for a given set of objects but still not know whether it is hot or cold. Likewise, with an uncalibrated measure of democracy, it is possible to know that one country is more democratic than another or more democratic than average but still not know if it is more a democracy or an autocracy.

Calibration is especially important in situations where one condition sets or shapes the context for other conditions. For example, the relationship between the temperature and volume of H_2O changes qualitatively at 0 °C and then again at 100 °C. Volume decreases as temperature crosses 0 °C and then increases as temperature crosses

---

1. Perhaps the greatest calibration efforts have been exerted in the field of poverty research, where the task of establishing external standards (i.e., defining who is poor) has deep policy relevance. Another example of a calibrated measure is the Human Development Index developed by the United Nations and published in its *Human Development Report*. In economics, by contrast, *calibration* has a different meaning altogether. Researchers "calibrate" parameters in models by fixing them to particular values, so that the properties and behavior of other parameters in the model can be observed. This type of calibration is very different from the explicit calibration of measures, the central concern of this chapter.

100 °C. The Celsius scale is purposefully calibrated to indicate these "phase shifts," and researchers studying the properties of H_2O know not to examine the relationships between its properties without taking these two qualitative breakpoints into account. Knowledge of these phase shifts, which is external to the measurement of temperature per se, provides the basis for its calibration.[2]

Context-setting conditions that operate like phase shifts abound in the study of social phenomena. The most basic context-setting condition is the scope condition (Walker and Cohen 1985). When researchers state that a certain property or relationship holds or exists only for cases of a certain type (e.g., only for countries that are democracies), they have used a scope condition to define an enabling context. Another example of a context-setting condition in social science is the use of empirical populations as enabling conditions. For instance, when researchers argue that a property or relationship holds only for Latin American countries, they have used an empirically delineated population as a context-setting condition. While the distinction between scope conditions and populations is sometimes blurred, their use as context-setting conditions is parallel. In both usages, they act as conditions that enable or disable specific properties or relationships.

Tests for statistical interaction are usually motivated by this same concern for conditions that alter the relationships between other variables, that is, by this same concern for context-setting conditions. If the effect of X on Y increases from no effect to a substantial effect as the level of a third variable Z increases, then Z operates as a context-setting condition, enabling a relationship between X and Y. Unlike scope conditions and population boundaries, the interaction variable Z in this example varies by level and is not a simple presence/absence dichotomy. While having context-setting conditions vary by level or degree complicates their study, the logic is the same in all three situations. In fact, it could be argued that dichotomous context-setting conditions such as scope conditions are special cases of statistical interaction.

---

2. I thank Henry Brady for pointing out the importance of the idea of phase shifts as a way to elaborate my argument.

The fact that the interaction variable Z varies by level as a context-setting condition automatically raises the issue of calibration. At what level of Z does a relationship between X and Y become possible? At what level of Z does a strong connection exist between X and Y? To answer these questions, it is necessary to specify the relevant values of Z, which is a de facto calibration of Z. Over a specific range of values of Z, there is no relation between X and Y, while over another range there is a strong relation between X and Y. Perhaps over intermediate values of Z, there is a weak to moderate relation between X and Y. To specify these values or levels, it is necessary to bring in external, substantive knowledge in some way—to interpret these different levels as context-setting conditions. Researchers who test for statistical interaction have largely ignored this issue and have been content to conduct broad tests of statistical interaction, focusing on increments to explained variation in a dependent variable without attending to issues of calibration and context.

To set the stage for the discussion of fuzzy sets and their calibration, I first examine common measurement practices in quantitative and qualitative social research. After sketching these practices, I show that fuzzy sets resonate with both the measurement concerns of qualitative researchers, where the goal often is to distinguish between relevant and irrelevant variation (that is, to *interpret* variation), and with the measurement concerns of quantitative researchers, where the goal is the precise placement of cases relative to each other.

Common Measurement Practices in Quantitative Research

Measurement, as practiced in the social sciences today, remains relatively haphazard and unsystematic, despite the efforts and exhortations of many distinguished scholars (e.g., Duncan 1984; Pawson 1989). The dominant approach is the indicator approach, in which social scientists seek to identify the best possible empirical indicators of their theoretical concepts. For example, national income per capita (in constant U.S. dollars, adjusted for differences in purchasing power) is often used as an empirical indicator of the theoretical concept of development applied to countries. In the indicator approach, the main requirement is that the indicator must vary across cases, ordering them in a way that is consistent with the underlying concept. The values of national income per capita, for example, must distinguish less-developed from more-developed countries in a systematic manner.

In this approach, fine gradations and equal measurement intervals are preferred to coarse distinctions and mere ordinal rankings. Indicators such as income per capita are especially prized not only because they offer fine gradations (e.g., an income per capita value of $5,500 is exactly $100 less than a value of $5,600) but also because the distance between two cases is considered the "same" regardless of whether it is the difference between $1,000 and $2,000 or between $21,000 and $22,000 (i.e., a $1,000 difference).[3] Such interval- and ratio-scale indicators are well suited for the most widely used analytic techniques for assessing relationships between variables, such as multiple regression and related linear techniques.[4]

More sophisticated versions of the indicator model use multiple indicators and rely on psychometric theory (Nunnally and Bernstein 1994). The core idea in psychometric theory is that an index that is composed of multiple, correlated indicators of the same underlying concept is likely to be more accurate and more reliable than any single indicator. Consider this simple example: National income per capita could easily overstate the level of development of oil-exporting countries,

---

3. Actually, there is a world of difference between living in a country with a gross national product (GNP) per capita of $2,000 and living in one with a GNP per capita of $1,000; however, there is virtually no difference between living in one with a GNP per capita of $22,000 and living in one with a GNP per capita of $21,000. Such fine points are rarely addressed by researchers who use the conventional indicator approach, but they must be confronted directly in research that uses calibrated measures (e.g., fuzzy sets).

4. While most textbooks assert that ratio scales are the highest form of measurement because they are anchored by a meaningful zero point, it is important to note that fuzzy sets have three numerical anchors: 1.0 (full membership), 0.0 (full non-membership), and 0.5 (the crossover point separating cases that are more in versus more out of the set in question); see Ragin (2000). If it is accepted than such "anchoring" signals a higher level of measurement, then it follows that a fuzzy set is a higher level of measurement than a ratio-scale variable.

making them appear to be more developed than they "really are." Such anomalies challenge the face validity of income per capita as an indicator of the underlying concept. However, using an index of development composed of multiple indicators (e.g., including such factors as literacy, life expectancy, energy consumption, and labor force composition) would address these anomalies, because many oil-exporting countries have relatively lower scores on some of these alternate indicators of development. Ideally, the various indicators of an underlying concept should correlate very strongly with each other. If they do not, then they may be indicators of different underlying concepts (Nunnally and Bernstein 1994). Only cases with consistently high scores across all indicators obtain the highest scores on an index built from multiple indicators. Correspondingly, only those cases with consistently low scores across all indicators obtain the lowest scores on an index. Cases in the middle, of course, are a mixed bag.

Perhaps the most sophisticated implementation of the indicator approach is through an analytic technique known as structural equation modeling (SEM) (see Bollen 1989). SEM extends the use of multiple indicators of a single concept (the basic psychometric model) to multiple concepts and their interrelationships. In essence, the construction of indexes from multiple indicators takes place within the context of an analysis of the interrelationships among concepts. Thus, index construction is adjusted in ways that optimize hypothesized relationships. Using SEM, researchers can evaluate the coherence of their constructed indexes within the context of the model in which they are embedded. Simultaneously, they can evaluate the coherence of the model as a whole.

All techniques in the indicator family share a deep reliance upon observed variation, which in turn is almost always sample specific in its definition and construction. As mentioned previously, in the conventional approach, the key requirement that an indicator must meet is that it must order cases in a way that reflects the underlying concept. It is important to point out that these orderings are entirely relative in nature. That is, cases are defined *relative to each other* in the distribution of scores on the indicator (i.e., as having "higher" versus "lower" scores). For example, if the United States' national income per capita is $1,000 higher than Italy's, then the United States correspondingly is considered *relatively* more developed. The greater the gap between countries, the more different their relative positions in the development hierarchy. Furthermore, the definition of "high" versus "low" scores is defined *relative to the observed distribution of scores,* usually conceived as a sample of scores drawn from a well-defined population. Thus, a case with a score that is above the sample's central tendency (usually the mean) has a high score; the greater this positive gap, the higher the score. Likewise, a case with a score that is below the mean has a low score; the greater this negative gap, the lower the score. Notice that the use of deviations from sample-specific measures of central tendency offers a very crude but passive form of calibration. Its crudeness lies in the fact that the calibration standards (e.g., the mean and standard deviation) vary from one sample to the next and are inductively derived. By contrast, the routine practice in the physical sciences is to base calibration on external, dependably known standards (e.g., the boiling point of water).

At first glance, these conventional practices with respect to the use of indicators in the social sciences appear to be entirely straightforward and uncontroversial. It seems completely reasonable, for example, that countries should be ranked relative to each other and that some measure of central tendency, based on the sample or population in question, should be used to define high versus low scores. Again, the fundamental requirement of the indicator model is simply variation, which in turn requires only (1) a sample (or population) displaying a variety of scores and (2) a measure of central tendency based on the sample (or population). Note, however, that in this view all variation is considered equally *relevant.*[5] That is, variation in the entire range of the indicator is considered pertinent with respect to what it

---

5. Of course, researchers sometimes transform their variables (e.g., using logarithmic transformations of raw data) in order to reduce skew and shift the weight of the variation. However, such adjustments are relatively uncommon and, in any event, are usually understood mechanistically, as a way to improve the robustness of a model.

reveals about the underlying concept. For example, the two countries at the very top of the income distribution are both "highly developed countries." Yet, the difference that separates them indicates that one is still more highly developed than the other. In the indicator approach, this difference is usually taken at face value, meaning that usually no attempt is made to look at the cases and ask whether this difference— or any other difference, regardless of magnitude—is a relevant or meaningful difference with respect to the underlying concept.[6] By contrast, the interpretation of scores relative to agreed upon, external standards is central to measurement calibration. These external standards provide a context for the interpretation of scores.

Common Measurement Practices in Qualitative Research

In conventional quantitative research, measures are indicators of concepts, which in turn are components of models, which in turn are derived from theories. Thus, the quantitative approach to measurement is strongly theory centered. Much qualitative research, by contrast, is more knowledge and case centered and thus tends to be more grounded in empirical evidence and also more "iterative" in nature. That is, there is an interplay between concept formation and measurement on the one hand and research strategy on the other hand (see, e.g., Glaser and Strauss 1967). The researcher begins with orienting ideas and broad concepts and uses empirical cases to help refine and elaborate concepts (Becker 1958). This process of progressive refinement involves an iterative "back and forth" movement between ideas and evidence (Katz 1982; Ragin 1994). In this back-and-forth process, researchers specify and refine their empirical indicators and measures.

---

6. Notice also that the idea that variation at either end of a distribution should be deemphasized or truncated in some way is usually viewed with great suspicion by quantitative researchers because truncating such variation tends to attenuate correlations.

Consider this simple example: Macrolevel researchers often distinguish between countries that experienced "early" versus "late" state formation (see, e.g., Rokkan 1975). Those that developed early had certain advantages over those that developed late and vice versa. David Laitin (1992, xi), for example, notes that coercive nation-building practices available earlier to monarchs (e.g., the draconian imposition of a national language) are not available to leaders of new states today, in part because of the international censure these policies might generate. But what is early state formation? The occurrence of state formation, of course, can be dated. Thus, it is possible to develop a relatively precise ratio-scale measure of the "age" of a state. But most of the variation captured by this simple and direct measure is not relevant to the concept of early versus late state formation. Suppose, for example, that one state has been around for 500 years and another for 250 years. The first is twice as old as the second, but both are fully early when viewed through the lens of accumulated substantive and theoretical knowledge about state formation. Thus, much of the variation captured by the ratio-scale indicator age is simply irrelevant to the distinction between early and late state formation. Age in years must be adjusted on the basis of accumulated substantive knowledge in order to be able to interpret early versus late in a way that resonates appropriately with existing theory.

Such calibrations are routine in qualitative work, even though they are rarely modeled or even stated explicitly. Indeed, from the perspective of conventional quantitative research, it appears that qualitative researchers skew their measurements to fit their preconceptions. In fact, however, the qualitative researcher's goal is simply to interpret "mere indicators" such as age in years in the light of knowledge about cases and the interests of the investigator (e.g., whether a state is early or late from the standpoint of state formation theory).

A second essential feature of measurement in qualitative research is that it is more case oriented than measurement in quantitative research. This observation goes well beyond the previous observation that qualitative researchers pay more attention to the details of cases. In case-oriented research, the conceptual focus is on specific *kinds* of cases, for example, the developed countries. In variable-oriented research, by contrast, the focus is on dimensions of variation in a defined sample or population of cases, for example, variation in level of development across currently constituted nation-states. The distinction is subtle but important because cases can vary not only along a given dimension but also in how well they satisfy the requirements for membership in a category or set. For example, countries vary in how well they satisfy requirements for membership in the set of developed countries—some cases satisfy them fully, some partially, and some not at all. In order to assess how well cases satisfy membership requirements, it is necessary to invoke external standards, for example, regarding what it takes for a country to be considered developed. Thus, in the case-oriented view, the main focus is on sets of cases, the members of which can be identified and studied individually (e.g., the developed countries). In the variable-oriented view, by contrast, cases are usually understood simply as sites for taking measurements (that is, they are often seen as mere "observations"), which in turn provide the necessary raw material for studying relationships between variables, viewed as cross-case patterns.

It follows that the case-oriented view is more compatible with the idea that measures should be calibrated, for the focus is on the degree to which cases satisfy membership criteria, which in turn are usually externally determined, not inductively derived (e.g., using the sample mean). These membership criteria must reflect agreed upon standards; otherwise, the constitution of a category or set will be contested. In the variable-oriented view, the members of a population simply vary in the degree to which they express a given trait or phenomenon, and there is usually no special motivation for specifying the criteria for membership in a set or for identifying specific cases as instances. Thus, a fundamental difference between the qualitative approach to measurement and the quantitative approach is that, in the qualitative approach, meaning is attached to or imposed upon specific measurements, for example, what constitutes early state formation or what it takes to warrant designation as a developed country. In short, measurement in qualitative research is interpreted.

The qualitative sociologist Aaron Cicourel was an early proponent of the understanding of measurement described here. In his classic text, *Method and Measurement in Sociology,* Cicourel (1964, 24) argues that it is necessary to consider the three "media" through which social scientists develop categories and link them to observable properties of objects and events: language, cultural meaning, and the properties of measurement systems. In his view, the problem of establishing equivalence classes (like "democracies" or "developed countries") cannot be seen as independent from or separate from problems of language and cultural meaning. Cicourel (1964, 33) argues, "Viewing variables as quantitative because available data are expressed in numerical form or because it is considered more 'scientific' does not provide a solution to the problems of measurement but avoids them in favor of measurement by fiat. Measurement by fiat is not a substitute for examining and re-examining the structure of our theories so that our observations, descriptions, and measures of the properties of social objects and events have a literal correspondence with what we believe to be the structure of social reality." In simple terms, Cicourel argues that measures and their properties must be evaluated in the context of both theoretical and substantive knowledge. The fact that social scientists may possess a ratio-scale indicator of a theoretical concept does not mean that this aspect of "social reality" has the mathematical properties of this type of scale.

Thus, in qualitative research, the idea that social scientists should use external standards to evaluate and interpret their measures has much greater currency than it does in conventional quantitative research. An important difference with quantitative research, however, is that measurement in qualitative research is typically lacking in precision, and the context-sensitive and case-oriented way of measuring that is typical of qualitative research often appears haphazard and unscientific.

Fuzzy Sets: A Bridge between the Two Approaches

With fuzzy sets, it is possible to have the best of both worlds, namely, the precision that is prized by quantitative researchers and the use of substantive knowledge to calibrate measures that is central to qualitative research. With fuzzy sets, precision comes in the form of quantitative assessments of degree of set membership, which can range from a score of 0.0 (full exclusion from a set) to 1.0 (full inclusion). Substantive knowledge provides the external criteria that make it possible to calibrate measures. This knowledge indicates what constitutes full membership, full nonmembership, and the point at which cases are more in a given set than out (Ragin 2000; Smithson and Verkuilen 2006; see also chapter 2).

The external criteria that are used to calibrate measures and translate them into set membership scores may reflect standards based on social knowledge (e.g., the fact that twelve years of education constitutes an important educational threshold), collective social scientific knowledge (e.g., about variation in economic development and what it takes to be considered fully in the set of developed countries), or the researcher's own accumulated knowledge, derived from the study of specific cases. These external criteria should be stated explicitly, and they also must be applied systematically and transparently. This requirement separates the use of fuzzy sets from conventional qualitative work, where the standards that are applied usually remain implicit.

Fuzzy sets bridge quantitative and qualitative approaches to measurement because they are simultaneously qualitative and quantitative. Full membership and full nonmembership are qualitative states. In between these two qualitative states are varying degrees of membership ranging from more out (closer to 0.0) to more in (closer to 1.0). Fuzzy sets are also simultaneously qualitative and quantitative because they are both case oriented and variable oriented. They are case oriented in their focus on sets and set membership. In case-oriented work, the identity of cases matters, as do the sets to which a case may belong (e.g., the set of democracies). Fuzzy sets are also variable oriented in their allowance for degrees of membership and thus for fine-grained variation across cases. This aspect of fuzzy sets also provides a basis for precise measurement, which is greatly prized in quantitative research.

Differences between Fuzzy Sets and Conventional Variables

A key difference between a fuzzy set and a conventional variable is how they are conceptualized and labeled. For example, while it is possible to construct a generic variable such as "years of education," it is impossible to transform this variable directly into a fuzzy set without first designating and defining a target set of cases. In this instance, the researcher might be interested in the set of individuals with at least a high school education or perhaps the set of individuals who are college educated. This example makes it clear that the designation of different target sets dictates different calibration schemes. A person who has one year of college education, for example, has full membership (1.0) in the set of people who are at least high school educated, but this same person clearly has less than full membership in the set of people who are college educated. In a parallel fashion, it is clear that "level of economic development" makes sense as a generic variable, but in order to calibrate it as a fuzzy set, a target set must be specified, for example, the set of developed countries. Notice that this requirement—that the researcher designate a target set—not only structures the calibration of the set but it also provides a direct connection between theoretical discourse and empirical analysis. After all, it is more common for theoretical discourse to be organized around designated sets of cases (e.g., developed countries) than it is for it to be organized around generic variables (e.g., level of economic development).

These examples clarify a crucial feature of fuzzy sets central to their calibration—the fact that in order to calibrate a fuzzy set it is necessary for researchers to distinguish between relevant and irrelevant variation. For example, the difference between an individual who has completed one year of college and an individual who has completed two years of college is irrelevant to the set of individuals with at least a high school education, for both of these individuals are fully in this set (membership = 1.0). Their one-year difference is simply not relevant to the target set as conceptualized and labeled. When calibrating a fuzzy set, variation that is irrelevant to the set must be truncated so that the resulting membership scores faithfully reflect the target set's label. This requirement also establishes a close connection between theoretical discourse and empirical analysis.

In line with the general theme of this book, a great benefit of using carefully calibrated fuzzy sets is that they permit the utilization of set-theoretic principles in social research. These principles include subset relations (which are central to the analysis of necessity and sufficiency), set intersection (which is central to the study of cases as configurations), set union (which is central to the examination of alternate paths to the same outcome), truth tables (which are used to unravel causal complexity), and so on. These set-theoretic operations are off-limits to researchers who use uncalibrated measures, such as conventional interval- and ratio-scale variables.

Looking Ahead

Chapter 5 explores the calibration of fuzzy sets in more detail, with a practical emphasis. It focuses on the calibration of interval- and ratio-scale variables as fuzzy sets and describes two general methods. The first, the direct method, is based on researcher-specified benchmarks for full membership, full nonmembership, and the crossover point. The second, labeled the indirect method, is based on the researcher's sorting of cases into six categories and the use of a regression estimation procedure to translate raw scores into fuzzy membership scores.

5: Calibrating Fuzzy Sets

This chapter sketches two techniques for calibrating conventional interval-scale variables as fuzzy sets, using external standards to structure the calibration. As noted in chapter 4, conventional variables are either uncalibrated or only implicitly calibrated using inductively derived, sample-specific standards—the mean and standard deviation. Fuzzy sets, by contrast, are calibrated using external criteria, which in turn must follow from and conform to the researcher's conceptualization, definition, and labeling of the set in question. External standards can be implemented in two different ways. Using the first, *direct,* method, the researcher specifies the values of an interval scale that correspond to the three qualitative breakpoints that structure a fuzzy set: full membership, full nonmembership, and the crossover point. These three benchmarks are then used to transform the original interval-scale values to fuzzy membership scores. Using the second, *indirect,* method, the external standard used is the researcher's qualitative assessment of the degree to which cases with given scores on an interval scale are members of the target set. The researcher assigns each case into one of six categories and then uses a simple estimation technique to rescale the original measure so that it conforms to these qualitative assessments. The end product of both methods is the fine-grained calibration of the degree of membership of cases in sets, with scores ranging from 0.0 to 1.0. The examples provided in this chapter illustrate the responsiveness of these calibration methods to the researcher's conceptualization of the target set.

Transforming Interval-Scale Variables into Fuzzy Sets

Ideally, the calibration of degree of membership in a set should be based entirely on the researcher's substantive and theoretical knowledge. That is, the collective knowledge base of social scientists should provide the basis for the specification of precise calibrations. For example, armed with an adequate knowledge of development, social scientists should be able to specify the per capita income level that signals full membership in the set of developed countries. However, the social sciences are still in their infancy, and this knowledge base does not exist. Furthermore, the dominance of variable-oriented research, with its paramount focus on mean-centered variation and on covariation as the key to assessing relationships between case aspects, undermines scholarly interest in substantively based thresholds and benchmarks. While the problem of specifying thresholds and benchmarks has not attracted the attention it deserves, it is not a daunting task. The primary requirement for useful calibration is simply sustained attention to the substantive issues at hand (e.g., establishing what constitutes full membership in the set of developed countries).

Despite the imperfections of the existing knowledge base, it is still possible to demonstrate techniques of calibration. All that is lacking are precise "agreed upon standards" for calibrating measures. To the extent possible, the calibrations presented in this chapter are based on the existing theoretical and substantive literature. Still, the focus is on techniques of calibration, and not on the specific empirical benchmarks used to structure calibration.

The techniques presented assume that researchers already have at their disposal conventional interval-scale indicators of their concepts, for example, per capita national income as an indicator of development. The techniques also assume that the underlying concept can be structured and labeled in set-theoretic terms, for example, degree of membership in the set of developed countries. Notice that this labeling requirement moves the investigation in a decidedly case-oriented direction. The set of developed countries identifies specific countries, while level of development does not. The latter simply identifies a dimension of cross-national variation.

The direct method uses estimates of the log of the odds of full membership in a set as an intermediate step. While this translation route—using estimates of the log odds of full membership—may seem roundabout, the value of the approach will become clear as the demonstration proceeds. For now, consider table 5.1, which shows the different metrics that are used in the demonstration of the direct method. The first column shows various verbal labels that can be attached to differing degrees of set membership, ranging from full nonmembership to full membership. The second column shows the degree of set membership linked to each verbal label. For convenience, degree of membership is rounded to three decimal places. The third column shows the odds of full membership that result from the transformation of the set membership scores (column 2) into the odds of full membership, using the following formula:

$$\text{odds of membership} = (\text{degree of membership})/$$
$$[1 - (\text{degree of membership})]$$

The last column shows the natural log of the odds reported in column 3. In effect, columns 2 through 4 are different representations of the same numerical values, using different metrics. For example, the membership score attached to "threshold of full membership" is 0.953. Converting it to an odds value yields 20.09. Calculating the natural log of 20.09 yields a score of 3.0.[1]

Working in the metric of log odds is useful because this metric is completely symmetric around 0.0 (an odds of 50/50) and suffers neither floor nor ceiling effects. Thus, for example, if a calibration technique returns a value in the log of odds that is either a very large positive number or a very large negative number, its translation to degree of membership stays within the 0.0 to 1.0 bounds, which is a core requirement of fuzzy membership scores. The essential task of calibration

---

1. The values shown for degree of membership in column 2 have been adjusted (e.g., using 0.993 instead of 0.99 for full membership) so that they correspond to simple, single-digit entries in column 4.

Table 5.1: Mathematical translations of verbal labels

Verbal label	Degree of membership	Associated odds	Log odds of full membership
Full membership	0.993	148.41	5.0
Threshold of full membership	0.953	20.09	3.0
Mostly in	0.881	7.39	2.0
More in than out	0.622	1.65	0.5
Crossover point	0.500	1.00	0.0
More out than in	0.378	0.61	−0.5
Mostly out	0.119	0.14	−2.0
Threshold of full nonmembership	0.047	0.05	−3.0
Full nonmembership	0.007	0.01	−5.0

using the direct method is to transform interval-scale variables into the log odds metric in a way that respects the verbal labels shown in column 1 of table 5.1.[2]

It is important to note that the set membership scores that result from these transformations (ranging from 0.0 to 1.0) are *not* probabilities, but instead should be seen simply as transformations of interval scales into degree of membership in the target set. In essence, a fuzzy membership score attaches a *truth value,* not a probability, to a statement (e.g., the statement that a country is in the set of developed countries). The difference between a truth value and a probability is easy to grasp, and it is surprising that so many scholars confuse the two. For example, the *truth value* of the statement "beer is a deadly poison" is perhaps about 0.05—that is, this statement is almost but not completely out of the set of true statements, and beer is consumed freely, without concern, by millions and millions of people every day. However, these same millions would be quite unlikely to consume a liquid that has a 0.05 *probability* of being a deadly poison, with death the outcome, on average, in one in twenty beers.

---

2. The procedures for calibrating fuzzy membership scores presented in this chapter are mathematically incapable of producing set membership scores of exactly 1.0 or 0.0. These two membership scores would correspond to positive and negative infinity, respectively, for the log of the odds. Instead, scores that are greater than 0.95 may be interpreted as (virtually) full membership in the target set, and scores that are less than 0.05 may be interpreted as (virtually) full nonmembership.

The Direct Method of Calibration

The starting point of any set calibration is clear specification of the target set. The focus of this demonstration is the set of developed countries, and the goal is to use per capita national income data to calibrate degree of membership in this set. Altogether, 136 countries are included in the demonstration; table 5.2 presents data on 24 of these 136 countries, which were chosen to represent a wide range of national income values.

Table 5.2: Calibrating degree of membership in the set of developed countries: Direct method

Country	National income (US$)	Deviations from crossover	Scalars	Product	Degree of membership
Switzerland	40,110	35,110.00	.0002	7.02	1.00
United States	34,400	29,400.00	.0002	5.88	1.00
Netherlands	25,200	20,200.00	.0002	4.04	0.98
Finland	24,920	19,920.00	.0002	3.98	0.98
Australia	20,060	15,060.00	.0002	3.01	0.95
Israel	17,090	12,090.00	.0002	2.42	0.92
Spain	15,320	10,320.00	.0002	2.06	0.89
New Zealand	13,680	8,680.00	.0002	1.74	0.85
Cyprus	11,720	6,720.00	.0002	1.34	0.79
Greece	11,290	6,290.00	.0002	1.26	0.78
Portugal	10,940	5,940.00	.0002	1.19	0.77
Korea, Rep.	9,800	4,800.00	.0002	.96	0.72
Argentina	7,470	2,470.00	.0002	.49	0.62
Hungary	4,670	−330.00	.0012	−0.40	0.40
Venezuela	4,100	−900.00	.0012	−1.08	0.25
Estonia	4,070	−930.00	.0012	−1.12	0.25
Panama	3,740	−1,260.00	.0012	−1.51	0.18
Mauritius	3,690	−1,310.00	.0012	−1.57	0.17
Brazil	3,590	−1,410.00	.0012	−1.69	0.16
Turkey	2,980	−2,020.00	.0012	−2.42	0.08
Bolivia	1,000	−4,000.00	.0012	−4.80	0.01
Cote d'Ivoire	650	−4,350.00	.0012	−5.22	0.01
Senegal	450	−4,550.00	.0012	−5.46	0.00
Burundi	110	−4,890.00	.0012	−5.87	0.00

The direct method uses three important qualitative anchors to structure calibration: the threshold for full membership, the threshold for full nonmembership, and the crossover point (see Ragin 2000 and chapter 2 of this book). The crossover point is the value of the interval-scale variable where there is maximum ambiguity as to whether a case is more in or more out of the target set. For the purpose of this demonstration, I use a per capita national income value of $5,000 as the crossover point. An important step in the direct method of calibration is to calculate the deviations of raw scores (shown in column 1) from the crossover point designated by the investigator ($5,000 in this example). These values are shown in column 2 of table 5.2. Negative scores indicate that a case is more out than in the target set, while positive scores signal that a case is more in than out.

For the threshold of full membership in the target set, I use a per capita national income value of $20,000, which is a deviation score of $15,000 (compare columns 1 and 2 of table 5.2). This value corresponds to a set membership score of .95 and a log odds of 3.0. Thus, cases with national income per capita of $20,000 or greater (i.e., deviation scores of $15,000 or greater) are considered fully in the target set, with set membership scores ≥ 0.95 and log odds of membership ≥ 3.0. In the reverse direction, the threshold for full nonmembership in the target set is $2,500, which is a deviation score of –$2,500. This national income value corresponds to a set membership score of .05 and a log odds of –3.0. Thus, cases with national income per capita of $2,500 or lower (i.e., deviation scores of –$2,500 or lower) are considered fully out of the target set, with set membership scores $\leq .05$ and log odds of membership ≤ -3.0.

Once these three values (the two thresholds and the crossover point) have been selected, it is possible to calibrate degree of membership in the target set. The main task at this point is to translate the crossover centered national income data (column 2) into the metric of log odds, utilizing the external criteria that have been operationalized in the three qualitative anchors. For deviation scores *above* the crossover point, this translation can be accomplished by multiplying the relevant deviation scores (in column 2 of table 5.2) by the ratio of the log odds associated with the verbal label for the threshold of full membership (3.0) to the deviation score designated as the threshold of full membership (i.e., $20,000 – $5,000 = $15,000). This ratio is 3/15,000, or 0.0002. For deviation scores *below* the crossover point, this translation can be accomplished by multiplying the relevant deviation scores (in column 2 of table 5.2) by the ratio of the log odds associated with the verbal label for the threshold of full nonmembership (–3.0) to the deviation score designated as the threshold of full nonmembership ($2,500 – $5,000 = –$2,500). This ratio is –3/–2,500, or 0.0012. These two scalars are shown in column 3, and the products of columns 2 and 3 are shown in column 4.[3] Thus, column 4 shows the translation of income deviation scores into the log odds metric, using the three qualitative anchors to structure the transformation via the two scalars.

The values in column 4, in effect, are per capita national income values that have been rescaled into values reflecting the log odds of membership in the set of developed countries, in a manner that strictly conforms to the values attached to the three qualitative anchors—the threshold of full membership, the threshold of full nonmembership, and the crossover point. Thus, the values in column 4 are not mere mechanistic rescalings of national income, for they reflect the imposition of external criteria via the three qualitative anchors. The use of such external criteria is the hallmark of measurement calibration (see chapter 4).

It is a small step from the log odds reported in column 4 to the degree of membership values reported in column 5. It is necessary simply to apply the standard formula for converting log odds to scores that range from 0.0 to 1.0, namely:

degree of membership = exp(log odds)/[1 + exp(log odds)]

where exp represents the exponentiation of log odds to simple odds.[4] Note that the membership values reported in the last column of table

---

3. These two scalars constitute the slopes of the two lines extending from the origin (0,0) to the two threshold points (15,000,3) and (–2,500,–3) in the plot of the deviations of national income from the crossover point (X axis) against the log odds of full membership in the set of developed countries (Y axis).

4. These procedures may seem forbidding. For the mathematically disinclined, I note that the complex set of computational steps depicted in table 5.2 can be accomplished

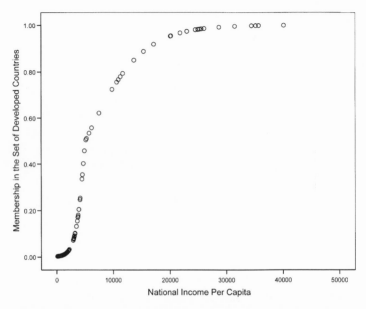

Figure 5.1 Plot of degree of membership in the set of developed countries against national income per capita: Direct method

5.2 strictly conform to the distribution dictated by the three qualitative anchors. That is, the threshold for full membership (0.95) is pegged to an income per capita value of $20,000; the crossover point (0.50) is pegged to an income of $5,000; and so on. For further illustration of the results of the direct method, consider figure 5.1, which shows a plot of degree of membership in the set of developed countries against per capita national income, using data on all 136 countries included in this demonstration. As the plot shows, the line flattens as it approaches 0.0 (full nonmembership) and 1.0 (full membership), consistent with the conceptualization of degree of set membership. What the plot does not reveal is that most of the world's countries are in the lower-left corner of the plot, with low national incomes and full exclusion from the set of developed countries (i.e., set membership scores < 0.05).

---

with a simple *compute* command using the software package fsQCA (Ragin, Drass, and Davey 2007).

Table 5.3: Calibrating degree of membership in the set of moderately developed dountries: Direct method

Country	National income (US$)	Deviations from crossover	Scalars	Product	Degree of membership
Switzerland	40,110	37,610	0.0006	22.57	1.00
United States	34,400	31,900	0.0006	19.14	1.00
Netherlands	25,200	22,700	0.0006	13.62	1.00
Finland	24,920	22,420	0.0006	13.45	1.00
Australia	20,060	17,560	0.0006	10.54	1.00
Israel	17,090	14,590	0.0006	8.75	1.00
Spain	15,320	12,820	0.0006	7.69	1.00
New Zealand	13,680	11,180	0.0006	6.71	1.00
Cyprus	11,720	9,220	0.0006	5.53	1.00
Greece	11,290	8,790	0.0006	5.27	0.99
Portugal	10,940	8,440	0.0006	5.06	0.99
Korea, Rep	9,800	7,300	0.0006	4.38	0.99
Argentina	7,470	4,970	0.0006	2.98	0.95
Hungary	4,670	2,170	0.0006	1.30	0.79
Venezuela	4,100	1,600	0.0006	0.96	0.72
Estonia	4,070	1,570	0.0006	0.94	0.72
Panama	3,740	1,240	0.0006	0.74	0.68
Mauritius	3,690	1,190	0.0006	0.71	0.67
Brazil	3,590	1,090	0.0006	0.65	0.66
Turkey	2,980	480	0.0006	0.29	0.57
Bolivia	1,000	−1,500	0.0020	−3.00	0.05
Cote d'Ivoire	650	−1,850	0.0020	−3.70	0.02
Senegal	450	−2,050	0.0020	−4.10	0.02
Burundi	110	−2,390	0.0020	−4.78	0.01

To illustrate the importance of external criteria to calibration, consider using the same national income data (column 1 of table 5.2) to calibrate degree of membership in the set of countries that are "at least moderately developed." Because the definition of the target set has changed, so, too, must the three qualitative anchors. Appropriate anchors for the set of at least moderately developed countries are a crossover value of $2,500; a threshold of full membership value of $7,500; and a threshold of full nonmembership value of $1,000. The appropriate scalars in this example are 3/5,000 for cases above the crossover value and $-3/-1,500$ for cases below the crossover value. The complete procedure is shown in table 5.3, using the same cases as in table 5.2.

The key point of contrast between tables 5.2 and 5.3 is shown in the last column, the calibrated membership scores. For example, with a national income per capita of $2,980, Turkey has a membership of 0.08 in the set of developed countries. Its membership in the set of at least moderately developed countries, however, is 0.57, which places it above the crossover point. Notice, more generally, that in table 5.3 many more cases register set membership scores close to 1.0, consistent with the simple fact that more countries have high membership in the set of countries that are at least moderately developed than in the set of countries that are fully developed. The contrast between tables 5.2 and 5.3 underscores both the knowledge-dependent nature of calibration and the impact of applying different external standards to the same measure (per capita national income). Again, the key to understanding calibration is to grasp the importance of external criteria, which are based, in turn, on the substantive and theoretical knowledge that researchers bring to their research.

The Indirect Method of Calibration

In contrast to the direct method, which relies on the specification of the numerical values linked to three qualitative anchors, the indirect method relies on the researcher's broad groupings of cases according to their degree of membership in the target set. In essence, the researcher performs an initial sorting of cases into different levels of membership, assigns these different levels preliminary membership scores, and then refines these membership scores using the interval-scale data.

Consider again the data on per capita national income, this time presented in table 5.4. The first and most important step in the indirect method is to categorize cases in a qualitative manner, according to their presumed degree of membership in the target set. These qualitative groupings can be preliminary and open to revision. However, they should be based as much as possible on existing theoretical and

Table 5.4: Calibrating degree of membership in the set of developed countries: Indirect method

Country	National income (US$)	Qualitative coding	Predicted value
Switzerland	40,110	1.00	1.000
United States	34,400	1.00	1.000
Netherlands	25,200	1.00	1.000
Finland	24,920	1.00	1.000
Australia	20,060	1.00	0.999
Israel	17,090	0.80	0.991
Spain	15,320	0.80	0.977
New Zealand	13,680	0.80	0.991
Cyprus	11,720	0.80	0.887
Greece	11,290	0.80	0.868
Portugal	10,940	0.80	0.852
Korea, Rep	9,800	0.60	0.793
Argentina	7,470	0.60	0.653
Hungary	4,670	0.40	0.495
Venezuela	4,100	0.40	0.465
Estonia	4,070	0.40	0.463
Panama	3,740	0.20	0.445
Mauritius	3,690	0.20	0.442
Brazil	3,590	0.20	0.436
Turkey	2,980	0.20	0.397
Bolivia	1,000	0.00	0.053
Cote d'Ivoire	650	0.00	0.002
Senegal	450	0.00	0.000
Burundi	110	0.00	0.000

substantive knowledge. The six key qualitative categories used in this demonstration are the following:[5]

1. In the target set (membership = 1.0)
2. Mostly but not fully in the target set (membership = 0.8)
3. More in than out of the target set (membership = 0.6)

---

5. Of course, other coding schemes are possible, using as few as three qualitative categories. The important point is that the scoring of these categories should reflect the researcher's initial estimate of each case's degree of set membership. These qualitative assessments provide the foundation for finer-grained calibration.

4. More out than in the target set (membership = 0.4)

5. Mostly but not fully out of the target set (membership = 0.2)

6. Out of the target set (membership = 0.0)

These categorizations are shown in column 2 of table 5.4, using explicit numerical values to reflect preliminary estimates of degree of set membership. These six numerical values are not arbitrary, of course, but are chosen as rough estimates of degree of membership specific to each qualitative grouping. The goal of the indirect method is to rescale the interval-scale indicator to reflect knowledge-based, qualitative groupings of cases, categorized according to degree of set membership. These qualitative interpretations of cases must be grounded in substantive knowledge. The stronger the empirical basis for making qualitative assessments of set membership, the more precise the calibration of the values of the interval-scale indicator as set membership scores.

Note that the qualitative groupings implemented in table 5.4 have been structured so that they utilize roughly the same criteria used to structure the calibrations shown in table 5.2. That is, countries with national income per capita greater than $20,000 have been coded as fully in the set of developed countries; countries with income per capita greater than $5,000 have been coded as more in than out; and so on. By maintaining fidelity to the qualitative anchors used in table 5.2, it is possible to compare the results of the two methods. The direct method utilizes precise specifications of the key benchmarks, while the indirect method requires only a broad classification of cases.

The next step is to use the two series reported in columns 1 and 2 of table 5.4 to estimate the predicted qualitative coding of each case, using per capita national income as the independent variable and the qualitative codings as the dependent variable. The best technique for this task is a fractional logit model, which is implemented in Stata software in the fracpoly (fractional polynomial) regression procedure.[6]

---

6. In Stata, this estimation procedure can be implemented using the commands *fracpoly glm qualcode intervv, family(binomial) link(logit)* and then *predict fzpred*, where qualcode is the variable that implements the researcher's six-value coding of set membership, as shown in table 5.4; intervv is the name of the interval-scale variable

The predicted values resulting from this analysis are reported in column 3 of table 5.4. The reported values are based on an analysis using all 136 cases, not the subset of 24 presented in the table. The predicted values, in essence, constitute estimates of fuzzy membership in the set of developed countries based on per capita national income (column 1) and the qualitative analysis that produced the codings shown in column 2.

Comparison of the set membership scores in column 5 of table 5.2 (direct method) and column 3 of table 5.4 (indirect method) reveals great similarities, but also some important differences. First, notice that table 5.2 faithfully implements $20,000 as the threshold for full membership in the set of developed countries (0.95). In table 5.4, however, this threshold value drops well below New Zealand's score ($13,680). Second, observe that the indirect method reveals a large gap separating Turkey (0.397) and the next case, Bolivia (0.053). Using the direct method, however, this gap is much narrower, with Turkey at 0.08 and Bolivia at 0.01. These differences, which arise despite the use of the same general criteria, follow from the indirectness of the second method and its necessary reliance on regression estimation. Still, if researchers lack the external criteria used in the direct method, the comparison of tables 5.2 and 5.4 confirms that the indirect method produces useful set membership scores.

Using Calibrated Measures

Calibrated measures have many uses. They are especially useful in evaluating theory that is formulated in terms of set relations. As noted in chapter 1, while some social science theory is strictly mathematical, the vast majority of it is verbal. Verbal theory, in turn, is formulated almost entirely in terms of set relations (Ragin 2000, 2006b). Unfortunately, social scientists have been slow to recognize this fact. Consider,

---

that is used to generate fuzzy membership scores; and fzpred is the predicted value showing the resulting fuzzy membership scores. I thank Steve Vaisey for pointing out the robustness of this estimation technique.

for example, the statement, "the developed countries are democratic." As in many statements of this type, the assertion is essentially that instances of the set mentioned first (developed countries) constitute a *subset* of instances of the set mentioned second (democracies). (It is common in English to state the subset first, as in the statement "ravens are black.") Close examination of most social science theories reveals that they are composed largely of statements describing set relations, such as the subset relation. These set relations, in turn, may involve a variety of different types of empirical connections—descriptive, constitutive, or causal, among others.

The set relation with developed countries as a subset of democratic countries, described above, is also compatible with a specific type of causal argument, namely, that development is sufficient but not necessary for democracy. In arguments of this type, if the cause (development) is present, then the outcome (democracy) should also be present. However, instances of the outcome (democracy) without the cause (development) do not count against or undermine the argument that development is sufficient for democracy (even though such cases dramatically undermine the correlation). Rather, these instances of the outcome without the cause are due to the existence of alternate routes or recipes for that outcome (e.g., the imposition of a democratic form of government by a departing colonial power). Thus, in situations where instances of a causal condition constitute a subset of instances of the outcome, a researcher may claim that the cause is sufficient but not necessary for the outcome.[7]

Before the advent of fuzzy sets (Zadeh 1965, 1972, 2002; Lakoff 1973), many social scientists disdained the analysis of set-theoretic relations because such analyses required the use of categorical-scale variables (i.e., conventional binary or crisp sets), which, in turn, often necessitated the dichotomization of interval and ratio scales. For example, using crisp sets to assess a set-theoretic statement about de-

---

7. As always, claims of this type cannot be based simply on the demonstration of the subset relation. Researchers should marshal as much corroborating evidence as possible when making any type of causal claim.

veloped countries, a researcher might be required to categorize countries into two groups, developed and not developed, using per capita national income. Such practices are often criticized because researchers may manipulate breakpoints when dichotomizing interval- and ratio-scale variables in ways that enhance the consistency of the evidence with a set-theoretic claim. However, as demonstrated here, it is possible to calibrate degree of membership in sets and thereby avoid arbitrary dichotomizations.

As shown in chapter 2, the fuzzy subset relation is established by demonstrating that membership scores in one set are consistently less than or equal to membership scores in another. In other words, if, for every case, degree of membership in set X is less than or equal to degree of membership in set Y, then set X is a subset of set Y. Of course, social science data are rarely perfect, and some allowance must be made for these imperfections. It is possible to assess the *degree* of consistency of empirical evidence with the subset relation using the simple formula described in chapter 3:

$$\text{Consistency } (X_i \leq Y_i) = \Sigma[\min(X_i, Y_i)]/\Sigma(X_i)$$

where X_i is degree of membership in set X; Y_i is degree of membership in set Y; $(X_i \leq Y_i)$ is the subset relation in question; and min dictates selection of the lower of the two scores.

For illustration, consider the consistency of the empirical evidence with the claim that the set of developed countries (as calibrated in table 5.2) constitutes a subset of the set of democracies, using data on all 136 countries. For this demonstration, the Polity IV democracy/autocracy measure is used, which ranges from −10 to +10. (This measure is used because of its popularity, despite its many shortcomings. See, e.g., Goertz 2006, ch. 4.) The calibration of membership in the set of democracies, using the direct method, is shown in table 5.5. Polity scores for 24 of the 136 countries included in the calibration are presented in column 1 of table 5.5. These specific cases were selected in order to provide a range of polity scores. Column 2 shows deviations from the crossover point (a polity score of 2), and the column 3 shows the scalars used to transform the polity deviation scores into the metric of log odds of membership in the set of democracies. The threshold

Table 5.5: Calibrating degree of membership in the set of democratic countries: Direct method

Country	Polity score	Deviations from crossover	Scalars	Product	Degree of membership
Norway	10	8.00	0.43	3.43	0.97
United States	10	8.00	0.43	3.43	0.97
France	9	7.00	0.43	3.00	0.95
Korea, Rep.	8	6.00	0.43	2.57	0.93
Colombia	7	5.00	0.43	2.14	0.89
Croatia	7	5.00	0.43	2.14	0.89
Bangladesh	6	4.00	0.43	1.71	0.85
Ecuador	6	4.00	0.43	1.71	0.85
Albania	5	3.00	0.43	1.29	0.78
Armenia	5	3.00	0.43	1.29	0.78
Nigeria	4	2.00	0.43	0.86	0.70
Malaysia	3	1.00	0.43	0.43	0.61
Cambodia	2	0.00	0.60	0.00	0.50
Tanzania	2	0.00	0.60	0.00	0.50
Zambia	1	−1.00	0.60	−0.60	0.35
Liberia	0	−2.00	0.60	−1.20	0.23
Tajikistan	−1	−3.00	0.60	−1.80	0.14
Jordan	−2	−4.00	0.60	−2.40	0.08
Algeria	−3	−5.00	0.60	−3.00	0.05
Rwanda	−4	−6.00	0.60	−3.60	0.03
Gambia	−5	−7.00	0.60	−4.20	0.01
Egypt	−6	−8.00	0.60	−4.80	0.01
Azerbaijan	−7	−9.00	0.60	−5.40	0.00
Bhutan	−8	−10.00	0.60	−6.00	0.00

of full membership in the set of democracies is a polity score of 9, yielding a scalar of 3/7 for cases above the crossover point; the threshold of full nonmembership in the set of democracies is a polity score of −3, yielding a scalar of −3/−5 for cases below the crossover point. Column 4 shows the product of the deviation scores and the scalars, while column 5 reports the calibrated membership scores, using the procedures previously described (see the discussion surrounding table 5.2).

Applying the formula for set-theoretic consistency described above to all 136 countries, the consistency of the evidence with the argument that the set of developed countries constitutes a subset of the set of democracies is 0.99. (1.0 indicates perfect consistency). Likewise, the consistency of the evidence with the argument that the set of at least moderately developed countries (as calibrated in table 5.3) constitutes a subset of the set of democratic countries is 0.95. In short, both subset relations are highly consistent, providing ample support for both statements ("developed countries are democratic" and "countries that are at least moderately developed are democratic"). Likewise, both analyses support the argument that development is sufficient but not necessary for democracy. Note, however, that the set of at least moderately developed countries is a much more inclusive set, with higher average membership scores than the set of developed countries. It thus offers a more demanding test of the underlying argument. The greater the average membership in a causal condition, the more difficult it is to satisfy the inequality indicating the subset relation ($X_i \leq Y_i$). The two formulations also differ substantially in their set theoretic "coverage." *Coverage* is a gauge of empirical importance or weight (see Ragin 2006b and chapter 3 of this book). It shows the proportion of the sum of the outcome membership scores (in this example, the set of democratic countries) that is "covered" by a causal condition. The coverage of democratic countries by developed countries is 0.35, while the coverage of democratic countries by at least moderately developed countries is substantially more, 0.52. These results indicate that the latter gives a much better account of degree of membership in the set of democratic countries. Thus, using set-theoretic methods, it is possible to demonstrate that membership in the set of countries with a moderate level of development is sufficient for democracy; membership in the set of fully developed countries is not required.

As explained in chapter 1, it is very difficult to evaluate set-theoretic arguments using correlational methods. The three main sources of this difficulty are as follows:

1. Set-theoretic statements are about kinds of cases; correlations concern relationships between variables. The statement that developed countries are democratic (i.e., that they constitute a subset of democratic countries) invokes cases, not dimensions of cross-national

variation. This focus on cases as instances of concepts follows directly from the set-theoretic nature of social science theory. The computation of a correlation, by contrast, is premised on an interest in assessing how well dimensions of variation parallel each other across a sample or population, not on an interest in a set of cases per se. To push the argument even further, a data set might not include a single developed country or a single democratic country, yet a correlational researcher could still compute a correlation between degree of development and degree of democracy. Note, however, that this data set would be completely inappropriate for a test of the argument that the developed countries are democratic, for it contains neither developed countries nor democratic countries.

2. Correlational arguments are fully symmetric, while set-theoretic arguments are almost always asymmetric. The correlation between development and democracy (treating both as conventional variables) is weakened by the fact that there are many less-developed countries that are democratic. However, such cases do not challenge the set-theoretic claim or weaken its consistency. The theoretical argument in question addresses the qualities of developed countries—that they are democratic—and does not make *specific* claims about relative differences between less-developed and more-developed countries in their degree of democracy. Again, set-theoretic analysis is faithful to verbal formulations, which are typically asymmetric; correlation is not.

3. Correlations are insensitive to the calibrations implemented by researchers. The contrast between tables 5.2 and 5.3 is meaningful from a set theoretic point of view. The set represented in table 5.3 is more inclusive and thus provides a more demanding set-theoretic test of the connection between development and democracy. From a correlational perspective, however, there is little difference between the two ways of representing development. Indeed, the Pearson correlation between fuzzy membership in the set of developed countries and fuzzy membership in the set of at least moderately developed countries is 0.911. Thus, from a strictly correlational viewpoint, the difference between these two fuzzy sets is slight. From a set-theoretic viewpoint, however, they are quite different, for the set-theoretic cov-

erage of democracy by developed is only 0.35, while the coverage of democracy by at least moderately developed is 0.52. The insensitivity of correlation to calibration follows directly from the fact that correlation is computationally reliant on deviations from an inductively derived, sample-specific measure of central tendency—the mean. For this reason, correlation is incapable of analyzing set-theoretic relations and, correspondingly, cannot be used to assess causal sufficiency or necessity.

Conclusion

This chapter demonstrates both the power of fuzzy sets and the centrality of calibration to their fruitful use. It is important to be able to assess not only "more versus less" (uncalibrated measurement) but also "a lot versus a little" (calibrated measurement). The use of calibrated measures grounds social science in substantive knowledge and enhances the relevance of the results of social research to practical and policy issues. Fuzzy sets are especially powerful as carriers of calibration. They offer measurement tools that transcend the quantitative/qualitative divide in the social sciences.

Current practices in quantitative social science undercut serious attention to calibration. These difficulties stem from reliance on the indicator approach to measurement, which requires only variation across sample points and treats all variation as equally meaningful. The limitations of the indicator approach are compounded and reinforced by correlational methods, which are insensitive to calibrations implemented by researchers. Reliance on deviations from the mean tends to neutralize the impact of any direct calibration implemented by the researcher. A further difficulty arises when it is acknowledged that almost all social science theory is set theoretic in nature and that correlational methods are incapable of assessing set-theoretic relations.

The set-theoretic nature of most social science theory is not generally recognized by social scientists today, nor is the fact that the assessment of set-theoretic arguments and set calibration go hand in hand.

Set theoretic analysis without careful calibration of set membership is an exercise in futility. It follows that researchers need to be faithful to their theories by clearly identifying the target sets that correspond to the concepts central to their theories and by specifying useful external criteria that can be used to guide the calibration of set membership.

Practical Appendix: Using fsQCA to Calibrate Fuzzy Sets (Direct Method)

1. In fuzzy-set qualitative comparative analysis (fsQCA), create or retrieve your data set. For example, you might have an SPSS or Excel file with the relevant interval- or ratio-scale data. Save these files as comma-delimited or tab-delimited files with simple variable names on the first row of the file. Make sure missing data are blank and not assigned a special code (e.g., –999).

2. With your data in the data spreadsheet window of fsQCA, click the Variables menu; then click Compute.

3. In the compute dialogue box, name the target fuzzy set. Select a simple name (two to eight characters), using standard alphanumeric characters and no spaces, dashes, or punctuation.

4. Click calibrate(x,n1,n2,n3) in the Functions menu and then click the up arrow that is next to the word Functions. Next, calibrate(,,,) will appear in the Expression field of the dialogue box.

5. Edit the expression so that calibrate(,,,) becomes something like calibrate(intvar,25,10,2), where intvar is the name of the existing interval- or ratio-scale variable already in the file, the first number is the value of intvar you have chosen as the threshold for full membership in the target set (fuzzy score = 0.95); the second number is the value of intvar that you have selected for the crossover point (fuzzy score = 0.5), and the third number is the value of intvar that you have selected for the threshold for full nonmembership in the target set (fuzzy score = 0.05).

6. Click OK. Check the data spreadsheet to make sure it came out as you expected. It is possible to sort the original interval-scale vari-

able in descending or ascending order using the pull-down menus. Click any case in the column you want to sort, then click Cases, and then Sort Ascending or Sort Descending. You can then check the corresponding fuzzy scores to see if they conform with your interval- or ratio-scale variable in the manner you intended.

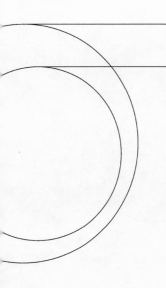

PART III

Configurations of Conditions
versus "Independent" Variables

6: Configurational Thinking

This chapter sketches the main features of configurational thinking, which is the basis for many forms of analysis in the social sciences. Qualitative researchers especially tend to think in terms of combinations and configurations because of their interest in context and in understanding social phenomena holistically. In case-oriented research, investigators often think of causal conditions in terms of what might be called *causal recipes*—the causally relevant conditions that combine to produce a given outcome. This interest in combinations of causes dovetails with a focus on "how" things happen. To think in terms of recipes is to think holistically and to understand causally relevant conditions as intersections of forces and events.

This chapter first examines configurational thinking in the case study and then shows how research can build on the study of a single case, using the idea of causal recipes. After briefly discussing the problems that the study of causal recipes pose for conventional quantitative research, the chapter turns to a key issue in configurational thinking using fuzzy sets—how to assess the degree of membership of a case in a configuration. Assessing degree of membership in a configuration is the foundation for the assessment of causal recipes. Further, the chapter shows how to use the measures of set-theoretic consistency and coverage presented in chapter 3 to compare recipes and evaluate their relative explanatory power.

Configurational Thinking and Case-Oriented Research

The centrality of configurational thinking to social research is most apparent in one of its most elemental forms—the case study. Suppose, for example, that a researcher argues that Peru experienced waves of mass protest against austerity programs mandated by the International Monetary Fund (IMF) because of (1) the severity of these austerity measures, (2) the high concentration of the poor in urban slums, (3) the perceived corruption of government officials, and (4) the substantial prior level of political mobilization and contention. This explanation of austerity protest cites a specific *combination* of conditions, some relatively long-standing (e.g., the concentration of the poor in urban slums) and some temporally proximate (e.g., the severity of the austerity measures mandated by the IMF). The explanation has the character of a recipe—all four conditions were met simultaneously in the case of Peru, and together they explain the explosion of protest following the imposition of stiff austerity measures by the IMF in the 1980s.

Like almost all arguments based on the study of a single case, the argument that this combination of causal conditions accounts for austerity protest in Peru is an *asymmetric* argument, that is, it is an explanation of a positive instance of austerity protest and is not necessarily intended as either a complete explanation of all austerity protest or as an explanation of the absence of austerity protest. By contrast, if the argument had been presented in a *symmetric* manner, the expectation would be that in order to avoid austerity protest, satisfying this recipe would have to be avoided. But several or even many recipes may exist for austerity protest, and avoiding Peru's recipe may not offer much protection. In the language of set theory, the recipe for austerity protest observed in Peru is a member of the larger set of recipes for austerity protest. Viewing all instances of austerity protest as a set, there may be cases displaying the same recipe as Peru, but there may be many cases displaying alternate recipes. The fact that there are alternate recipes (and thus many instances of the outcome, austerity protest, which fail to display the same combination of causal conditions displayed by

Peru) does not invalidate Peru's recipe as a sufficient (but not necessary) combination of conditions for mass austerity protest.

Using the analysis of Peru as a springboard, a researcher could move in either of two main research directions. The first possible direction would be to find other instances of austerity protest and examine the extent to which they agree in displaying the same recipe, the same combination of four causal ingredients, found in Peru, that is, do all (or virtually all) instances of austerity protest display these four antecedent conditions? This strategy employs the common qualitative research strategy of selecting on the dependent variable, an approach that is almost universally, but mistakenly, condemned by quantitative researchers (see, e.g., King, Keohane, and Verba 1994). The second direction would be to try to find other instances of Peru's recipe and examine whether these cases also experienced austerity protest. In essence, the researcher would select cases on the basis of their scores on the independent variable. In this example, however, the independent variable is a recipe with its four main conditions all satisfied. The goal of the second strategy would be to assess the recipe, Does it invariably (or at least with substantial consistency) lead to austerity protest?

Both of these strategies are set theoretic in nature and conform to the two general set-theoretic approaches described in chapter 1 (see also Ragin and Rihoux 2004). The first is an examination of whether instances of the outcome (austerity protest) constitute a subset of instances of a combination of causal conditions (i.e., Peru's recipe). This demonstration would establish that the causal conditions in question are necessary. The second is an examination of whether instances of a specific combination of causal conditions (Peru's recipe) constitute a subset of instances of an outcome (austerity protest). This demonstration would establish that the combination of causal conditions is sufficient. Of course, both strategies could be used, and if both subset relations were confirmed, then the two sets (the set of cases with Peru's recipe and the set of cases with austerity protest) would coincide. While it might appear that the two strategies together constitute a correlational analysis, recall that correlations are strong when there are many "null-null" instances—cases that lack both the causal recipe and the outcome.

Neither of these two research strategies depends on such cases in any direct manner.

One of the most important aspects of configurational thinking is that it links directly to cases, causal processes, and causal mechanisms (Boswell and Brown 1999). That is, usually a direct correspondence exists in configurational work between causal arguments and case-level analysis. The argument that a specific combination of conditions generates some outcome directs attention not only toward specific cases, as in the Peru austerity protest example, but also toward specific features of these cases. Further, the combination of conditions cited by the investigator should have an internal coherence—the combination should make sense as a causal recipe. Ultimately, causation can be observed only at the case level; a combinatorial causal argument provides explicit guidance regarding what to observe in an empirical case and very often also implies specific causal mechanisms that both link the different ingredients together and indicate the nature of their connections to the outcome.

Configurations and Conventional Quantitative Analysis

In conventional quantitative research, independent variables are seen as analytically separable causes of the outcome under investigation. Typically, each causal variable is thought to have an autonomous or independent capacity to influence the level, intensity, or probability of the dependent variable. Most applications of conventional quantitative methods assume that the effects of the independent variables are both linear and additive, which means that the impact of a given independent variable on the dependent variable is assumed to be the same regardless of the values of the other independent variables. Estimates of net effects assume that the impact of a given independent variable is the same not only across all the values of the other independent variables but also across all their different combinations (see Ragin 2006a and chapter 10 in this book.)

To estimate the net effect of a given independent variable, the researcher offsets the impact of competing causal conditions by subtracting from the estimate of the effect of each variable any explained variation in the dependent variable it shares with other causal variables. This is the core meaning of *net effects*—the calculation of the non-overlapping contribution of each independent variable to explained variation in the dependent variable. Degree of overlap is a direct function of correlation. Generally, the greater the correlation of an independent variable with its competitors, the less its net effect.

When confronted with arguments that cite combined conditions (e.g., that a recipe of some sort must be satisfied), the usual recommendation is that researchers model combinations of conditions as interaction effects and test for the significance of the incremental contribution of "statistical interaction" to explained variation in the dependent variable. When there is interaction, the size of the effect of an independent variable (e.g., the severity of IMF-mandated austerity) on a dependent variable (e.g., intensity of austerity protest) depends upon the values of one or more other independent variables (e.g., the perceived level of corruption of government officials). For example, a researcher might argue that the perception of corruption might make the social and political fallout from the imposition of severe austerity measures much more explosive.

However, as explained in detail in Ragin (1987) and related publications, estimation techniques designed for linear-additive models often come up short when assigned the task of estimating complex interaction effects. The data requirements alone are substantial, especially when the goal is to estimate higher-order interactions (e.g., the four-way interaction that constitutes Peru's recipe). Furthermore, many controversies and difficulties surround the use of any variable that lacks a meaningful zero point in multiplicative interaction models (see, e.g., Allison 1977). More generally, it is unreasonable to expect techniques that are specifically designed to estimate the net effects of independent variables in linear-additive models to do a good job of assessing causal recipes, especially in situations where multiple recipes may be involved.

The challenge posed by configurational thinking is to see causal conditions not as adversaries in the struggle to explain variation in dependent variables but as potential collaborators in the production of outcomes. The key issue is not which variable is the strongest (i.e., has the biggest net effect) but how different conditions combine and whether there is only one combination or several different combinations of conditions (causal recipes) capable of generating the same outcome. Once these combinations are identified, it is possible to specify the contexts that enable or disable specific causes. For example, a researcher might find that the combination of severe IMF-mandated austerity and perceived government corruption yields severe IMF protest only in countries with a history of political contention. Thus, a history of contention "enables" explosive consequences when austerity and corruption combine.

Assessing Degree of Membership in a Configuration

As an alternative to testing for statistical interaction, consider addressing the problem of causal configurations as a measurement issue. That is, rather than testing interaction effects against additive effects in linear models, as recommended in texts on quantitative methods, simply measure the degree to which specific recipes are present (i.e., have been met or satisfied) in relevant cases. Fuzzy sets are especially useful for this task.

With fuzzy sets, the degree to which a case exhibits a combination of conditions is determined by the condition that registers the lowest score or lowest degree of expression (i.e., the minimum membership score). This "weakest link" thinking argues, in effect, that the degree to which a case expresses a combination of conditions (or configuration) is only as strong as its degree of expression of its weakest element. Fuzzy sets provide a direct way to operationalize this principle as a measurement strategy (see Ragin 2000, 309–33), using fuzzy-set intersection. All relevant case aspects are calibrated in the same manner, with degree of membership in the relevant sets ranging from 0.0 (full nonmembership) to 1.0 (full membership). Degree of membership in a combination of memberships (i.e., a configuration) is simply the minimum (lowest) fuzzy membership score among the causal conditions and other case aspects that are combined in a recipe (see chapter 2 for a discussion of the basics of fuzzy-set analysis and fuzzy algebra).

For example, assume a researcher is interested in the degree to which different countries exhibit Peru's recipe for austerity protest. The four ingredients in this recipe are (1) severe IMF austerity measures (A), (2) the concentration of the poor in urban slums (S), (3) the perception of government corruption (P), and (4) a recent history of political mobilization and contention (M). Once these conditions are calibrated as fuzzy sets showing the degree of membership of cases in each of these sets, it is possible to use these fuzzy sets to construct a simple measure of the degree to which cases combine these four conditions:

$$R_i = \min(A_i, S_i, P_i, M_i)$$

where R is degree of membership in the recipe (the combination of four conditions), min indicates the selection of the lowest of the four fuzzy scores, and i indicates that the formula is applied to cases individually. After using fuzzy sets to calculate the degree to which different countries conform to this recipe, the researcher could then assess the connection between how strongly cases exhibit (or conform to) this recipe and their degree of membership in the outcome (degree of membership in the set of countries with mass protest against the International Monetary Fund), also operationalized as a fuzzy set. If Peru's recipe is one of several possible recipes (and thus sufficient but not necessary), then the expectation is that cases conforming to this recipe should constitute a subset of the cases with mass protest. This relationship, if plotted, would appear as an upper-left triangle in the plot of degree of membership the set of cases with austerity protest (Y axis) against degree of membership in the given causal recipe (X axis).

Comparing Causal Recipes

Using fuzzy sets to address recipes is quite flexible, and it is a simple matter to formulate and compare competing recipes. It is also possible to compare simpler versions of a recipe against more complex versions. For example, a researcher might argue that the perception of government corruption (**P**) is not an essential ingredient in the recipe for mass austerity protest and propose an alternate formulation that omits this causal condition from the recipe. The simplified, three-condition recipe in this example would be:

$$R_i = \min(A_i, S_i, M_i)$$

In order to compare the two recipes, the researcher would measure the degree of membership of relevant cases in both recipes and then assess the set-theoretic connection between the two recipes on the one hand and the outcome on the other hand, using the measures of set-theoretic consistency and coverage presented in chapter 3.

In this example, the comparison is between a four-condition causal recipe and a three-condition recipe, where the three-condition recipe is a simplified and therefore more inclusive version of the four-condition recipe. Note that the degree of membership in the four-condition recipe is a subset of degree of membership in the three-condition recipe. That is, each case's degree of membership in the four-condition recipe must be less than or equal to its degree of membership in the three-condition recipe. A simple way to understand this mathematical property is to recognize that with four conditions, there is an additional opportunity for cases to receive a low score in the recipe because of the inclusion of condition **P** (perception of government corruption). From a set-theoretic viewpoint, it is always true that compounding sets (as when condition **P** is added to the combination of **A**, **S**, and **M**) produces subsets via set intersection (see chapter 2).

The expectation in this example is that Peru's recipe is only one of several routes to mass protest against the IMF; therefore, degree of membership in Peru's recipe should be a subset of degree of membership in IMF protest. The set-theoretic analysis, therefore, would proceed as follows:

1. Measure each case's degree of membership in the four-condition recipe.

2. Measure each case's degree of membership in the three-condition recipe.

3. Measure each case's degree of membership in the outcome, mass protest against the IMF.

4. Assess the consistency of the four-condition recipe as a subset of the outcome. If it is consistent, assess its coverage.

5. Assess the consistency of the three-condition recipe as a subset of the outcome. If it is consistent, assess its coverage.

6. Compare the two sets of results.

As noted in chapter 3, often a trade-off occurs between consistency and coverage. Because membership scores in the four-condition recipe must be less than or equal to membership scores in the three-condition recipe, the consistency of the four-condition recipe generally will be greater than or equal to the consistency of the three-condition recipe.[1] By contrast, the reverse is true for coverage. Because membership scores in the three-condition recipe must be greater than or equal to membership scores in the four-condition recipe, then the coverage of the three-condition recipe generally will be greater than or equal to the coverage of the four-condition recipe.

The relevant patterns are illustrated in figures 6.1 and 6.2, using hypothetical data. Figure 6.1 shows the plot of the four-condition recipe against the outcome (IMF protest), along with relevant consistency and coverage measures. Figure 6.2 provides the same information using the three-condition recipe. Notice that in the first plot, most points are consistently above the diagonal; the few that stray are not far below the diagonal. Thus, this plot registers a high consistency score, 0.93, indicating that the evidence supports the claim that membership in the four-condition recipe is a subset of membership in the outcome, which indicates in turn that it would be reasonable to attempt an interpretation of causal sufficiency for this recipe. This relatively high consistency score also permits interpretation of the coverage score, which is 0.53. Thus, the coverage of the outcome by the four-condition recipe is substantial, accounting for more than half of the sum of the

---

1. It is possible to construct a data set in which the set-theoretic consistency of a simpler recipe, using a subset of ingredients, is greater than the set-theoretic consistency of a more complex recipe, but this situation is rare empirically.

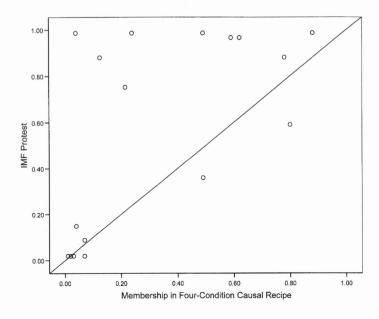

Set-theoretic consistency: 0.93
Set-theoretic coverage: 0.53

Figure 6.1 Plot of membership in IMF protest against membership in the four-condition causal recipe

memberships in the outcome. By contrast, the three-condition recipe has more cases below the diagonal and a correspondingly lower consistency score, 0.79. The gap between the two scores (0.93 to 0.79) indicates a substantial increase in inconsistency when condition **P** (perception of government corruption) is removed from the recipe. Correspondingly, this borderline consistency score (0.79) indicates that it would be hazardous to interpret the coverage measure reported for figure 6.2 (0.66). (See chapter 3 on the use and interpretation of measures of set-theoretic consistency and coverage.)

The procedure just outlined can be extended so that researchers can assess all possible versions of a given recipe (that is, all possible subsets of the ingredients specified in the "full" version of the recipe). In the example shown in figure 6.2, only one causal condition has been removed (**P**), yielding a single three-condition recipe. Altogether, in addition to the four-condition recipe, there are four three-condition recipes (when using the four-condition recipe as the starting point), six two-condition recipes, and four one-condition recipes. Using fuzzy-set methods, the degree of membership of cases in each of these fifteen possible recipes can be assessed, and these scores, in turn, can be used to assess the consistency and coverage of each recipe as a subset of the outcome. In this way, researchers can compare simpler versions of a given recipe with more complex versions. If a simpler version has comparable consistency but greater coverage than a more complex version, then it might be preferred. As an example of this type of analysis, suppose the examination of the fifteen recipes revealed that degree of membership in a two-condition recipe, say the

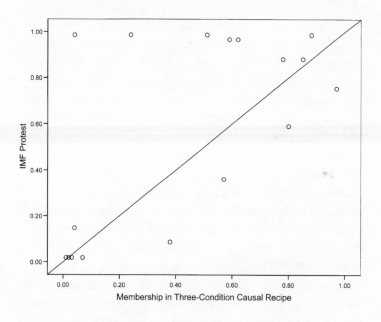

| Set-theoretic consistency: | 0.79 |
| Set-theoretic coverage: | 0.66 |

Figure 6.2 Plot of membership in IMF protest against membership in the three-condition causal recipe

combination of severe IMF austerity measures (**A**) and the perception of government corruption (**P**), formed a consistent subset of the outcome, IMF protest, with a consistency score of 0.90 and a coverage score of 0.71. The researcher might well prefer this more parsimonious explanation to the original, four-condition recipe. While a small amount of set-theoretic consistency has been sacrificed (0.93 for the four-condition recipe versus 0.90 for the two-condition recipe), there is a substantial increase in set-theoretic coverage (0.71 for the two-condition recipe versus 0.53 for the four-condition recipe). A coverage score of 0.71 indicates that the two-condition recipe accounts for 71 percent of the sum of the membership scores in the outcome.

Still, it is important to avoid becoming infatuated with parsimony. Consider the following results: a four-condition recipe has a consistency score of 0.93 and a coverage score of 0.80, while a three-condition recipe (using three of the four conditions in the previous recipe) has only slightly different scores, consistency = 0.91 and coverage = 0.81. In other words, the difference between the two recipes with respect to these set-theoretic measures is substantively trivial. The scientifically based impulse is to favor the more parsimonious three-condition recipe. But consider the fact that from a configurational perspective, the four-condition recipe might make more sense. That is, when using it as a guide for understanding cases, the four-condition recipe might offer a more complete account, connect better to the observed causal processes, and offer a better basis for understanding the causal mechanisms at work. In short, if a more complex explanation scores roughly the same as a more parsimonious explanation, the more complex explanation might be preferred to the more parsimonious explanation on substantive and theoretical grounds.

Some readers no doubt are hungry, at this point, for some probabilistic tests, applied especially to measures of consistency. Because consistency is a proportion, these tests can be readily applied. For example, as shown in *Fuzzy-Set Social Science* (Ragin 2000), it is possible to set a benchmark consistency score and an alpha level before calculating consistency scores, and then find out which observed consistency scores are significantly greater than the benchmark value, given the number of cases included in the study. Is a consistency score of 0.93 significantly greater than a benchmark score of 0.75, using an alpha level of 0.05 and an N of 50? It is easy enough to find out. It is also possible to determine if one observed consistency score is significantly greater than another observed consistency score for a given number of cases and a given alpha. This same test can be computed for two observed coverage scores, which are also proportions. This marriage of set-theoretic analysis and probabilistic analysis is useful, and others are encouraged to explore the possibilities. The emphasis here, however, is on a descriptive understanding of consistency and coverage.

Finally, it is important to emphasize again that the real test of any recipe is how well it resonates with case knowledge. An important part of any set-theoretic analysis is a return to the cases. As noted at the outset, configurational reasoning in general, and the idea of causal recipes specifically, facilitates the dialogue between cross-case analysis and within-case analysis that is central to this return. When formulated as causal recipes (and not as the net effects of independent variables), the connection between analytic findings and empirical cases is greatly strengthened.

Practical Appendix: How to Assess a Causal Recipe

Sometimes researchers have a specific recipe in mind or may want to compare a small number of different recipes with respect to their set-theoretic consistency and coverage. Using fuzzy-set qualitative comparative analysis (fsQCA), the steps are as follows:

1. Define the recipe. Typically, the recipe is a specific combination of conditions, and the first objective is to assess the conformity of each case to this specific combination. For example, a researcher might specify a causal recipe that combines four conditions (ingredients).

2. Determine the degree of membership of each case in each of the conditions included in the recipe, conceiving each condition as a fuzzy set. If necessary, use the procedures detailed in chapter 5 to transform interval- and ratio-scale variables into well-calibrated fuzzy sets.

3. Calculate the degree of membership of each case in the recipe. To do this, first retrieve your data set (with well-calibrated fuzzy sets) into fsQCA. With your data set in the data spreadsheet window, click *Variables,* then click *Compute,* and the *Compute Variable* dialogue box will appear. Name the target fuzzy set. Select a simple name (two to eight characters), using standard alphanumeric characters and no spaces, dashes, or punctuation (e.g., "recipe1").

4. Click *fuzzyand(x, . . . ,)* in the *Functions* menu and then click the up arrow that is next to the word *Functions.* Next, *fuzzyand()* will appear in the *Expression* field of the dialogue box. The fuzzyand function performs fuzzy-set intersection, which means that it selects the lowest membership score for each case from the fuzzy sets that are listed inside the parentheses. With fuzzy-set intersection, the degree to which a case displays a given causal recipe is only as strong as its expression of its weakest constituent ingredient.

5. Edit the expression so that *fuzzyand()* becomes something like *fuzzyand(fvar1,fvar2,fvar3,fvar4),* where fvar1 to fvar4 are the variable names of the conditions that make up the recipe (in this example, there are four ingredients), using fuzzy-set variable names in the existing data file. Click *OK.*

6. Check the data spreadsheet to make sure it came out as you expected. It is possible to sort degree of membership in the newly computed recipe in descending or ascending order using the pull-down menus. Click any case in the column you want to sort, then click *Cases,* and then *Sort Ascending* or *Sort Descending.*

7. A simple way to assess the set-theoretic connection between the recipe just computed and a fuzzy-set outcome is to use the XY plot procedure. From the data spreadsheet window, click *Graphs,* then *Fuzzy,* then *XY Plot.* Specify the fuzzy sets to be plotted on the X and Y axes by clicking the adjacent down arrows and then clicking the relevant variable names. For the Y axis, click the fuzzy set for degree of membership in the outcome. For the X axis, click degree of membership in the causal recipe. Specify an optional *Case Id Variable* so that the case or cases that reside on specific points in the plot can be identified.

8. Click *Plot*. If the expectation is that membership in the recipe is sufficient but not necessary for membership in the outcome, then the points should be on or above the main diagonal of the plot. The number shown in the box that is above the upper-left corner of the plot shows the degree of consistency of the plot with the subset relation ($X_i \leq Y_i$). The number that is in the box below the lower-right corner of the plot is the degree of set-theoretic coverage of the outcome by the specified recipe (see chapter 3).

7: Configurational Analysis Using Fuzzy Sets and Truth Tables

An especially useful aspect of configurational thinking is its attention to causal complexity. *Causal complexity* is defined as a situation in which a given outcome may follow from several different combinations of causal conditions—from different causal "recipes." For example, as suggested in chapter 6, a researcher may have good reason to suspect that several different recipes lead to mass protest against International Monetary Fund (IMF)-mandated austerity measures. By examining the fate of cases with different combinations of causally relevant conditions, it is possible to identify the decisive recipes and thereby unravel causal complexity.

As explained in chapter 1 (see also Ragin 1987, 2000), the key tool for systematic analysis of causal complexity is the "truth table." Crisp truth tables list the logically possible combinations of dichotomous causal conditions (e.g., presence/absence of severe IMF-mandated austerity measures, presence/absence of high concentrations of the poor in urban slums, presence/absence of perceived corruption of government officials, and presence/absence of substantial prior level of political mobilization and contention), along with the outcome exhibited by the cases conforming to each combination of causal conditions (e.g., whether austerity protest is consistently present among the cases displaying each combination of conditions). A truth table using this four-condition recipe would have sixteen rows, one for each logically possible combination of causal conditions. In more complex truth tables, the rows (each representing a different combination of causal conditions) may be numerous, for the number of causal combinations is an exponential function of the number of causal conditions (number of combinations = 2^k, where k is the number of causal conditions). In effect, a crisp truth table turns k presence/absence causal conditions into 2^k configurations, as illustrated in table 1.4.

The truth table approach to causal complexity is much more rigorous and exacting than the one sketched in chapter 6. The concern in chapter 6 was for a given causal recipe and the various simplified versions of that recipe that could be constructed from subsets of the conditions specified in the initial recipe. By contrast, the truth table approach is based on all logically possible combinations of the causal conditions specified by the investigator, which typically includes conditions drawn from different perspectives and thus different recipes. Further, rather than looking at different subsets of a given set of conditions (with conditions either present or irrelevant), the truth table approach considers all logically possible combinations of conditions, considering both their presence and their absence. Thus, the truth table approach allows for the possibility that different casual recipes may operate when a given condition (e.g., the perception of corruption in the austerity protest example) is present versus absent (as opposed to irrelevant). For example, one recipe for austerity protest might require an *absence* of a perception of corruption—that is, that government officials be perceived as *not* corrupt. Examining all logically possible combinations of causal conditions makes it possible to construct experiment design–like contrasts (where only one causal condition at a time is allowed to vary) and thus offers a thorough analysis of the effects of relevant causal conditions. In effect, the impact of each cause is examined in all logically possible contexts (the 2^k configurations of conditions).

The goal of truth table construction is to identify explicit connections between combinations of causal conditions and outcomes. Using the truth table, it is possible to assess the sufficiency of all logically possible combinations of presence/absence conditions (the 2^k causal configurations) that can be constructed from a given set of k causal conditions. The combinations that pass sufficiency are then logically simplified in a bottom-up fashion. For example, in the analysis of conditions linked to mass protest against the IMF, if the cases with all four conditions present all experience austerity protest and the cases with three of four of the conditions present (and one absent) also all experience protest, then the researcher can conclude that the causal condition that varies across these two combinations is irrelevant in this context. (Readers interested in the specific procedures used to simplify truth tables and thereby unravel causal complexity should consult Ragin 1987, 2000).

Truth tables also discipline the process of learning about cases and the effort to generalize about them. For example, suppose a truth table for austerity protest based on conclusions drawn from the Peruvian case (see chapter 6) revealed substantial inconsistency in Peru's row—that is, suppose there are several cases in the row that failed to exhibit austerity protest, in addition to the ones, like Peru, that did. This inconsistency in outcomes signals to the investigator that more in-depth study of cases is needed. For example, by comparing the cases in this row lacking austerity protest with those exhibiting protest, it would be possible to elaborate the recipe. Suppose this comparison revealed that the cases lacking austerity protest all had regimes with extensive repressive capacities and histories of severe political repression. This ingredient (the *absence* of extensive repressive capacities) could then be added to the recipe, and the truth table could be reformulated accordingly with five causal conditions. Notice that it would have been difficult to know, based on knowledge of only the Peruvian case, that this factor (absence of extensive repressive capacity) is an important part of the recipe because it is (hypothetically) absent in Peru and in cases like Peru. This point underscores the value of comparative analysis more generally, for it is often difficult to identify causal ingredients that must be absent when studying only positive instances of an outcome.

Fuzzy Sets and Truth Tables

This chapter builds bridges between fuzzy sets, configurations, and truth table analysis, demonstrating how to construct a conventional Boolean truth table from fuzzy-set data and then how to use it to

Table 7.1: Fuzzy-set data on class voting in the advanced industrial societies

Country	Weak class voting (W)	Affluent (A)	Income inequality (I)	Manufac- turing (M)	Strong unions (U)
Australia	0.6	0.8	0.6	0.4	0.6
Belgium	0.6	0.6	0.2	0.2	0.8
Denmark	0.2	0.6	0.4	0.2	0.8
France	0.8	0.6	0.8	0.2	0.2
Germany	0.6	0.6	0.8	0.4	0.4
Ireland	0.8	0.2	0.6	0.8	0.8
Italy	0.6	0.4	0.8	0.2	0.6
Netherlands	0.8	0.6	0.4	0.2	0.4
Norway	0.2	0.6	0.4	0.6	0.8
Sweden	0.0	0.8	0.4	0.8	1.0
United Kingdom	0.4	0.6	0.6	0.8	0.6
United States	1.0	1.0	0.8	0.4	0.2

unravel causal complexity. This technique takes full advantage of the gradations in set membership central to the constitution of fuzzy sets and is not predicated upon a dichotomization of fuzzy membership scores. To illustrate these procedures, the chapter uses data on class voting in the advanced industrial societies compiled by Paul Nieuw-beerta (see, e.g., Nieuwbeerta 1995; Nieuwbeerta and De Graaf 1999; Nieuwbeerta and Ultee 1999; Nieuwbeerta, De Graaf and Ultee 2000), the same data set introduced in chapter 2. This simple data set is re-produced in table 7.1. Degree of membership in the set of advanced industrial democracies with weak class voting (**W**) is the outcome; the causal conditions are degree of membership in the set of highly affluent countries (**A**), degree of membership in the set of countries with substantial income inequality (**I**), degree of membership in the set of countries with substantial manufacturing employment (**M**), and degree of membership in the set of countries with strong unions (**U**). The fuzzy membership scores reflect general characterizations of these countries over the second half of the twentieth century.

It is important to point out that the approach sketched in this chapter offers an entirely new way to conduct fuzzy-set analysis of social data, an analytic strategy that is superior in several respects to the one sketched in *Fuzzy-Set Social Science* (Ragin 2000). While both approaches have strengths and weaknesses, the one presented here uses the truth table as the key analytic device. A further advantage of the fuzzy-set truth table approach presented in this chapter is that it is more transparent, and thus the researcher has more direct control over the analysis. This type of control is central to the practice of case-oriented research.

The bridge from fuzzy sets to truth tables has three main pillars. The first pillar is the *direct correspondence* that exists between the rows of a truth table and the corners of the vector space defined by fuzzy-set causal conditions (Ragin 2000). The second pillar is the assessment of the *distribution of cases* across the different logically possible combinations of causal conditions (i.e., the distribution of cases across sectors of the vector space defined by the fuzzy-set causal conditions). The third pillar is the assessment of the *consistency of the evidence* for each causal combination with the argument that it is a subset of the outcome. As explained in chapter 1, the subset relation is important because it signals an explicit connection between a combination of causal conditions and an outcome. Once these three pillars are in place, it is possible to construct a truth table that summarizes the results of analyses of fuzzy-set relations and then to analyze this truth table. In effect, the analysis of the truth table synthesizes the results of multiple fuzzy-set analyses.

The Correspondence between Vector Space Corners and Truth Table Rows

A multidimensional vector space constructed from fuzzy-set causal conditions has 2^k corners, just as a crisp truth table has 2^k rows (where k is the number of causal conditions). A direct correspondence exists between causal combinations, truth table rows, and vector space corners (Ragin 2000). For example, a simple truth table with two crisp-set causal conditions has four rows: 00, 01, 10, and 11; a vector space formed from two fuzzy-set causal conditions has four corners: (0,0),

(0,1), (1,0), and (1,1). In crisp-set analyses, cases are sorted into truth table rows according to their specific combinations of presence/absence scores on the causal conditions. Thus, each case is assigned to a unique row, and each row embraces a unique subset of the cases included in the study. With fuzzy sets, however, cases may have varying degrees of membership in the different corners of the vector space and thus varying degrees of membership in the corresponding truth table rows. The degree of membership of a case in a given corner of the fuzzy-set vector space is determined by its membership scores. For example, a case with a membership of 0.7 in set **B** and a membership of 0.9 in set **C** has a membership of 0.7 in the (1,1) corner (**B·C**) of the vector space formed by these two fuzzy sets (the minimum of 0.7 and 0.9 is 0.7). This same case has a membership of 0.1 in the (0,0) corner (~**B·**~**C**) of the vector space,[1] where ~ signals fuzzy-set negation, which corresponds to absence using crisp sets, and · denotes set intersections (logical *and*).

Despite this feature of fuzzy sets, truth tables can still be used to aid fuzzy-set analysis. Specifically, the researcher can use truth table rows as specifications of the corners of the vector space and use the truth table *to summarize statements about the characteristics of the causal combination represented by each corner.* For example, the researcher might calculate degree of membership in the ~**A·**~**I·M·U** corner of the vector space (the combination of low membership in highly affluent, low membership in substantial inequality, high membership in substantial manufacturing employment, and high membership in strong unions) and assess whether degree of membership in this corner of the vector space is a consistent subset of degree of membership in the outcome (weak class voting, **W**). (See chapters 2 and 6 on the calculation of degree of membership in a combination of conditions.) The researcher would then use the techniques sketched in chapter 3 for assessing fuzzy subset relations and use the membership scores for *all* cases in this assessment, not just those with strong membership

---

1. The membership of this case in ~**B·**~**C** = min(~**B**,~**C**) = min(1 − 0.7, 1 − 0.9) = min(0.3,0.1) = 0.1. See chapter 1 for a discussion of basic operations on fuzzy sets.

scores. If degree of membership in this corner of the vector space (which corresponds to one of the sixteen combinations of causal conditions) is consistently less than or equal to degree of membership in the outcome across all cases, then the researcher can conclude that membership in the causal combination is a subset of membership in the outcome. The researcher would then append information about the results of this assessment to the truth table row corresponding to the relevant corner of the vector space. In this way, the entire truth table can be used to summarize the results of 2^k fuzzy-set analyses.

Thus, in the translation of fuzzy sets to truth tables, the truth table represents *statements* about the corners of the vector space formed by the fuzzy-set causal conditions. Two pieces of information about each vector space corner are especially important: (1) the *number* of cases with strong membership in each corner (i.e., in each combination of causal conditions) and (2) the *consistency* of the empirical evidence for each corner with the argument that degree of membership in the corner is a subset of degree of membership in the outcome.

The Distribution of Cases across Causal Combinations

The distribution of cases across causal combinations is easy to assess when causal conditions are represented with crisp sets, for it is a simple matter to construct a truth table from such data and to examine the number of cases crisply sorted into each row. When causal conditions are fuzzy sets, however, this analysis is less straightforward because each case may have partial membership in every truth table row (i.e., in every corner of the vector space). Still, it is important to assess the distribution of cases' membership scores across causal combinations in fuzzy-set analyses because some causal combinations may be empirically trivial. In other words, if most cases have very low or zero membership in a combination, then it is pointless to assess that combination's link to the outcome. The empirical basis for such an assessment would be too weak to warrant it. Some corners of the vector space may have many cases with strong membership; other corners may have only a few cases with any degree of membership at all. When constructing a truth table from fuzzy sets, it is important to take these differences into account.

Table 7.2 shows the distribution of the membership scores of the twelve countries across the sixteen logically possible combinations of the four causal conditions shown in table 7.1. Lowercase letters in this table signal the negation of a condition ($\mathbf{a} = \sim\mathbf{A}$). In essence, the table lists the sixteen corners of the four-dimensional vector space that is formed by the four fuzzy sets and shows as well the degree of membership of each case in each corner. This table demonstrates an important property of intersections of fuzzy sets, namely, that each case can have (at most) only a single membership score greater than 0.5 in the logically possible combinations formed from a given set of causal conditions.[2] A membership score greater than 0.5 in a causal combination signals that a case is more in than out of the causal combination in question. A score greater than 0.5 also indicates to which corner of the multidimensional vector space a given case is closest. This property of fuzzy sets allows investigators to determine how many cases are close to each corner of the vector space, based on their degree of membership. The last row of table 7.2 shows the number of cases with greater than 0.5 membership in each corner.

The key task in this phase of the analysis is to establish a number-of-cases threshold, that is, to develop a rule for classifying some combinations of conditions as relevant and others as *remainders* based on the number of cases with greater than 0.5 membership in each combination. (A remainder row in fuzzy-set qualitative comparative analysis, or fsQCA, is a logically possible combination of conditions lacking empirical instances—either because the researcher has inadequate information about such cases or because the cases simply do not exist.) The rule established by the investigator must reflect the nature of the

---

2. Note that if a case has 0.5 membership in a causal condition, then its maximum membership in any causal combination that includes that condition is only 0.5. Thus, any case with a code of 0.5 on a causal condition will not be "closest" to any single corner of the vector space defined by the causal conditions. Thus, it is good practice to avoid, if possible, using the 0.5 membership score (which signals maximum ambiguity) when assessing degree of membership in a causal condition.

Table 7.2: Assessing the distribution of cases across combinations of causal conditions

Country	a·i·m·u	a·i·m·U	a·i·M·u	a·i·M·U	a·I·m·u	a·I·m·U	a·I·M·u	a·I·M·U	A·i·m·u	A·i·m·U	A·i·M·u	A·i·M·U	A·I·m·u	A·I·m·U	A·I·M·u	A·I·M·U
Australia	0.200	0.200	0.200	0.200	0.200	0.200	0.200	0.200	0.400	0.400	0.400	0.400	0.400	0.600	0.400	0.400
Belgium	0.200	0.400	0.200	0.200	0.200	0.200	0.200	0.200	0.200	0.600	0.200	0.200	0.200	0.200	0.200	0.200
Denmark	0.200	0.400	0.200	0.200	0.200	0.400	0.200	0.200	0.200	0.600	0.200	0.200	0.200	0.400	0.200	0.200
France	0.200	0.200	0.200	0.200	0.400	0.200	0.200	0.200	0.200	0.200	0.200	0.200	0.600	0.200	0.200	0.200
Germany	0.200	0.200	0.200	0.200	0.400	0.400	0.400	0.400	0.200	0.200	0.200	0.200	0.600	0.400	0.400	0.400
Ireland	0.200	0.200	0.400	0.400	0.200	0.200	0.400	0.600	0.200	0.200	0.200	0.200	0.200	0.200	0.200	0.200
Italy	0.200	0.200	0.200	0.200	0.400	0.600	0.200	0.200	0.200	0.200	0.200	0.200	0.400	0.400	0.200	0.200
Netherlands	0.400	0.400	0.200	0.200	0.400	0.400	0.200	0.200	0.600	0.400	0.200	0.200	0.400	0.400	0.200	0.200
Norway	0.200	0.400	0.200	0.400	0.200	0.400	0.200	0.400	0.200	0.400	0.200	0.600	0.200	0.400	0.200	0.400
Sweden	0.000	0.200	0.000	0.200	0.000	0.200	0.000	0.200	0.000	0.200	0.000	0.600	0.000	0.200	0.000	0.400
United Kingdom	0.200	0.200	0.400	0.400	0.200	0.200	0.400	0.400	0.200	0.200	0.400	0.400	0.200	0.200	0.400	0.600
United States	0.000	0.000	0.000	0.000	0.000	0.000	0.000	0.000	0.200	0.200	0.200	0.200	0.600	0.200	0.400	0.200
Number: score > 0.5	0	0	0	0	1	1	0	1	1	2	0	2	3	1	0	1

evidence and the character of the study. Important considerations include the total number of cases, the number of causal conditions, the degree of familiarity of the researcher with each case, the degree of precision that is possible in the calibration of fuzzy sets, the extent of measurement and assignment error, whether the researcher is interested in coarse versus fine-grained patterns in the results, and so on. The data set used in this demonstration is composed of twelve cases and sixteen logically possible combinations of conditions. In this situation, a reasonable frequency threshold is one case. Thus, the eight combinations of conditions lacking a single case with greater than 0.5 membership are treated as remainders in the analysis that follows, for there are no strong empirical instances of any of these combinations. The causal combinations with at least one case with greater than 0.5 membership are retained for further examination.[3]

When the total number of cases included in an analysis is large (e.g., hundreds), it is important to establish a *frequency threshold* for the relevance or viability of causal combinations. In such analyses, some corners may have several cases with greater than 0.5 membership due to measurement or coding errors. It would be prudent, therefore, to treat low-frequency causal combinations the same as those lacking strong empirical instances altogether (i.e., the same as those with frequency = 0). When the total number of cases in a study is large, the issue is not which combinations have instances (i.e., at least one case with greater than 0.5 membership), but which combinations have enough instances to warrant conducting an assessment of the subset relation with the outcome. For example, a researcher might use a frequency threshold of at least ten cases with greater than 0.5 membership.

Assessing the Consistency of Fuzzy Subset Relations

Once the empirically relevant causal combinations have been identified based on the distribution of cases across causal combinations, the

---

3. The treatment of remainders is a very important issue in QCA. This topic is the central focus of chapters 8 and 9.

Table 7.3: Assessing the consistency of causal combinations with the fuzzy subset relation

Affluence	Inequality	Manufacturing	Unions	Consistency	Outcome
1	0	0	0	1.00	1
1	1	0	0	1.00	1
0	1	1	1	0.87	0
1	1	0	1	0.84	0
0	1	0	1	0.82	0
1	0	0	1	0.79	0
1	1	1	1	0.78	0
1	0	1	1	0.72	0

next step is to evaluate each combination's *consistency* with the set-theoretic relation in question. Which causal combinations are subsets of the outcome? What different combinations of conditions are linked to strong membership in the outcome? Chapter 3 describes in detail the measure of set-theoretic consistency used to evaluate the link between causal combinations and outcomes. The formula is:

$$\text{Consistency } (X_i \leq Y_i) = \Sigma[\min(X_i, Y_i)]/\Sigma(X_i)$$

where min indicates the selection of the lower of the two values; X_i is degree of membership in a causal combination; and Y_i is degree of membership in the outcome (see also Kosko 1993; Smithson and Verkuilen 2006). When the X_i values are all less than or equal to their corresponding Y_i values, the consistency score is 1.00; when only a few near misses are present, the score is slightly less than 1.00; when many inconsistent scores are present, with some X_i values greatly exceeding their corresponding Y_i values, consistency can drop below 0.50.

Table 7.3 shows the degree to which the eight relevant causal combinations (those with at least one case with greater than 0.5 membership) are consistent subsets of the outcome (weak class voting) using data on all twelve countries for each assessment. The consistency scores reported in the table are based on the set-theoretic consistency formula presented above. For ease of interpretation, the causal combinations have been sorted in descending order according to their consistency scores. It is important to remember that table 7.3, in effect, presents summary *statements* about the corners of the vector space defined by the four fuzzy-set causal conditions used in this analysis. Each row essentially answers the question: Is degree of membership in this corner of the vector space a consistent subset of degree of membership in the outcome? The analysis of the evidence in table 7.3 is thus a logical synthesis of statements about vector space corners.

Analyzing the Truth Table

It is a short step from tables like table 7.3 to truth tables appropriate for the Quine procedure of fsQCA. The key determination that must be made is the consistency score to be used as a cutoff value for determining which causal combinations pass fuzzy set–theoretic consistency and which do not. Causal combinations with consistency scores above the cutoff value are designated fuzzy subsets of the outcome and are coded 1; those below the cutoff value are not fuzzy subsets and are coded 0.[4] In effect, the causal combinations that are fuzzy subsets of the outcome delineate the kinds of cases in which the outcome is found (e.g., the kinds of countries that have weak class voting). Simple inspection of the consistency values in table 7.3 reveals a substantial gap in consistency scores between the second and third causal combinations; degree of consistency with the subset relation drops from 1.00 (perfect consistency) to 0.87. This gap provides an easy basis for differentiating consistent causal combinations from inconsistent combinations, as shown in the last column of table 7.3, outcome. In most analyses of this type, however, the consistency cutoff value will be less than 1.0, for perfect set-theoretic consistency is not common with fuzzy-set data.

Ragin (2000) demonstrates how to incorporate probabilistic criteria into the assessment of the consistency of subset relations, and

---

4. Rows that do not meet the frequency threshold selected by the investigator (based on the number of cases with greater than 0.5 membership) are treated as remainder rows. Designating such rows as remainders is justified on the grounds that the empirical evidence relevant to these combinations is not substantial enough to permit an evaluation of set-theoretic consistency.

these same criteria can be modified for use here. The probabilistic test requires a benchmark value (e.g., 0.75 consistency) and an alpha (e.g., 0.05 significance). In the interest of staying close to the evidence, it is often useful simply to sort the consistency scores in descending order, as in table 7.3, and observe whether a substantial gap occurs in the upper ranges of consistency scores. With the large gap between rows two and three of table 7.3, it is clear that using probabilistic criteria to aid the selection of a cutoff value would simply obfuscate the obvious. In general, the cutoff value should not be less than 0.75; a cutoff value $\geq$ 0.85 is recommended, especially for macrolevel data. While the measure of consistency can range from 0.0 to 1.0, scores between 0.0 and 0.75 indicate the existence of substantial inconsistency.

The truth table resulting from these procedures is contained within table 7.3. The first four columns show the codings of the causal conditions; the last column shows the crisp-set outcome (consistent versus not-consistent) attached to each truth table row (vector space corner). The eight combinations of causal conditions *not* listed in table 7.3 are remainders. The results of the analysis of this truth table with the remainder combinations defined as false (i.e., no simplifying assumptions allowed) show:

$$A{\cdot}{\sim}M{\cdot}{\sim}U \leq W$$

where W = membership in the set of countries with weak class voting, A = affluent country, M = high manufacturing employment, U = strong unions, $\sim$ indicates negated fuzzy sets, and $\leq$ signals the subset relation. The set-theoretic consistency of this solution is 1.0; its coverage of the outcome (weak class voting) is 0.636 (see chapter 3). The results indicate that weak class voting (W) occurs in countries where affluence is combined with both weak membership in the set of countries with high manufacturing employment and weak membership in the set of countries with strong unions. Inspection of table 7.1 reveals that the best instances of this combination of conditions are the United States, France, Germany, and the Netherlands.

When simplifying assumptions are drawn from the pool of eight remainders (by fsQCA), a more parsimonious solution results:

$$\sim U \leq W$$

(see also figure 2.1). According to these results, weak class voting has a single source, weak unions (~U). The set-theoretic consistency of this solution is 1.0; its coverage of the outcome is 0.727. As table 7.1 shows, the countries with the lowest membership scores in strong unions are the United States and France. This solution of the truth table is dependent on six simplifying assumptions (see Ragin 1987, 2000 and chapter 9 of this book) describing unobserved combinations of causal conditions. The six assumptions are drawn from the eight combinations of causal conditions lacking strong empirical instances (i.e., those lacking cases with membership scores greater than 0.5, shown in the last row of table 7.2).[5]

At this juncture, it is important to point out a property of fuzzy sets that sharply distinguishes them from crisp sets. Briefly stated, with fuzzy sets it is mathematically possible for a causal condition or causal combination to be a subset of both an outcome (e.g., weak class voting) and the negation of the outcome (e.g., not-weak class voting). This result is mathematically possible because degree of membership in a causal condition or combination (e.g., a score of 0.3) can be less than the outcome (e.g., 0.6) and less than the negation of the outcome (1.0 – 0.6 = 0.4). It is also possible for a causal condition or combination to be *inconsistent* with both the outcome and its *negation* by exceeding both (e.g., causal combination score = 0.8, outcome membership score = 0.7; negation of the outcome membership score = 0.3). The important point is that with fuzzy sets, no mathematical reason exists to expect consistency scores calculated for the negation of an outcome to be perfectly negatively correlated with consistency scores for the original outcome, as they are in crisp-set analyses. This property of fuzzy sets provides an additional reason for conducting an analysis of the negation of the outcome (e.g., not-weak class voting) separately from the analysis of the outcome (e.g., weak class voting). Conducting

---

5. Ragin and Sonnett (2004; see also chapters 8 and 9 of this work) demonstrate how to use these two solutions to conduct counterfactual analyses. The first solution maximizes complexity; the second maximizes parsimony. Chapters 8 and 9 describe how theoretical and substantive knowledge can be used to travel various middle paths between parsimony and complexity.

these two analyses separately allows for *asymmetry* between the results of the analysis of the causes of an outcome and the analysis of the causes of its negation.[6]

From the viewpoint of correlational methods, this property of set-theoretic analysis is perplexing. From the viewpoint of social theory, however, it is not. Consider the solution using simplifying assumptions presented above. This analysis shows that persistently low levels of class voting are found in countries with weak unions. In effect, this analysis reveals a main impediment to class voting. The question of which conditions are *impediments* to class voting is not the same as the question of which conditions are *productive* of class voting (see also Lieberson 1985 on the asymmetry of social causation). The answers to these two questions could easily differ. Thus, the asymmetry of set-theoretic analysis dovetails with theoretical expectations of asymmetric causation.

Why Not Simply Dichotomize Fuzzy Sets?

The construction of a truth table from fuzzy-set data, as just sketched, is cognitively taxing. It involves two analyses: (1) the assessment of the distribution of cases across causal combinations and (2) the assessment of the degree of consistency of each causal combination with the subset relation vis-à-vis the outcome. Further, both assessments involve the selection of cutoff values, which may seem arbitrary.[7] Why not simply recode fuzzy sets to crisp sets and conduct a conventional crisp-set analysis using the dichotomized membership scores? After all, a fuzzy score of 0.5 differentiates cases that are more in versus more out of a given fuzzy set. The use of the crossover value to create crisp sets from fuzzy sets appears at first glance to be a straightforward extension of the approach.

---

6. Separate analysis of an outcome and its negation is also standard practice using crisp-set QCA.

7. Actually, the range of plausible cutoff values is relatively narrow, and the range can be narrowed further when researchers are familiar with their cases and with relevant theoretical and substantive literatures.

Table 7.4: Crisp-set data on class voting in the advanced industrial societies

Country	Weak class voting (W)	Affluent (A)	Income inequality (I)	Manufac-turing (M)	Strong unions (U)
Australia	1	1	1	0	1
Belgium	1	1	0	0	1
Denmark	0	1	0	0	1
France	1	1	1	0	0
Germany	1	1	1	0	0
Ireland	1	0	1	1	1
Italy	1	0	1	0	1
Netherlands	1	1	0	0	0
Norway	0	1	0	1	1
Sweden	0	1	0	1	1
United Kingdom	0	1	1	1	1
United States	1	1	1	0	0

The best way to evaluate the viability of this option is simply to re-analyze the fuzzy-set data presented in table 7.1, first converting the fuzzy sets to crisp sets. Table 7.4 shows the crisp-set data that result from the application of the crossover rule (which dichotomizes fuzzy data at the 0.5 membership score) to the fuzzy-set data presented in table 7.1. Clearly a gain in simplicity is obtained when comparing tables 7.4 and 7.1. The cases in table 7.4 are either fully in (1) or fully out (0) of the relevant sets; in table 7.1, their memberships are graded. However, some costs are involved in obtaining that simplicity. Notice, for example, that the data set now includes a "contradiction" (identical cases with contrary outcomes). Belgium and Denmark have the same scores on the four crisp causal conditions (**A, I, M,** and **U**), yet they have different scores on the outcome (**W**). In a conventional crisp-set analysis, it is necessary to address this contradiction in some way before the analysis can proceed.

With one contradictory causal combination and eight remainders, there are several ways to analyze the evidence in table 7.4. In an effort to match the second fuzzy-set solution as closely as possible, the contradiction is set to "false" and the eight remainders are used as "don't care" combinations, which makes them available for use as simplifying assumptions. (A don't care row may be assigned either 1 or 0 on the outcome by fsQCA, depending on which assignment yields a more parsimonious solution.) The results of the crisp-set analysis show:

$$\sim U + \sim A + I \cdot \sim M \leq W$$

where W = membership in the set of countries with weak class voting, U = strong unions, A = highly affluent country, I = substantial income inequality, M = high manufacturing employment, $\sim$ signals negation, $\cdot$ indicates logical *and* (combinations of conditions), + indicates logical *or* (alternate causal conditions or alternate causal combinations), and $\leq$ indicates the subset relation. The results indicate that there are three alternate bases for weak class voting (W): weak unions ($\sim U$), a relative lack of affluence ($\sim A$), or the combination of income inequality and lower levels of employment in manufacturing ($I \cdot \sim M$). This solution is dependent on a number of simplifying assumptions (not examined here) because eight of the sixteen truth table rows lack cases. The key difference between the crisp-set solution and the second fuzzy-set solution (the more parsimonious solution) is that the crisp-set solution adds two new terms: $\sim A$ (not highly affluent) and $I \cdot \sim M$ (substantial income inequality combined with lower levels of employment in manufacturing). Thus, the crisp-set solution is both more complex and more inclusive than the second fuzzy-set solution.

The two new terms, $\sim A$ and $I \cdot \sim M$, appear in the crisp-set solution because of its *lower standard of set-theoretic consistency*. Perfect set-theoretic consistency is achieved with fuzzy sets when the cases all reside above the main diagonal of the fuzzy scatterplot. With crisp sets, however, perfect set-theoretic consistency is much easier to achieve. As long as no cases appear in the fourth quadrant of the fuzzy scatterplot (the lower-right quadrant), then the set plotted on the horizontal axis can be described as a subset of the set plotted on the vertical axis. The lower-right quadrant of a scatterplot of two fuzzy sets is a subset of and only half the size of the triangle below the main diagonal. This lower consistency standard defines more cases and thus more causal combinations as consistent. For example, both Norway and Denmark score 0.4 on $\sim A$ (not highly affluent, one of the crisp-set solution terms) and 0.2 on W (weak class voting). In the fuzzy-set analysis, these cases are *inconsistent* because their scores on the causal condition exceed their scores on the outcome. These fuzzy-set inconsistencies directly undermine the argument that ~**A** is a subset of **W**. From a crisp-set perspective, however, these cases are entirely *consistent* because they display both an absence of affluence (their 0.4 scores are recoded to 0s) and an absence of weak class voting (their 0.2 scores on the outcome are also recoded to 0s). A similar pattern emerges for **I·~M**: some of the cases defined as consistent in the crisp-set analysis are inconsistent in the fuzzy-set analysis. Thus, the additional causal terms appearing in the crisp-set solution are due to its lower consistency standard.

Given these results, it appears that the practice of dichotomizing fuzzy sets (and, by implication, interval and ratio scales) to create crisp sets for conventional crisp-set analysis is *not* an attractive option. Researchers should use the procedures described in chapters 4 and 5 to calibrate fuzzy sets from interval and ratio scales and conduct fuzzy-set analyses instead. Using fuzzy sets is also preferable to multivalue sets (Cronqvist 2004) because multivalue sets tend to exacerbate the problem of limited diversity (see chapters 8 and 9 and Rihoux and Ragin 2008). More generally, these results indicate that if researchers can represent their causal conditions and outcomes as fuzzy sets, they should not use crisp sets. The use of crisp sets should be reserved for phenomena that are categorical in nature.

Conclusion

The goal of fsQCA is to aid causal interpretation, in concert with knowledge of cases. The practical goal of the techniques presented in this chapter, and of fsQCA more generally, is to explore evidence descriptively and configurationally, with an eye toward the different ways causally relevant conditions may combine to produce a given outcome. This chapter provides researchers interested in complex causation a variety of strategies and tools for uncovering and analyzing it, while at the same time bringing researchers closer to their cases and their evidence.

Practical Appendix: The Fuzzy-Set Truth Table Procedure

The primary focus of this chapter is the process of constructing truth tables that summarize the results of analyses of fuzzy-set relations. The basic steps are as follows:

1. Create a data set with fuzzy-set membership scores. (Crisp sets may be included among the causal conditions.) The fuzzy sets must be carefully labeled and defined (e.g., degree of membership in the set of countries with persistently low levels of class voting). Pay close attention to the calibration of fuzzy membership scores, especially with respect to the three qualitative anchors: full membership, full nonmembership, and the crossover point. Fuzzy sets are often unimodal at 1.0 or 0.0, or bimodal at both 0.0 and 1.0. In general, calibration requires good grounding in theoretical and substantive knowledge, as well as in-depth understanding of cases (see chapters 4 and 5). The procedures described in this chapter work best when the 0.5 membership score and membership scores close to 0.5 are used sparingly—preferably not at all—when coding the causal conditions.

2. Input the fuzzy-set data directly into fsQCA or into a program that can save data files in a format compatible with fsQCA (e.g., Excel, using comma-delimited files, or SPSS, using tab-delimited files; simple variable names with no embedded spaces or punctuation constitute the first row of the data file). The data set should include both the outcome and relevant causal conditions. Open the data file using fsQCA version 2.0 or later. (Click *Help* on the startup screen to identify fsQCA version and date; the most up-to-date version can be downloaded from www.fsqca.com.)

3. Select a preliminary list of causal conditions. In general, the number of causal conditions should be modest, in the range of three to eight. Often, causal conditions can be combined in some way to create "macrovariables" using the procedures described in chapter 11 of Ragin (2000). These macrovariables can be used in place of their components to reduce the dimensionality of the vector space. For example, a single macrovariable might be used to replace three substitutable causal conditions joined together by logical *or*, which dictates

using their maximum membership score. (In the *Data Sheet* window of fsQCA, click *Variables*, then *Compute*, and then use the *fuzzyor* function to create this type of macrovariable.)

4. Create a truth table by specifying the outcome and the causal conditions. In fsQCA, this function is accessed by clicking *Analyze, Fuzzy Sets*, and *Truth Table Algorithm*. The resulting truth table will have 2^k rows, reflecting the different corners of the vector space. (The 1s and 0s for the causal conditions identify the different corners of the vector space.) For each row, the program reports the number of cases with greater than 0.5 membership in the vector space corner (in the column labeled *number*). Two columns to the right of *number* is a column labeled *consistency*, the consistency measure assessing the degree to which membership in each corner is a subset of membership in the outcome for all cases.

5. The researcher must select a frequency threshold to apply to the data listed in the *number* column. When the total number of cases included in a study is relatively small, the frequency threshold should be 1 or 2. When the total *N* is large, however, a more substantial threshold should be selected. It is very important to inspect the distribution of the cases when deciding upon a frequency threshold. This can be accomplished simply by clicking on any case in the *number* column and then clicking the *Sort* menu and then *Descending*. The resulting list of the number of cases with greater than 0.5 membership in each corner will provide a snapshot of the distribution and also may reveal important discontinuities or gaps. After selecting a threshold, delete all rows that do not meet it. This can be accomplished (for tables that have been sorted according to number) by clicking on the first case that falls below the threshold (in the *number* column), clicking the *Edit* menu, and then clicking *Delete current row to last*. The truth table will now list only the corners of the vector space that meet the frequency threshold.

6. Next is the selection of a *consistency* threshold for distinguishing causal combinations that are subsets of the outcome from those that are not. This determination is made using the measure of set-theoretic consistency reported in the consistency column. In general,

values below 0.75 in this column indicate substantial inconsistency. It is always useful to sort the consistency scores in descending order so that it is possible to evaluate their distribution. This should be done *after* rows that fall below the frequency threshold have been deleted from the table (step 5). Click on any value in the *consistency* column; click the *Sort* menu; and then click *Descending.* Identify any gaps in the upper range of consistency that might be useful for establishing a threshold, keeping in mind that it is always possible to examine several different thresholds and assess the consequences of lowering and raising the consistency cutoff. Often, it is useful to present two analyses, one with a relatively permissive consistency threshold (e.g., around 0.8) and another with a more restrictive consistency threshold (e.g., around 0.9).

7. Next, manually input 1s and 0s into the empty outcome column, which is labeled with the name of the outcome and listed to the left of the *consistency* column. Using the threshold value selected in the previous step, enter a value of 1 when the consistency value meets or exceeds the consistency threshold, and 0 otherwise. If the truth table spreadsheet has more than twenty rows, code the outcome column using the *Delete and code* function in the *Edit* menu.

8. Click the *Standard Analyses* button at the bottom of the screen to produce three solutions: the complex, the parsimonious, and the intermediate. These different solutions are explained in chapters 8 and 9. The intermediate solution is based on information about the causal conditions that the user inputs, based on his or her substantive knowledge (see chapter 9).

PART IV

Analysis of Causal
Complexity versus
Analysis of Net Effects

8: Limited Diversity and Counterfactual Cases
coauthored with John Sonnett

Naturally occurring social phenomena are profoundly limited in their diversity. In fact, it could be argued that limited diversity is one of their trademark features. It is no accident that social hierarchies such as occupational prestige, education, and income coincide, just as it is not happenstance that high scores on virtually all nation-level indicators of wealth and well-being are clustered in the advanced industrial countries. Social diversity is limited not only by overlapping inequities of wealth and power but also by history. For example, the colonization of almost all of South and Central America by Spain and Portugal is a historical and cultural "given" for social scientists who study this region. Likewise, the concentration of African Americans in the U.S. South and in northern cities reflects their history, first as slaves and then as economic migrants. Some regions of the United States have relatively few African Americans, just as others have relatively few Hispanics, and so on. History matters; its fingerprints are everywhere.

While limited diversity is central to the constitution of social phenomena, it also severely complicates their analysis. If the empirical world would only cooperate and present social scientists with cases exhibiting all logically possible combinations of relevant causal conditions, then social research would be much more straightforward. For example, by matching cases that differ on only a single causal condition, it would be possible to construct structured, focused comparisons (George 1979), which in turn would greatly facilitate the assessment of causation. Unfortunately, the empirical world offers relatively few opportunities for constructing fully articulated, experiment-like comparisons.

Table 8.1: Simple example of the impact of limited diversity

Strong unions (U)	Strong left parties (L)	Generous welfare state (G)	N
Yes	Yes	Yes	6
Yes	No	No	8
No	No	No	5
No	Yes	?	0

Even very simple forms of causal analysis are stymied by limited diversity. Consider, for example, table 8.1, which shows hypothetical country-level data on two causal conditions, strong left parties (yes/no) and strong unions (yes/no), and one outcome, generous welfare state (yes/no). The table presents all four combinations of the two presence/absence causal conditions, but only three of the four exist. Specifically, no existing countries combine the presence of a strong left party with the absence of strong unions. Simple inspection of the table reveals a perfect correlation between presence of strong left parties and presence of generous welfare states, suggesting a simple, parsimonious explanation.

Notice, however, that an alternate approach to the evidence yields a different explanation. If the question is, What are the causally relevant conditions shared by all instances of the outcome (generous welfare states)? there are two shared conditions, strong left parties *and* strong unions. Further, none of the negative cases (instances of the absence of a generous welfare state) share this combination. This second analytic strategy indicates that it is the combination of strong left parties *and* strong unions that explains the emergence of generous welfare states, not strong left parties by itself.

Which explanation is "correct"? A conventional quantitative analysis of these data points to the first explanation because it is not only more parsimonious, it also is "complete" from an explained variance viewpoint—there are no unexplained cases. Case-oriented researchers, however, are not so enamored of parsimony and prefer causal explanations that resonate with what is known about the cases themselves. Typically, when cases are examined in an in-depth manner, re-searchers find that causation is complex and very often involves spe-cific combinations of causal conditions (or causal "recipes"). Thus, they would no doubt favor the second explanation over the first. The second explanation also would be preferred by case-oriented re-searchers on analytic grounds. The search for causally relevant com-monalities shared by a set of cases with the same outcome is often the very first analytic move in case-oriented inquiry, despite the fact that this practice of "selecting on the dependent variable" is almost universally condemned by quantitative researchers who think only in terms of correlations.

At a more formal level, which answer is correct depends on the outcome that would be observed for cases exhibiting the presence of strong left parties combined with the absence of strong unions—that is, if such cases could be found. If these cases displayed generous wel-fare states, then the conclusion would be that having strong left par-ties, by itself, causes generous welfare states. If these cases failed to display generous welfare states, then the conclusion would be that it is the combination of strong left parties and strong unions that explains generous welfare states. If relevant cases combining strong left parties and weak unions could not be identified, then researchers must specu-late: What would happen in such cases? Would generous welfare states emerge? To answer these questions, researchers must rely on their sub-stantive and theoretical knowledge, which in turn would provide the basis for deciding between the two explanations, the parsimonious (single cause) account versus the more complex (combined causes) account. In short, *the choice of explanations is theory and knowledge dependent.*

Notice that even though the example is very simple—there are only two causal conditions, and only one of the four causal combi-nations lacks cases—it is impossible to draw a firm conclusion about causation directly from the evidence presented because of the lim-ited diversity of empirical cases. Furthermore, which answer is cor-rect, in the eyes of contemporary social science, could be a matter of taste. Scholars who favor parsimony might prefer the first answer;

scholars who seek a closer connection to cases might prefer the second.[1]

Counterfactual Cases

Assessing the plausible outcome of a combination of conditions that does not exist and instead must be imagined may seem esoteric. However, this analytic strategy has a long and distinguished tradition in the history of social science. A causal combination that lacks empirical instances and therefore must be imagined is a *counterfactual case;* evaluating its plausible outcome is *counterfactual analysis* (see, e.g., Hicks, Misra, and Ng 1995).

To some, counterfactual analysis is central to case-oriented inquiry because such research typically embraces only a handful of empirical cases (Fearon 1991). If only a few instances exist (e.g., of social revolution), then researchers must compare empirical cases to hypothetical cases. The affinity between counterfactual analysis and case-oriented research, however, derives not simply from its focus on small Ns, but from its configurational nature. Case-oriented explanations of outcomes are often combinatorial in nature, stressing specific configurations of causal conditions. Counterfactual cases thus often differ from empirical cases by a single causal condition, thus creating a decisive, though partially imaginary, comparison.

The consideration of counterfactual cases is often explicit in case-oriented comparative research. In *The Social Origins of Dictatorship and Democracy,* for example, Barrington Moore, Jr. (1966) invites readers to imagine a United States in which the South had prevailed over the North in the U.S. Civil War. His intention was not literary; rather, he wanted to support his larger theoretical point that a "revolutionary break with the past" (e.g., the U.S. Civil War) is an essential ingredient in the recipe for the emergence of modern democratic po-

---

1. It is important to point out that this ambiguity regarding which is the correct explanation is not a consequence of using dichotomous causal conditions. For illustration, see chapters 10 and 11.

litical systems. This explicit use of hypothetical cases is well known in comparative and case-study research; it is also common in historical research, where counterfactual cases are used to accomplish both rhetorical and analytic ends.

Max Weber (1949) is commonly cited as the first social scientist to advocate the use of thought experiments in social research. He argued that researchers can gain insight on the causal significance of individual components of events by conducting thought experiments, which imagine "unreal" cases. Weber's view is based on an explicitly configurational approach to causal analysis, in that "a concrete result cannot be viewed as the product of a struggle of certain causes favoring it and others opposing it. The situation must, instead, be seen as follows: the totality of *all* the conditions back to which the causal chain from the 'effect' leads had to 'act jointly' in a certain way and in no other for the concrete effect to be realized" (Weber 1949, 187).

Contemporary comparative researchers have continued to debate how to construct and use counterfactuals in research and theory development (Elster 1978; Fearon 1991; Hawthorn 1991; Tetlock and Belkin 1996a). In the introduction to a volume on counterfactual thought experiments, Tetlock and Belkin (1996b, 4) describe five styles of counterfactual argumentation and suggest six criteria researchers use for judging these arguments. Although the described styles of counterfactual argument range widely, none formalizes the use of counterfactuals within an explicitly configurational understanding of causality. As will be demonstrated below, the configurational framework of qualitative comparative analysis (QCA) offers a helpful guide for using counterfactuals in social research. In QCA, counterfactual cases are conceived as substitutes for matched empirical cases. These hypothetical matched cases are identified by their configurations of causal conditions.

At a more abstract level, counterfactual analysis is implicated whenever a researcher makes a causal inference based on the analysis of "naturally occurring" (i.e., nonexperimental) social data—data in which limited diversity is the norm. For example, when cross-national researchers state that "strength of left party" is an important cause of "welfare state generosity" net of other relevant causes, they are arguing, in effect, that countries with weak or nonexistent left parties such as the United States would have more generous welfare states if only this one feature were different. Thus, the interpretation of the observed effect invokes hypothetical countries, for example, a country that is like the United States in all causally relevant respects except that it has a strong left party.

Obviously, as nonexperimentalists, social scientists cannot create this country. They cannot assign causal conditions to their cases as an experimenter would distribute treatments across randomized subjects. They are stuck with nonexperimental data and must contend with the fact that a variety of observed and unobserved factors usually enter into naturally occurring selection processes (e.g., which account for why the United States has a nonexistent left party). These naturally occurring selection processes, in turn, distort the estimation of causal effects (e.g., the impact of left party strength on the generosity of welfare states).

The problem of selection has led econometricians and statisticians to develop a general framework for understanding causation in terms of the difference between each case's value on the dependent variable when it is in the "control" versus "treatment" conditions (e.g., the United States with and without strong left parties).[2] Because only one of these two conditions is observable, the other must be estimated statistically, taking into account the effects of selection processes (Holland 1986; Sobel 1995; Winship and Morgan 1999; Winship and Sobel 2004; see also Brady 2003). While sophisticated in their approach to

---

2. Winship and Morgan (1999, 660) argue that the language of "treatment" and "control" variables is generally applicable: "In almost any situation where a researcher attempts to estimate a causal effect, the analysis can be described, at least in terms of a thought experiment, as an experiment." A more direct implication of using experimental language, which they do not discuss in detail, is the restriction that "the treatment must be manipulable" (Winship and Morgan 1999, 663, fn. 2). Citing Holland (1986), they argue that "it makes no sense to talk about the causal effect of gender or any other nonmanipulable individual trait alone. One must explicitly model the manipulable mechanism that generates an apparent causal effect of a nonmanipulable attribute" (Winship and Morgan 1999, 663, fn. 2).

the problem of selection, counterfactual regression procedures are feasible only when (1) there is a very large N and (2) it is plausible a priori that each case could be in either the control or the treatment group (see Winship and Morgan 1999). Also, these procedures, like conventional statistical analyses, remain linear and additive, so they do not examine problems of limited diversity and matched cases directly.[3]

A Formal Approach to the Problem of Matched Cases

To support an argument emphasizing combinations of causal conditions, researchers must compare cases that are closely matched with each other. The ideal comparison, following Mill (1967), is between pairs of cases that differ on only one causal condition. Such comparisons help researchers establish whether or not a specific causal condition is an integral part of the combination of conditions that generates the outcome in question. It is very difficult to match empirical cases in this manner, however, due to the limited diversity of empirical social phenomena. For example, to interpret the impact of having a strong left party on the generosity of the U.S. welfare state, the ideal matched case would be a country similar to the United States with respect to the causes of welfare state generosity but with a strong left party. The search for matched cases is profoundly theory dependent because the process of matching must focus on causal conditions that are identified as relevant by the investigator, based on his or her substantive and theoretical knowledge.

To illustrate the role of matched empirical cases, consider a case-oriented researcher who argues that four causal conditions combine to produce generous welfare states: sociocultural homogeneity, corporatist institutions, a strong left party, and strong unions.[4] The researcher cites the Nordic countries as relevant instances of this argument. This

3. An attempt to address limited diversity, or "the curse of dimensionality," with Boolean logit and probit regression is offered by Braumoeller (2003).

4. This may or may not be the only pathway to having a generous welfare state. The focus here is simply on the evaluation of the sufficiency of this pathway, not its necessity.

causal argument calls for (at least) four kinds of closely matched cases: countries similar to the Nordic countries but without sociocultural homogeneity, countries similar to the Nordic countries but without corporatist institutions, and so on (the comparison cases match the Nordic countries on three of the four causal conditions). These matched cases can be represented using Boolean algebra as follows: the Nordic cases

$$H \cdot C \cdot L \cdot U \leq G$$

the four matched cases

$$\sim H \cdot C \cdot L \cdot U + H \cdot \sim C \cdot L \cdot U + H \cdot C \cdot \sim L \cdot U + H \cdot C \cdot L \cdot \sim U \leq \sim G$$

where, H = sociocultural homogeneity; C = corporatist institutions; L = strong left party, U = strong unions; G = generous welfare state; $\sim$ indicates absence or negation; the midlevel dot ($\cdot$) indicates combined conditions (logical *and*), + indicates alternate combinations of conditions (logical *or*), and $\leq$ indicates "is sufficient for." If the researcher is able to demonstrate that generous welfare states failed to develop in the four matched cases, this finding would greatly bolster his or her causal argument. In effect, the absence of the outcome in these four matched cases would allow the researcher to claim that each of the four causal conditions is an "INUS" condition: "an insufficient but necessary part of a condition which is itself unnecessary but sufficient for the result" (Mackie 1965, 245).

Ideal matched cases are very often hard to find, for some combinations of causal conditions are unlikely and others may be empirically impossible. For example, it might prove very difficult to identify a country with sociocultural homogeneity, strong unions, a strong left party, but *no* corporatism. Furthermore, when causal arguments are combinatorially complex (which is a common result when researchers examine cases in an in-depth manner), the array of matched cases needed to support a causal argument can be substantial. The empirical world is profoundly limited in its diversity, and cases that are matched on all relevant causal conditions save one are relatively rare. Thus, comparative researchers usually cannot identify relevant matched empirical cases and must substitute counterfactual cases.

Counterfactual Cases and Qualitative Comparative Analysis

Qualitative comparative analysis is one of the few techniques available today that directly addresses the limited diversity of naturally occurring social phenomena. Unlike conventional techniques, QCA starts by assuming that causation is configurationally complex, rather than simple. Most conventional techniques assume that causal conditions are "independent" variables whose effects on outcomes are both linear and additive. The key to QCA is that it sees cases as configurations of conditions and uses truth tables to represent and analyze them logically. Table 8.1 is, in fact, a very simple truth table with two causal conditions and four causal combinations.

In the language of QCA, the fourth row of the truth table shown in table 8.1 is a *remainder*—a combination of causal conditions that lacks empirical instances. In QCA, the solution to this truth table depends on how this remainder is treated. The most conservative strategy is to treat it as *false* (excluded) when assessing the conditions for the emergence of generous welfare states and also as *false* (excluded) when assessing the conditions for the absence of generous welfare states, as follows:

presence of generous welfare state

$$L \cdot U \leq G$$

absence of generous welfare state

$$\sim L \cdot U + \sim L \cdot \sim U \leq \sim G$$
$$\sim L \cdot (U + \sim U) \leq \sim G$$
$$\sim L \leq \sim G$$

where the notations are the same as in the previous example. The first statement summarizes the first row of table 8.1; the second statement summarizes the second and third rows; the third and fourth statements simplify the second, using Boolean algebra. According to this analysis, the combination of strong left parties and strong unions is sufficient for the emergence of generous welfare states. The absence of strong left parties is sufficient for the absence of generous welfare states.

In QCA, an alternate strategy is to treat remainders as *don't care* combinations. (The don't care label reflects the origin of the truth table approach in the design and analysis of switching circuits.) When treated as a don't care, a remainder is available as a potential "simplifying assumption." That is, it will be treated as an instance of the outcome if doing so results in a logically simpler solution. Likewise, it also can be treated as an instance of the absence of the outcome, again, if doing so results in a logically simpler solution for the absence of the outcome. This use of don't cares can be represented in symbolic form as follows, with the remainder term $L·{\sim}U$ added to both statements:

presence of generous welfare state
$$L·U + L·{\sim}U \leq G$$
$$L·(U + {\sim}U) \leq G$$
$$L \leq G$$

absence of generous welfare state
$${\sim}L·U + {\sim}L·{\sim}U + L·{\sim}U \leq {\sim}G$$
$${\sim}L·(U + {\sim}U) + {\sim}U·(L + {\sim}L) \leq {\sim}G$$
$${\sim}L + {\sim}U \leq {\sim}G$$

It is clear from these results that using the remainder as a don't care combination in the solution for the presence of generous welfare states leads to a logically simpler solution, while it leads to a more complex solution for the absence of generous welfare states. Thus, a researcher interested in deriving a more parsimonious solution might prefer the use of the remainder (the fourth row of the truth table) as a don't care combination in the solution for the presence of generous welfare states. Notice that the use of the remainder as a don't care combination in the analysis of the presence of generous welfare states offers the same result as a conventional statistical analysis of the same data.

Using QCA, it is incumbent upon the researcher to evaluate the plausibility of any don't care combination that is incorporated into a solution. Assume that the researcher in this example chose the more parsimonious solution for the presence of generous welfare states— concluding that this outcome is due entirely to the presence of strong left parties. It would then be necessary for the researcher to evaluate the plausibility of the simplifying assumption that this solution incorporates, namely, that if instances of the presence of strong left parties combined with the absence of strong unions did in fact exist, these cases would display generous welfare states. This is a very strong assumption. Many researchers would find it implausible in light of existing substantive and theoretical knowledge. That "existing knowledge," in part, would be the simple fact that all known instances of generous welfare states (in this hypothetical example) occur in countries with strong unions. Existing knowledge would also include in-depth, case-level analyses of the emergence of generous welfare states. This knowledge might indicate, for example, that strong unions have been centrally involved in the establishment of generous welfare states.

The important point here is not the specific conclusion of the study or whether or not having a strong left party is sufficient by itself for the establishment of a generous welfare state. Rather, the issue is the status of assumptions about combinations of conditions that lack empirical instances. In QCA, these assumptions must be evaluated; don't care combinations (remainders) should not be grafted onto solutions in a mechanistic fashion because, after all, we *do* care.

Contrasts with Conventional Quantitative Research

In conventional quantitative research, the issue of limited diversity is obscured because researchers use techniques and models that embody very specific assumptions about the nature of causation. Typically, investigators begin their research by developing lists of potential causal factors relevant to the outcome in question, using a variety of theoretical perspectives. By default, they usually treat each causal condition as an independent cause of the outcome and view their primary analytic task as one of assessing which among the listed causal conditions are the most important. That is, they try to identify the best "predictors" of the outcome, based on statistical estimates of the net effect of each variable. The estimate of net effects, in turn, is based on the assumption that each cause, by itself, is capable of influencing the outcome; that is, it is assumed that the causes are independent and additive in their effects. Thus, conventional quantitative research circumvents the problem of limited diversity by assuming that causation is unrealistically simple. QCA, by contrast, remains true to the combinatorial emphasis of case-oriented research—to the idea that causation may be complex and that the same outcome may result from different combinations of conditions. This idea is implemented in truth tables, which consider all logically possible combinations of relevant causal conditions.

When the number of cases is small to moderate, it is common even for a truth table with only sixteen rows (based on four causal conditions) to have rows without cases (i.e., remainder rows), which are all potential counterfactual cases. Having a large number of cases is no guarantee, however, that remainders can be avoided. Again, limited diversity (i.e., an abundance of remainder rows) is the rule, not the exception, in the study of naturally occurring social phenomena. Ragin (2003b), for example, demonstrates that a large-N, individual-level data set ($N = 758$) populates only twenty-four rows of a thirty-two-row truth table (five causal conditions) and that thirteen of these thirty-two rows contain almost all the cases (96.7 percent of the total N). In an analysis of individual-level data on musical tastes ($N = 1,606$), Sonnett (2004) similarly finds that twenty-two of sixty-four rows in the truth table (34 percent of the rows) contain the bulk of the respondents in the sample (90 percent). Braumoeller (2003, 229) also finds evidence of "complex covariation" (what Braumoeller [2003] calls limited diversity) in a data set with 8,328 observations. From this viewpoint, it is easy to see why counterfactual analysis is essential to social research. Any analysis that allows combinatorial complexity will almost certainly confront an abundance of remainders and thus a wealth of potential counterfactual cases.

The key question is what to do about it. One route is to retreat to the laboratory and avoid nonexperimental data altogether. This path seeks to create matched cases through experimental manipulation. Another route is to use statistical techniques such as those discussed by Winship and Morgan (1999) to estimate unknown data (i.e., the value of either the control or treatment condition), based on a statistical model that attempts to control for underlying selection processes.

The third route is to engage in counterfactual analysis (i.e., thought experiments). The laboratory route entails severe restrictions on the kinds of questions social scientists may ask. The statistical route requires not only a large number of cases and a specific type of causal variable—a condition that can be manipulated—but also a number of strong, simplifying assumptions about the nature of causation. The thought experiment route may seem unattractive because it involves dealing with hypothetical cases. In chapter 9, however, I demonstrate that many counterfactual cases can be considered "easy" as long as researchers have well-developed theoretical and substantive knowledge at their disposal.

9: Easy versus Difficult Counterfactuals

Imagine a researcher who postulates, based on existing theoretical and substantive knowledge, that causal conditions **A**, **B**, **C**, and **D** are all relevant to outcome **Y**. The available evidence indicates that many instances of **Y** are coupled with the presence of causal conditions **A**, **B**, and **C**, along with the absence of condition **D** (i.e., **A·B·C·~D** ≤ **Y**).[1] The researcher suspects, however, that all that really matters is the presence of the first three causes, **A**, **B**, and **C**, and that the fourth condition (**~D**) is superfluous in the presence of **A·B·C**. However, there are no instances of **A**, **B**, and **C** combined with the presence of **D** (i.e., no instances of **A·B·C·D**). Thus, the decisive matched case for determining whether or not the *absence* of **D** is an essential part of the causal mix simply does not exist.

Through counterfactual analysis (i.e., a thought experiment, as described in chapter 8), the researcher could declare this hypothetical combination (**A·B·C·D**) to be a *likely instance* of the outcome. That is, the researcher might assert that **A·B·C·D**, if it existed, would lead to **Y**. This counterfactual analysis would allow the following logical simplification:

$$A·B·C·\text{\textasciitilde}D + A·B·C·D \le Y$$
$$A·B·C·(\text{\textasciitilde}D + D) \le Y$$
$$A·B·C \le Y$$

---

1. There can be other, unspecified combinations of causal conditions linked to outcome **Y** in this example. There is no assumption that this is the only combination linked to the outcome (**Y**).

How plausible is this simplification? The answer to this question depends on the state of the relevant theoretical and substantive knowledge concerning the connection between **D** and **Y** in the combined presence of the other three causal conditions (**A·B·C**). If the researcher can establish on the basis of existing knowledge that there is every reason to expect that the *presence* of **D** would contribute to outcome **Y** under these conditions (or conversely, that the absence of **D** should *not* be a contributing factor), then the counterfactual analysis presented above is both plausible and reasonable. In other words, existing knowledge makes the assertion **A·B·C·D** ≤ **Y** an "easy" counterfactual, because the researcher would be adding a redundant contributing cause (the presence of **D**) to a configuration that is already thought to lead to the outcome (**A·B·C**).

It is important to point out that what has been accomplished in this example (using Boolean algebra) is routine, though often implicit, in much case-oriented research. If conventional case-oriented researchers were to examine the empirical instance **A·B·C·~D** ≤ **Y**, they would likely develop their causal argument or narrative based on factors thought to be linked to the outcome (that is, the presence of **A**, **B**, and **C**). Along the way, they might well consider the possibility that the absence of **D** (i.e., ~**D**) observed in these cases might be integral in some way to the production of **Y** by **A·B·C**. They would be quite likely to conclude otherwise, given the presumed state of existing knowledge about the four causal conditions, namely that it is the presence of these causal factors, not their absence, that is linked to the occurrence of the outcome. Thus, they would quickly arrive at the more parsimonious conclusion, that **A·B·C** ≤ **Y**. The point here is that counterfactual analysis is not always explicit or even articulated in case-oriented research, especially when the counterfactuals are so easy. Such analyses are routinely conducted by case-oriented researchers "on the fly"—in the process of constructing explanations of a case or a specific category of cases.

Now consider the opposite situation. The researcher observes instances of **A·B·C·D** ≤ **Y** but believes that **D** is superfluous or redundant in the production of outcome **Y** given the presence of **A·B·C**. What would happen if **D** were absent? Unfortunately, in this instance, there are no cases of **A·B·C·~D**, and the investigator must resort to counterfactual analysis. Existing theoretical and substantive knowledge, however, connects the *presence* of **D** to outcome **Y**. Is it reasonable to assert that **A·B·C·~D**, if it existed, would lead to **Y**? This counterfactual, which would allow the simplification of **A·B·C·D** to **A·B·C**, is "difficult." The researcher would have to mount a concerted effort, with detailed argumentation and empirical support, to make the case.[2] The point here is not that difficult counterfactual cases should be avoided; rather, the point is that that they require careful explication and justification. Sometimes researchers succeed in justifying their difficult counterfactuals, and such efforts can lead to important theoretical insights and advances.

The easy versus difficult distinction is not a rigid dichotomy, but rather a continuum of plausibility. At one end are easy counterfactuals, which assume that adding a redundant causal condition to a configuration known to produce the outcome (e.g., condition **D** to combination **A·B·C**) would still produce the outcome. At the other end are more difficult counterfactuals, which attempt to remove a contributing causal condition from a configuration displaying the outcome, on the assumption that this cause is redundant and the reduced configuration would still produce the outcome. The exact placement of any specific use of a counterfactual on the easy/difficult continuum depends primarily on the state of existing theoretical and substantive knowledge in the social scientific community at large. This knowledge helps the researcher decide which causes may be redundant or irrelevant by giving theoretical or empirical support for counterfactual arguments about the importance or irrelevance of a particular causal condition (Tetlock and Belkin 1996b). This aspect of counterfactual

---

2. Note that methodological discussions of counterfactuals often assume a nonconfigurational variant of the difficult form, as in Fearon (1996, 39): "When trying to argue or assess whether some factor A caused event B, social scientists frequently use counterfactuals. That is, they either ask whether or claim that 'if A had not occurred, B would not have occurred.'"

analysis also highlights the theory and knowledge dependence of social scientific inquiry in general, as well as its fundamentally social and collective nature (Merton 1973).

Because limited diversity is the rule and not the exception in the study of naturally occurring social phenomena, there will be many logically possible combinations of causal conditions lacking empirical instances in most social scientific investigations. These counterfactual cases can be used to simplify results, as just demonstrated. Some of these counterfactuals will be relatively easy (and thus more or less routine); some will be difficult (and thus perhaps should be avoided). The key consideration is the stock of theoretical and substantive knowledge underlying each use.

Easy Counterfactuals and QCA

Researchers using qualitative comparative analysis (QCA) have two main options when confronted with limited diversity and an abundance of remainders (and thus many potential counterfactual cases): (1) they can avoid using any remainders to simplify a truth table or (2) they can permit the incorporation of the subset of remainders that yields the most parsimonious solution of the truth table. The first option bars counterfactual cases altogether; the second permits the inclusion of both easy and difficult counterfactuals, without any evaluation of their plausibility. At first glance, neither of these options seems attractive. The first is likely to lead to results that are needlessly complex, as in the first example described above, where the simple addition of an easy counterfactual would permit the simplification of A·B·C·~D to A·B·C. The second may lead to results that are unrealistically parsimonious due to the incorporation of difficult counterfactuals, as in the second example, where A·B·C·D is simplified to A·B·C. Rather than rejecting these two options out of hand, however, it is important to view them as the endpoints of a single continuum of possible results. One end of the continuum privileges complexity (no counterfactual cases allowed); the other end privileges parsimony (easy and difficult counterfactual cases are both allowed). Both endpoints are rooted in evidence; they differ in their tolerance for the incorporation of counterfactual cases.

Most social scientists prefer explanations that strike a balance between complexity and parsimony. That is, they prefer explanations that are somewhere in between these two extremes. Consider, for example, Barrington Moore, Jr.'s (1966) *The Social Origins of Dictatorship and Democracy,* a comparative case-oriented investigation of political development in eight countries. An explanation allowing maximum complexity would conclude with perhaps eight different causal combinations linked to eight distinct outcomes. An explanation privileging parsimony, by contrast, would focus on one or a very small number of causal conditions. A researcher, for example, might cite the strength of the urban bourgeoisie as the key causal factor, arguing that the stronger and more numerous this class, the more democratic the outcome. By contrast, an explanation balancing parsimony and complexity (e.g., the explanation Moore offers) would focus on distinct paths of political development and group countries according to a relatively small number of paths.

One strength of QCA is that it not only provides tools for deriving the two endpoints of the complexity/parsimony continuum but it also provides tools for specifying *intermediate* solutions. Consider, for example, the truth table presented in table 9.1, which uses **A**, **B**, **C**, and **D** as causal conditions and **Y** as the outcome. Assume, as before, that existing theoretical and substantive knowledge maintains that it is the presence of these causal conditions, not their absence, that is linked to the outcome. The results of the analysis, barring counterfactual cases from the solution, reveals that combination **A·B·~C** explains **Y**. That is, the presence of **A** combined with the presence of **B** and the absence of **C** (i.e., ~**C**) accounts for the presence of **Y**. The analysis of this same evidence, permitting any counterfactual that will yield a more parsimonious result, leads to the conclusion that **A** by itself accounts for the presence of **Y**.

Conceive of these two results as the endpoints of the complexity/parsimony continuum, as follows:

<u>**A·B·~C**   **A**</u>

Table 9.1: Truth table with four causal conditions (A, B, C, and D) and one outcome (Y)

A	B	C	D	Y
no	no	no	no	no
no	no	no	yes	?
no	no	yes	no	?
no	no	yes	yes	?
no	yes	no	no	no
no	yes	no	yes	no
no	yes	yes	no	?
no	yes	yes	yes	no
yes	no	no	no	?
yes	no	no	yes	?
yes	no	yes	no	?
yes	no	yes	yes	?
yes	yes	no	no	yes
yes	yes	no	yes	yes
yes	yes	yes	no	?
yes	yes	yes	yes	?

Observe that the solution privileging complexity (**A·B·~C**) is a subset of the solution privileging parsimony (**A**). This follows logically from the fact that both solutions must cover the rows of the truth table with **Y** present; the parsimonious solution also incorporates some of the remainder rows as counterfactual cases and thus embraces additional rows. Along the complexity/parsimony continuum are other possible solutions to this same truth table, for example, the combination **A·B**. These intermediate solutions are produced when different subsets of the remainders that are used to produce the parsimonious solution are incorporated into the complex solution. These intermediate solutions constitute subsets of the most parsimonious solution (**A** in this example) and supersets of the solution allowing maximum complexity (**A·B·~C**). The subset relation between solutions is maintained along the complexity/parsimony continuum. The implication in this example is that any causal combination that uses at least some of the causal conditions specified in the complex solution (**A·B·~C**) is a valid solution of the truth table as long as it contains the causal conditions specified in the parsimonious solution (**A**). It follows that there are two valid intermediate solutions to the truth table in table 9.1:

$$\text{A·B}$$

A·B·~C	A·~C	A

Both intermediate solutions are subsets of the solution privileging parsimony and supersets of the solution privileging complexity. The first (**A·B**) permits counterfactuals **A·B·C·D** and **A·B·C·~D** as combinations linked to outcome **Y**. The second links counterfactuals **A·~B·~C·D** and **A·~B·~C·~D** to outcome **Y**.

The relative viability of these two intermediate solutions depends on the plausibility of the counterfactuals that have been incorporated into them. The counterfactuals incorporated into the first intermediate solution are easy because they are used to eliminate ~**C** from the combination **A·B·~C**, and in this example, existing knowledge supports the idea that it is the *presence* of **C**, not its absence (~**C**), that is linked to outcome **Y**. The counterfactuals incorporated into the second intermediate solution, however, are difficult because they are used to eliminate **B** from **A·B·~C**, and according to existing knowledge, the presence of **B** should be linked to the presence of outcome **Y**. The principle that only easy counterfactuals should be incorporated supports the selection of **A·B** as the optimal intermediate solution. Observe that this solution is the same as the one that a conventional case-oriented researcher would derive from this evidence, based on a straightforward interest in causal conditions that are (1) shared by the positive cases (or at least a subset of the positive cases), (2) believed to be linked to the outcome, and (3) not displayed by any negative cases.

As this example illustrates, incorporating different counterfactuals yields different solutions. However, these different solutions are all supersets of the solution privileging complexity and subsets of the solution privileging parsimony. Further, I have demonstrated that it is possible to derive an optimal intermediate solution permitting only easy counterfactuals. This procedure is relatively simple to specify: the researcher removes causal conditions from the complex solution that are at odds with existing knowledge, while upholding the subset principle that underlies the complexity/parsimony continuum, meaning that the intermediate solution constructed by the researcher must be a subset of the most parsimonious solution. The counterfactuals that are incorporated into this optimal solution would be relatively routine in a conventional case-oriented investigation of the same evidence. One of the great strengths of QCA is that all counterfactuals, both easy and difficult, are made explicit, as is the process of incorporating them into results. QCA makes this process transparent and thus open to evaluation by the producers and consumers of social research.

The chapter turns now to a simple illustration of the approach—the formal incorporation of easy counterfactuals—using evidence on international fishing regimes published by Olav Schram Stokke (2004).

Demonstration

Stokke (2004) reports the results of a study of the conditions that promote successful "shaming" in international regimes, focusing explicitly on countries that violate international fishing agreements. He examines ten cases of attempted shaming—five successful (that is, the targets of shaming reformed their behaviors) and five unsuccessful. His causal conditions were the following:

1. Advice (**A**): Whether the shamers can substantiate their criticism with reference to explicit recommendations of the regime's scientific advisory body.

2. Commitment (**C**): Whether the target behavior explicitly violates a conservation measure adopted by the regime's decision-making body.

3. Shadow of the future (**S**): Perceived need of the target of shaming to strike new deals under the regime—such beneficial deals are likely to be jeopardized if criticism is ignored.

4. Inconvenience (**I**): The inconvenience (to the target of shaming) of the behavioral change that the shamers are trying to prompt.

5. Reverberation (**R**): The domestic political costs to the target of shaming for not complying (i.e., for being scandalized as a culprit).

Stokke's truth table is reported in table 9.2. This truth table is typical of small-N research. Many logically possible combinations of causal

Table 9.2: Partial truth table for causes of successful shaming in international regimes (remainders not shown)

Advice (A)	Commitment (C)	Shadow (S)	Inconvenience (I)	Reverberation (R)	Success (Y)
yes	no	yes	yes	yes	yes
yes	no	no	yes	no	no
yes	no	no	yes	yes	no
no	no	no	yes	no	no
yes	yes	yes	yes	yes	yes
yes	yes	yes	yes	no	no
yes	yes	yes	no	no	yes
yes	no	no	no	no	yes

conditions ($2^5 = 32$ rows) exist; only a handful (eight rows) have empirical instances; consequently, there is an abundance of remainders (twenty-four rows) and thus many potential counterfactuals that could be incorporated into the solution. It also follows that because diversity is severely limited, many different solutions to this truth table are possible, all within the bounds established by the endpoints of the complexity/parsimony continuum.

Analysis of this truth table without permitting the incorporation of any counterfactuals produces the following "complex" solution:

$$A \cdot S \cdot I \cdot R + A \cdot C \cdot S \cdot {\sim}I \cdot {\sim}R + A \cdot {\sim}C \cdot {\sim}S \cdot {\sim}I \cdot {\sim}R \leq Y$$

These complex results follows from the fact that only four of the thirty-two logically possible combinations display the outcome and none of the twenty-four remainders have been incorporated into the solution. Essentially, only one simplification has occurred: $A \cdot C \cdot S \cdot I \cdot R$ and $A \cdot {\sim}C \cdot S \cdot I \cdot R$ have been joined to produce $A \cdot S \cdot I \cdot R$. This solution is the most complex possible and thus establishes the first endpoint of the complexity/parsimony continuum.

By contrast, the use of all possible simplifying assumptions (i.e., any counterfactual—easy or difficult—that helps to produce a more parsimonious result) yields a dramatically simpler solution:

$$\sim I + S \cdot R \leq Y$$

This solution states that shaming works when it is not inconvenient (~I) for the targets of shaming to reform their behavior or when the shadow of the future and domestic reverberations combine (**S·R**) to produce a conforming response to shaming. While these are not unreasonable conclusions to draw from this evidence, and while they are truly succinct, they run slightly counter to the conclusions that a conventional case-oriented researcher would draw. Notice, for example, that all four causal combinations in table 9.2 linked to successful shaming include the presence of **A**, the support of the regime's scientific advisory board. This commonality, which could be seen as a necessary condition for successful shaming, would not escape the attention of either a case-oriented researcher or a practitioner interested in using shaming as a tactic for stimulating compliance.

This second analysis provides the other endpoint of the complexity/parsimony continuum, which can now be depicted as follows:

$$\text{A·~C·~S·~I·~R} +$$
$$\text{A·C·S·~I·~R} + \qquad\qquad\qquad\qquad \text{~I} +$$
$$\underline{\text{A·S·I·R} \qquad\qquad\qquad\qquad\qquad\qquad\qquad \text{S·R}}$$

The subset relation can be observed in the fact that **A·S·I·R** is a subset of **S·R** and both **A·C·S·~I·~R** and **A·~C·~S·~I·~R** are subsets of **~I**. (The causal combinations grouped at each end of the continuum are joined by logical *or*, as shown in the corresponding solutions, denoted by +.) The next step is to specify intermediate solutions and to evaluate them with respect to the counterfactuals they incorporate. As explained previously, an optimal intermediate solution incorporates only *easy* counterfactuals. To find such a solution, it is necessary simply to inspect each of the terms at the complex end of the continuum and determine which of the separate causal conditions, if any, can be removed from each combination.

Consider first the combination **A·S·I·R**. Causal conditions **S** and **R** cannot be removed because they appear in the corresponding parsimonious term at the other end of the continuum. To remove either would violate the subset relationship. The only candidates for removal are conditions **I** and **A**. The support of the regime's scientific advisory body (**A**) is certainly linked to the success of shaming. Thus, this causal condition should not be removed. However, the fact that it is inconvenient (**I**) for the targets of shaming to change their behavior does *not* promote successful shaming. Thus, inconvenience (**I**) can be dropped from the combination **A·S·I·R** because inconvenience of behavioral change to the target of shaming is not central to the success of **A·S·R** in generating conformity. Dropping condition **I** yields the intermediate combination **A·S·R**. This combination is a subset of **S·R** and a superset of **A·S·I·R**.

Next, consider combination **A·C·S·~I·~R**. Condition ~**I** (the behavioral change is not inconvenient) cannot be dropped because it appears in the corresponding parsimonious term at the other end of the continuum. As before, condition **A** (the support of the regime's scientific advisory board) should not be removed because this condition is clearly linked to the success of shaming. Condition **C** (the offending behavior clearly violates a prior commitment) also should not be dropped, for this, too, is something that should only contribute to the success of shaming. Condition **S** (shadow of the future—the violator will need to strike future deals with the regime) is also a factor that should only promote successful shaming. In fact, only condition ~**R** (absence of domestic reverberations for being shamed) can be removed. Clearly, the presence of domestic reverberation (**R**) would promote successful shaming; that is, these same instances of successful shaming still would have succeeded if there had been domestic reverberations (**R**). Thus, this combination can be simplified by only one condition, yielding the intermediate term **A·C·S·~I**.

Finally, consider combination **A·~C·~S·~I·~R**. Again, condition ~**I** must be retained because it appears in the corresponding parsimonious term, and condition **A** is retained as well, for the reasons stated in the analysis of the two previous combinations. Condition ~**R** (absence of domestic reverberations) can be removed, as it was from the previous combination, for the same reason provided. Condition ~**C** (absence of violation of a commitment) can be removed, for surely these instances of successful shaming would still have been successful if there had been an explicit violation of a commitment (**C**). Likewise, condition ~**S** (absence of a need to strike future deals with the regime) can be safely removed because only its presence (**S**) should contribute to the success of shaming. Altogether, three terms can be removed, yielding the intermediate term $A \cdot \sim I$.

These three intermediate terms can be joined into a single solution:

$$A \cdot S \cdot R + A \cdot C \cdot S \cdot \sim I + A \cdot \sim I \le Y$$

which can then be simplified to:

$$A \cdot S \cdot R + A \cdot \sim I \le Y$$

because the term $A \cdot C \cdot S \cdot \sim I$ is a subset of the term $A \cdot \sim I$ and is thus logically redundant (all cases of $A \cdot C \cdot S \cdot \sim I$ are also cases of $A \cdot \sim I$). These results indicate that two paths lead to successful shaming: (1) support from the regime's scientific advisory body (A) combined with the need to strike future deals (S) and domestic reverberations for being shamed (R) and (2) support from the regime's scientific advisory body (A) combined with the fact that the behavioral change is not inconvenient ($\sim I$). The intermediate solution can now be added to the complexity/parsimony continuum as follows:

$$A \cdot \sim C \cdot \sim S \cdot \sim I \cdot \sim R +$$

$A \cdot C \cdot S \cdot \sim I \cdot \sim R +$	$A \cdot \sim I +$	$\sim I +$
$A \cdot S \cdot I \cdot R$	$A \cdot S \cdot R$	$S \cdot R$

As indicated previously, the intermediate solution is a superset of the most complex solution and a subset of the most parsimonious. It is optimal because it incorporates only easy counterfactuals, eschewing the difficult ones that have been incorporated into the most parsimonious solution. The intermediate solution thus strikes a balance between complexity and parsimony, using procedures that mimic the practice of conventional case-oriented comparative research.[3]

Many researchers who use QCA either incorporate as many simplifying assumptions (counterfactuals) as possible or they avoid them altogether. They should instead strike a balance between complexity

---

3. Note that Stokke (2004) includes condition **A** in his results, based on the recommendation in Ragin (2000, 105, 254) to perform necessary conditions tests prior to sufficiency tests. The counterfactual procedure described in this chapter can be seen as an extension and reformulation of QCA techniques, one that locates the specification of necessary and sufficient conditions within a continuum of solutions defined by the most complex and the most parsimonious solutions.

and parsimony, using substantive and theoretical knowledge to conduct thought experiments, as just demonstrated. QCA can be used to derive the two ends of the complexity/parsimony continuum. Intermediate solutions can be constructed anywhere along this continuum, as long as the subset principle is maintained (that is, solutions closer to the complexity end of the continuum must be subsets of solutions closer to the parsimony end). An optimal intermediate solution can be obtained by removing individual causal conditions that are inconsistent with existing knowledge from combinations in the complex solution while maintaining the subset relation with the most parsimonious solution.

Counterfactual Analysis and Case-Oriented Research

When viewed from the perspective of conventional quantitative research, case-oriented comparative research seems impenetrable (Achen 2005b). Quantitative researchers know well that statistical analysis works best when Ns are large. Not only is statistical significance easier to attain, but large Ns also can save researchers the trouble of meeting many of the most demanding assumptions of the techniques they use. Violations of these underlying assumptions are all too common when Ns are small or even moderate in size, as they must be in case-oriented research. On top of the small-N problem is the additional difficulty that when researchers know their cases well, they tend to construct combinatorial causal arguments from their evidence. From the perspective of conventional quantitative research, this fixation on causal combinations places even more difficult demands on skimpy cross-case evidence. It also runs counter to the central logic of the most used and most popular quantitative techniques, which are geared primarily toward assessing the net, independent effects of causal variables, not their multiple combined effects.

Comparative case-oriented work, however, has its own logic and rigor. Because it is explicitly configurational, the examination of combinations of conditions is essential to this type of research. Such rigor is lacking in most quantitative research, where matching cases would undermine degrees of freedom and statistical power. As this chapter shows, however, the study of combinations of causes very often involves counterfactual analysis because naturally occurring social data are profoundly limited in their diversity, and researchers must engage in thought experiments using hypothetical cases. This practice may seem suspect, again especially to conventional quantitative researchers, because it runs counter to the norms of "empirical" social research. However, this chapter demonstrates that many of these counterfactual analyses can be considered routine because they involve easy hypothetical cases. This chapter further shows how to formalize and incorporate these easy counterfactuals into cross-case research within the configurational framework of QCA.

This chapter also highlights a very important feature of social research, namely, that it is built upon a foundation of substantive and theoretical knowledge, not just methodological technique. It is this substantive and theoretical knowledge that makes it possible to assess the plausibility of counterfactual cases. In essence, the methods outlined in this chapter show how existing knowledge can be woven into the fabric of empirical results, providing a knowledge-based method for addressing the problem of limited diversity.

Practical Appendix: Deriving Intermediate Solutions Using fsQCA

As noted in this chapter, the derivation of the complex and parsimonious solutions in fuzzy-set qualitative comparative analysis (fsQCA) is straightforward. The parsimonious solution follows from the designation of all remainder combinations (i.e., those without strong instances or with very few strong instances) as potential counterfactual cases. The resulting solution incorporates any counterfactual combination that yields a simpler solution, regardless of whether the counterfactual is easy or difficult. The complex solution, by contrast, does not permit any counterfactual cases and thus no simplifying assumptions regarding combinations of conditions that do not exist in the data. In effect, the complex solution defines all remainder combinations as false. The derivation of the intermediate solution, by contrast, is not automatic, for it requires utilization of the investigator's substantive and theoretical knowledge. This knowledge is the basis for distinguishing between easy counterfactuals (which can be incorporated into the intermediate solution) and difficult counterfactuals (which are barred).

In fsQCA, the intermediate solution is produced along with the complex and parsimonious solutions whenever the Truth Table Algorithm is selected, using either crisp or fuzzy sets. Once the truth table is fully coded by the user (see the practical appendix to chapter 7 for details), the user clicks the Standard Analyses button at the bottom of the truth table. First, the complex solution is derived, then the parsimonious solution. Next, users are queried regarding their expectations for each causal condition. This query takes the form of a dialogue box in which the user specifies whether it is the presence or the absence of the condition that should be linked to the presence of the outcome. Additionally, the researcher can input that either presence or absence of the condition may be linked to the outcome. For example, if the outcome is "avoiding poverty" and one of the causal conditions is "having at least a high school education," then the user would specify that this condition should be linked to the outcome, avoiding poverty, when present. This coding would be based on the well-known connection between low education and low income. By contrast, if the causal condition is "having low-income parents," then the user would specify that this condition should be linked to staying out of poverty when absent. Finally, if the causal condition is "urban residence," then the user would click present or absent, for there is considerable urban and rural poverty in the United States today and thus no clear expectation one way or the other. In fact, it might be reasonable to expect different configurations of conditions linked to staying out of poverty for urban versus rural residents.

These codings of the causal conditions provide the basis for distinguishing between easy and difficult counterfactuals. Consider a simple example: Suppose the combination "high school educated, married, without children" is found to be linked to poverty avoidance. Suppose further that there are no cases of "not high school educated, married, without children." If the user fails to code "at least high school educated" as a condition that is linked to poverty avoidance, then the counterfactual combination (not high school educated, married, without children) can be used to simplify the existing combination (high school educated, married, without children) to "married, without children." The simplified term would indicate that education is not relevant to staying out of poverty if a person is married and without children. Empirically, though, this is not true, for all relevant cases of married, without children are also at least high school educated. In other words, without the coding of at least high school educated as a condition that is linked to poverty avoidance, a difficult counterfactual would be incorporated into the solution. When properly coded, however, this unwarranted simplification is barred.

In general, intermediate solutions are preferred because they are often the most interpretable. When limited diversity is substantial, complex solutions can be exceedingly intricate because little or no simplification occurs. Likewise, under these same conditions, parsimonious solutions can be unrealistically simple, due to the incorporation of many (easy and difficult) counterfactual combinations. Intermediate solutions strike a balance between parsimony and complexity, based on the substantive and theoretical knowledge of the investigator.

10: The Limitations of Net-Effects Thinking

Conventional methods of data analysis such as multiple regression form the backbone of most quantitative research in the social sciences today. It should not be surprising that they do, for they are considered by many to be the most rigorous, the most disciplined, and the most scientific of the analytic methods available to social researchers. If the results of social research are to have an impact on the larger society, such findings should be produced using the most rigorous analytic methods available.

While conventional quantitative methods are clearly rigorous, they are organized around a specific kind of rigor. That is, they have their own rigor and their own discipline, not a *universal* rigor. There are several features of conventional quantitative methods that make them rigorous and therefore valuable as analytic tools; in this chapter I focus on a single, key aspect—the fact that they are typically centered on the task of estimating the "net effects" of "independent" variables on outcomes. I focus on this central aspect, which I characterize as *net-effects thinking*, because this feature of conventional methods limits their usefulness. While it is important to assess the relative importance of independent variables, this task should not be the exclusive focus of analytic social science. Instead, in addition to assessing net effects, researchers should examine how different causal conditions combine to produce a given outcome. This chapter presents a critique of net-effects thinking, focusing on its limitations, and describes key contrasts between net-effects thinking and the configurational approach of qualitative comparative analysis (QCA). Chapter 11 provides an example, using a large-N data set.

It is important to point out that the argument presented here is not that conventional analytic techniques are flawed—in fact, they are powerful and rigorous. Rather, the argument is that they are not well suited for analyzing causal complexity. Indeed, the assessment of net effects requires that the researcher assume that causation is uncomplicated.

Net-Effects Thinking

In what has become "normal" social science, researchers view their primary task as one of assessing the relative importance of causal variables drawn from competing theories. In the ideal situation, the relevant theories emphasize different variables and make clear, unambiguous statements about how these variables are connected to relevant empirical outcomes. In practice, however, most theories in the social sciences are vague when it comes to specifying both causal conditions and outcomes, and they tend to be even more reserved when it comes to stating *how* the causal conditions are connected to outcomes (e.g., specifying the conditions that must be met for a given causal variable to have its impact). Typically, researchers are able to develop only general lists of potentially relevant causal conditions based on the broad portraits of social phenomena they find in competing theories. The key analytic task is typically viewed as one of assessing the relative importance of the relevant variables. If the variables associated with a particular theory prove to be the best predictors of the outcome (i.e., the best "explainers" of its variation), then this theory wins the contest. This way of conducting quantitative analysis is the default procedure in the social sciences today—one that researchers fall back on time and time again, often for lack of knowledge of a clear alternative.

In the net-effects approach, estimates of the effects of independent variables are based on the assumption that each variable, by itself, is capable of influencing the level or probability of the outcome. While it is common to treat *causal* and *independent* as synonymous modifiers of the word *variable*, the core meaning of *independent* relates to the notion of autonomous capacity. Specifically, each independent variable is assumed to be capable of influencing the level or probability of the outcome *regardless of the values or levels of other variables* (i.e., regardless of the varied contexts defined by these variables). Estimates of net effects thus assume *additivity*, that the net impact of a given independent variable on an outcome is the same across all the values of the other independent variables and their different combinations. To estimate the net effect of a given variable, the researcher offsets the impact of competing causal conditions by subtracting from the estimate of the effect of each variable any explained variation in the dependent variable it shares with other causal variables. This is the core meaning of *net effects*—the calculation of the nonoverlapping contribution of each independent variable to explained variation in the outcome. Degree of overlap is a direct function of correlation. Generally, the greater the correlation of an independent variable with its competitors, the less its net effect.

An important underlying affinity exists between poorly specified theory and net-effects thinking. When theories are weak, they offer only general characterizations of social phenomena and do not address causal complexity. Clear specifications of relevant contexts and scope conditions are rare, as is consideration of how causal conditions may modify each other's relevance or impact (i.e., how they may display nonadditivity). Researchers are fortunate if they are able to derive coherent lists of potentially relevant causal conditions from most theories in the social sciences, for the typical theory offers very little specific guidance. This guidance void is filled by linear, additive models with their emphasis on estimating generic net effects. Researchers often declare that they estimate linear-additive models because they are the "simplest possible" models and make the "fewest assumptions" about the nature of causation. In this view, additivity (and thus causal simplicity) is the default state; any analysis of nonadditivity requires explicit theoretical authorization, which is usually lacking.

This common emphasis on the calculation of net effects dovetails with the notion that the foremost goal of social research is to assess the relative explanatory power of variables attached to competing theories. Net-effects analyses provide explicit quantitative assessments of the nonoverlapping explained variation that can be credited to each theory's variables. Thus, the calculation of net effects provides a strong basis for theory adjudication, providing further justification for the use of these methods. Often, however, theories do not contradict each other directly and thus do not really compete. After all, the typical social science theory is little more than a general portrait. The use of the net-effects approach thus may create the appearance of theory adjudication in research in which such adjudication may not be necessary or even possible.

Problems with Net-Effects Thinking

Several problems are associated with the net-effects approach, especially when it is treated as the exclusive or even the primary means of generating useful social scientific knowledge. These include both practical and conceptual problems.

A fundamental practical problem is the fact that the assessment of net effects is dependent upon model specification. The estimate of an independent variable's net effect is powerfully swayed by its correlations with competing variables. Limit the number of correlated competitors, and a chosen variable may have a substantial net effect on the outcome; pile them on, and its net effect may be reduced to nil. The specification dependence of the estimation of net effects is well known, which explains why quantitative researchers are thoroughly schooled in the importance of "correct" specification. However, correct specification is dependent upon strong theory and deep substantive knowledge, both of which are usually lacking in applications of net-effects methods.

The importance of model specification is apparent in the many analyses of the data set that is used in chapter 11, the National Longitudinal Survey of Youth, analyzed by Herrnstein and Murray (1994) in *The Bell Curve*. In this work, Herrnstein and Murray report a very strong net effect of test scores from the Armed Forces Qualifying Test (AFQT), which they treat as a test of general intelligence, on outcomes such as poverty. They find that the higher the AFQT score, the lower the odds of poverty. By contrast, Fischer et al. (1996) use the same data and the same estimation technique (logistic regression) but find a weak net effect of AFQT scores on poverty. The key difference between these two analyses is the fact that Herrnstein and Murray allow only a few variables to compete with AFQT, usually only one or two, while Fischer et al. allow many. Which estimate of the net effect of AFQT scores is correct? The answer depends upon which specification is considered correct. Thus, debates about net effects often stalemate in disagreements about model specification. While social scientists tend to think that having more variables is better than having few, as in Fischer et al.'s analysis, having too many independent variables can also be a crippling specification error and yield uninterpretable findings (Achen 2005a).

A related practical problem is the fact that many of the independent variables that interest social scientists are highly correlated with each other and thus can have only modest nonoverlapping effects on a given outcome. Again, *The Bell Curve* controversy is a case in point. Test scores and socioeconomic status of family of origin are strongly correlated, as are these two variables with a variety of other potentially relevant causal conditions (years of schooling, neighborhood and school characteristics, and so on, as Fischer et al. 1996 demonstrate). Because social inequalities overlap, cases' scores on independent variables tend to bunch together: high AFQT scores tend to go with better family backgrounds, better schools, better neighborhoods, and so on. Of course, these correlations are far from perfect; thus, it is possible to squeeze estimates of the net effects of these independent variables out of the data. Still, the overwhelming empirical pattern is one of confounded causes, of clusters of favorable versus unfavorable conditions, not of analytically separable independent variables. One thing social scientists know about social inequalities is that because they overlap, they reinforce. It is their overlapping nature that gives them their strength and durability. Given this characteristic feature of social phenomena, it seems somewhat counterintuitive for quantitative social scientists to rely almost exclusively on techniques that champion the estimation of the separate, unique net effect of each causal variable.

More generally, while it is useful to examine correlations between independent variables (e.g., the strength of the correlation between AFQT scores and family background) and to adjust the estimation of net effects accordingly, it is also useful to study cases holistically, as specific configurations of attributes. In this view, cases combine different causally relevant characteristics in different ways, and it is important to assess the consequences of these different combinations. Consider, for example, what it takes to avoid poverty. Does college education make a difference for married white males from families with good incomes? Probably not, or at least not much of a difference. But college education may make a huge difference for unmarried black females from low-income families. By examining cases as configurations, it is possible to conduct context-specific assessments, which are circumstantially delimited. Assessments of this type involve questions about the conditions that enable or disable specific connections between causes and outcomes (e.g., Amenta and Poulsen 1996). Under what conditions do test scores matter when it comes to avoiding poverty? Under what conditions does marriage matter? Are these connections different for white females and black males? These kinds of questions are outside the scope of conventional net-effects analyses, for those approaches are centered on the task of estimating context-independent net effects.

Such configurational assessments are directly relevant to policy debates in the larger society. Policy discourse often focuses on categories and kinds of people (or cases), not on variables and their net effects across heterogeneous populations. Consider, for example, phrases like "truly disadvantaged," "working poor," and "welfare mothers." Generally, such categories embrace combinations of characteristics. Consider also the fact that social policy is fundamentally concerned with social intervention. While it might be good to know that education, in general, decreases the odds of poverty (i.e., it has a significant, negative net effect on poverty), from a policy perspective it is far more useful to know under what conditions education has a decisive impact, shielding an otherwise vulnerable subpopulation from poverty. Typically, net effects are calculated across samples drawn from entire populations. They are not based on "structured, focused comparisons" (George 1979, 54–55) using specific kinds and categories of cases.

Finally, while the calculation of net-effects offers succinct assessments of the relative explanatory power of variables drawn from different theories, the adjudication between competing theories is not a central concern of social policy. Which theory prevails in the competition to explain variation in outcomes such as poverty is primarily an academic question. The issue that is important to the larger society, especially when the goal is intervention, is determining which causal conditions are decisive in which contexts, regardless of the (typically vague) theory from which the conditions are drawn.

To summarize, the net-effects approach, while powerful and rigorous, is limited. It is restrained by its own rigor, for its strength is also its weakness. It is particularly disadvantaged when used to study combinations of case characteristics, especially overlapping inequalities. Given these drawbacks, it is reasonable to explore an alternate approach, one with strengths that differ from those of net-effects methods. Specifically, the net-effects approach, with its heavy emphasis on calculating the uncontaminated effect of each independent variable in order to isolate its independent impact, can be counterbalanced and complemented with an approach that explicitly considers combinations and configurations of case aspects.

Shifting the Focus to Kinds of Cases

Underlying the broad expanse of social scientific methodology is a continuum that extends from small-N, case-oriented, qualitative techniques to large-N, variable-oriented, quantitative techniques. Generally, social scientists deplore the wide gulf that separates the two ends of this continuum, but they typically stick to only one end when they conduct research. With QCA, however, it is possible to bring some of the spirit and logic of case-oriented investigation to large-N research.

This technique offers researchers tools for studying cases as configurations and for exploring the connections between *combinations* of causally relevant conditions and outcomes. By studying combinations of conditions, it is possible to unravel the conditions and contexts that enable or disable specific connections (e.g., between education and the avoidance of poverty).

The starting point of QCA is the principle that cases should be viewed in terms of the combinations of causally relevant conditions they display. To represent combinations of conditions, researchers use truth tables, which list the logically possible combinations of causal conditions specified by the researcher, sort cases according to the combinations they display, and list an outcome value (typically coded either true or false) for each combination of causal conditions. A simple, hypothetical truth table with four crisp-set (i.e., dichotomous) causal conditions, one outcome, and 200 cases is presented in table 10.1. The four causal conditions are as follows:

1. Did the respondent earn a college degree?
2. Was the respondent raised in a household with at least a middle-class income?
3. Did at least one of the respondent's parents earn a college degree?
4. Did the respondent receive a high score on the AFQT?

With four causal conditions, there are sixteen logically possible combinations of conditions, the same as the number of rows in the table. The goal of QCA is to derive a logically simplified statement describing the different combinations of conditions linked to an outcome. In short, QCA summarizes the truth table in a logically shorthand manner.

The hypothetical data presented in table 10.1 display a characteristic feature of nonexperimental data: the 200 cases are unevenly distributed across the sixteen rows, and some combinations of conditions (i.e., rows) lack cases altogether. (The number of individuals with each combination of causal conditions is reported in the last column.) In the net-effects approach, this unevenness is understood as the result of correlated independent variables. Generally, the

Table 10.1: Hypothetical truth table with four causal conditions and one outcome

	College educated (C)	High parental income (I)	Parent college educated (P)	High AFQT score (S)	Poverty avoidance (A)	Number of cases
1	0	0	0	0	0	30
2	0	0	0	1	?	3
3	0	0	1	0	?	4
4	0	0	1	1	?	0
5	0	1	0	0	0	25
6	0	1	0	1	0	19
7	0	1	1	0	?	0
8	0	1	1	1	0	20
9	1	0	0	0	?	0
10	1	0	0	1	?	1
11	1	0	1	0	?	0
12	1	0	1	1	?	2
13	1	1	0	0	1	19
14	1	1	0	1	1	22
15	1	1	1	0	1	32
16	1	1	1	1	1	23

greater the correlations among the causal variables, the greater the unevenness of the distribution of cases across the different combinations of causal conditions. By contrast, in QCA, this unevenness is understood as "limited diversity." In this view, the four causal conditions define sixteen different kinds of cases, and the four dichotomies become, in effect, a single nominal-scale variable with sixteen possible categories. Because there are empirical instances of only a subset of the sixteen logically possible kinds of cases, the data set is understood as limited in its diversity (see chapters 8 and 9). Note also that the rows that embrace only a small number of cases do not have outcome codes assigned to them (see "poverty avoidance" column in table 10.1). When the empirical evidence is weak, no judgments about row outcomes can be made. (In the parlance of QCA, these rows are "remainders.")

In QCA, outcomes are coded using set-theoretic criteria. The key question for each row is the degree to which the individuals in the row constitute a subset of the individuals who are not in poverty. That is, to what degree do the cases in a given row agree in not displaying poverty? Of course, perfect subset relations are rare with individual-level data. Surprising cases are always present, for example, the person with every possible advantage who nevertheless manages to fall into poverty. With QCA, researchers establish rules for determining the degree to which the cases in each row are consistent with the subset relation. The researcher first establishes a threshold proportion for set-theoretic "consistency" (see chapters 3 and 7), which the observed proportions must exceed. For example, a researcher might argue that the observed proportion of cases in a row that are not in poverty must exceed a benchmark proportion of 0.90. Additionally, the researcher may also apply conventional probabilistic criteria to these assessments. For example, the researcher might state that the observed proportion of individuals not-in poverty must be significantly greater than a benchmark proportion of 0.80, using a significance level (alpha) of 0.05. The specific benchmarks and alphas used by researchers depend upon the state of existing substantive and theoretical knowledge.

The assessment of each row's set-theoretic consistency is straightforward when truth tables are constructed from crisp sets. When fuzzy sets are used, the set-theoretic principles that are invoked are the same, but the procedures are more complex (see chapters 3 and 7). The next-to-last column of table 10.1 ("poverty avoidance") shows the coding of the outcome of each row, based on the evaluation of consistency scores.

Comparing Configurations

The key difference between QCA and the net-effects approach is that the latter focuses on analytically separable independent variables and their degree of intercorrelation, whereas the former focuses on kinds of cases defined with respect to the combinations of causally relevant conditions they display. In short, the net-effects approach builds generalizations by examining the correlations between variables. QCA builds generalizations by comparing case configurations in a bottom-up fashion and constructing more inclusive specifications of the conditions under which a statement is "true." These contrasting views of the same evidence, correlational versus configurational, have very different implications for how the analysis proceeds. Notice, for example, that table 10.1 shows a perfect correlation between having a college degree and avoiding poverty. That is, whenever there is a 1 (yes) in the outcome column ("poverty avoidance"), there is also a 1 (yes) in the "college educated" column, and whenever there is a 0 (no) in the "poverty avoidance" column, there is also a 0 (no) in the "college educated" column. From a net-effects perspective, this pattern constitutes very strong evidence that the key to avoiding poverty is college education. Once the effect of college education is taken into account (using the hypothetical data in table 10.1), no variation in poverty avoidance remains for the other variables to explain.

This conclusion does not come so easily using QCA, however, for there are several combinations of conditions (i.e., kinds of cases) in the truth table where college education is present and the outcome (poverty avoidance) is unknown, due to an insufficiency of cases. For example, the ninth row combines presence of college education with absence of the other three resources. However, there are no cases with this combination of conditions and consequently no way to assess empirically whether this combination of conditions is linked to poverty avoidance. As explained in chapters 8 and 9, in conventional net-effects analyses, such remainder combinations are routinely incorporated into solutions; however, their incorporation is invisible to most researchers using that approach. In the conventional approach, remainders, in effect, are covertly incorporated into solutions via the assumption of additivity—the idea that the net effect of a variable is the same regardless of the values of the other independent variables. Thus, the issue of limited diversity and the need for counterfactual analysis are both veiled in the analytical effort to isolate the effect of each independent variable on the outcome.

From the viewpoint of QCA, it is noteworthy that the four rows coded 1 (yes) for poverty avoidance all include the presence of both college education and high parental income. Based on arguments presented in chapters 8 and 9, it would be unwise to accept the parsimonious conclusion that college education alone accounts for poverty avoidance, even though a perfect correspondence exists between college education and poverty avoidance in table 10.1. Using QCA, it is difficult to ignore the fact that two conditions—college education and high parental income—are always combined when poverty avoidance is the outcome. These two conditions would surely reinforce each other in their impact on poverty avoidance.

Fuzzy Sets and Configurational Analysis

Because of the mathematical continuities underlying crisp and fuzzy sets, table 10.1 could have been constructed from fuzzy-set data (see chapter 7). To do so, it would have been necessary to calibrate the degree of membership of each case in each of the sets defined by the causal conditions (e.g., degree of membership in the set of individuals with high AFQT scores) and then assess the degree of membership of each case in each of the sixteen combinations of causal conditions defining the rows of table 10.1. After calibrating degree of membership in the outcome (i.e., in the set of individuals successfully avoiding poverty), it would be possible to evaluate the degree to which membership in each combination of causal conditions is a fuzzy subset of membership in the outcome. In effect, these analyses assess the degree to which the individuals represented in each row consistently avoid poverty. Such assessments are conducted using fuzzy membership scores, not dichotomized scores, and they utilize a stricter and more demanding definition of the subset relation than is used in crisp-set analyses.

As shown in chapter 7, a truth table can be used to summarize the results of these fuzzy-set assessments. In this example, there would be sixteen fuzzy-set assessments because there are four fuzzy-set causal conditions and thus sixteen configuration membership scores. More generally, the number of fuzzy-set assessments is 2^k, where k is the number of causal conditions. The rows of the resulting truth table list the different combinations of conditions assessed. For example, row 4 of the truth table would summarize the results of the fuzzy-set analysis of degree of membership in the set of individuals who combine low membership in college educated, low membership in at least middle-class parental income, high membership in parents college educated, and high membership in high AFQT score.

Note that with fuzzy sets, the problem of limited diversity is transformed from one of "empty cells" in a k-way cross-tabulation of dichotomized causal conditions (i.e., remainder rows in a truth table), to one of vacant (or mostly vacant) sectors in a vector space with k fuzzy-set dimensions. The 2^k sectors of this space vary in the degree to which they are populated with cases, with some sectors lacking cases altogether. In other words, with naturally occurring social data, it is common for many sectors of the vector space defined by causal conditions to be void of cases, just as it is common for a k-way cross-tabulation of dichotomies to yield an abundance of empty cells. The same tools developed to address limited diversity in crisp-set analyses described in chapters 8 and 9 can be used to address limited diversity in fuzzy-set analyses, using the truth table that summarizes the results of the fuzzy-set analyses as an intermediary device.

The outcome column in a fuzzy-set truth table shows the results of the 2^k fuzzy-set assessments—that is, whether or not degree of membership in the configuration of causal conditions specified in a row can be considered a fuzzy subset of degree of membership in the outcome. The examination of the resulting truth table is, in effect, an analysis of *statements* summarizing the 2^k fuzzy-set analyses. The end product of the truth table analysis, in turn, is a logical synthesis of these statements. This synthesis specifies the different combinations of causal conditions linked to the outcome via the fuzzy subset relationship.

Looking Ahead

Chapter 11 offers a complete demonstration of the use of fuzzy sets in social research, using a large-N data set—the *Bell Curve* (Herrnstein and Murray 1994) data. It contrasts two analyses of the same data, a conventional net-effects analysis using logistic regression and a fuzzy-set analysis using the truth table approach just described. The contrast between these two analyses shows that the fuzzy-set approach offers what is bypassed in a net-effects analysis, namely, close attention to cases as configurations and to the different combinations of conditions that are linked to an outcome.

11: Net Effects versus Configurations:
An Empirical Demonstration
coauthored with Peer Fiss

This chapter presents a critique of net-effects thinking in a practical manner by contrasting a conventional net-effects analysis of a large-N, policy-relevant data set (the National Longitudinal Survey of Youth, or NLSY, also known as the *Bell Curve* data, from Herrnstein and Murray's 1994 publication *The Bell Curve*) with an alternate analysis of the same data, following the principles developed in this book. While the two approaches differ in several important respects, the key difference is that the net-effects approach focuses on the independent effects of causal variables on the outcome, while the configurational approach attends to combinations of causal conditions and attempts to establish explicit links between specific combinations of conditions and the outcome. This alternate method, known as fuzzy-set qualitative comparative analysis (fsQCA), combines the use of fuzzy sets with the analysis of cases as configurations, a central feature of case-oriented social research (Ragin 1987). In this approach, each case is examined in terms of its degree of membership in different *combinations* of causally relevant conditions. Using fsQCA, researchers can consider cases' varying degree of membership in all of the logically possible combinations of a given set of causal conditions and then use set-theoretic methods to analyze—in a logically disciplined manner—the varied connections between causal combinations and the outcome.

I offer this alternate approach not as a replacement for net-effects analysis but as a complementary technique. Fuzzy-set qualitative comparative analysis is best understood as an exploratory/interpretive technique, grounded in set theory. While probabilistic criteria can be incorporated into fsQCA, it is not an inferential technique, per se. It is an alternate way of analyzing evidence, starting from very different assumptions regarding the kinds of "findings" that social scientists seek. These alternate assumptions reflect the logic and spirit of qualitative research, where investigators study cases as configurations, with an eye toward how the different parts or aspects of cases fit together.

A Net-Effects Analysis of the Bell Curve Data

In *The Bell Curve*, Herrnstein and Murray (1994) compute rudimentary logistic regression analyses to gauge the importance of Armed Forces Qualification Test (AFQT) scores on a variety of outcomes. They control for the effects of only two competing variables in most of their main analyses, respondent's age (at the time the AFQT was administered) and parental socioeconomic status (SES). Their central finding is that AFQT score (which they interpret as a measure of general intelligence) is more important than parental SES when considering major life outcomes such as avoiding poverty. They interpret this and related findings as proof that, in modern society, "intelligence" (which they assert is inborn) has become the most important factor shaping life chances. Their explanation focuses on the fact that the nature of work has changed and that today a much higher labor market premium is attached to high cognitive ability.

Herrnstein and Murray's main findings with presence/absence of poverty as the outcome of interest are presented in table 11.1 (with absence of poverty = 1). The reported analysis uses standardized data (z scores) for both parental SES and AFQT score to facilitate comparison of effects. The analysis shown in table 11.1 is limited to black males with complete data on all the variables used in this analysis and in the subsequent analyses reported in this chapter, including the fuzzy-set analysis. The strong positive impact of AFQT scores, despite the statistical control for the effect of parental SES, mirrors the *Bell Curve* results.

A major rebuttal of the *Bell Curve* "thesis," as it became known, was presented by a team of University of California at Berkeley sociologists, Claude Fischer, Michael Hout, Martin Sanchez Jankowsk,

Table 11.1: Logistic regression of poverty avoidance on AFQT scores, parental SES, and age (Bell Curve model; black males only)

	B	S.E.	Sig.	Exp(B)
AFQT (z score)	0.651	0.139	0.000	1.917
Parental SES (z score)	0.376	0.117	0.001	1.457
Age	0.040	0.050	0.630	1.040
Constant	1.123	0.859	0.191	3.074

Note: Chi-squared = 53.973, df = 3. B = regression coefficient, S.E. = standard error of regression coefficient, Sig. = statistical significance.

Samuel Lucas, Ann Swidler, and Kim Voss (1996). In their book, *Inequality By Design,* they present a much more elaborate logistic regression analysis of the NLSY data. Step by step, they include more and more causal conditions (e.g., neighborhood and school characteristics) that they argue should be seen as competitors with AFQT scores. In their view, AFQT score has a substantial effect in the *Bell Curve* analysis only because the logistic regression analyses that Herrnstein and Murray report are radically underspecified. To remedy this problem, Fischer et al. include more than fifteen control variables in their analysis of the effects of AFQT scores on the odds of avoiding poverty. While this "everything but the kitchen sink" approach dramatically reduces the impact of AFQT scores on poverty, the authors leave themselves open to the charge that they have misspecified their analyses by being overinclusive.

Table 11.2 reports the results of a logistic regression analysis of poverty using only a moderate number of independent variables. Specifically, presence/absence of poverty (with absence = 1) is regressed on five independent variables: AFQT score, years of education, parental income, married versus not married, and one or more children versus no children. The three interval-scale variables are standardized (using z scores) to simplify the comparison of effects. Like the previous analysis, the table shows the results for black males only. The rationale for this specification, using five independent variables, is that the model is more fully specified than the radically spare model presented by Herrnstein and Murray and less elaborate and cumbersome than Fischer et al.'s kitchen-sink model. In other words, this logistic regression analysis attempts to strike a balance between the two specification extremes, while focusing on several of the most important causal conditions. The results presented in table 11.2 are consistent with both Herrnstein and Murray and Fischer et al. in that they show that AFQT score has an independent impact on poverty avoidance, but not nearly as strong as that reported by Herrnstein and Murray. Consistent with Fischer et al., table 11.2 shows very strong effects of competing causal conditions, especially years of education and marital status. These conditions were not included in the *Bell Curve* analysis.

More generally, table 11.2 confirms the specification dependence of net-effects analysis. For example, if years of education is "accepted" as a competing cause (and not considered derivative of AFQT scores), then it is clearly more important than test scores. Likewise, the impact of marriage on the odds of staying out of poverty is substantial for black males. According to table 11.2, married black males are more than five times more likely to avoid poverty that unmarried black males. Even though these results, like all net-effects analyses, are specification dependent, the fact that a very modest number of competing independent variables greatly reduces the estimate of the effect of AFQT scores on poverty casts substantial doubt on the *Bell Curve* thesis.

Table 11.2: Logistic regression of poverty avoidance on AFQT scores, parental income, years of education, marital status, and children (black male sample)

	B	S.E.	Sig.	Exp(B)
AFQT (z score)	0.391	0.154	0.011	1.479
Parental income (z score)	0.357	0.154	0.020	1.429
Education (z score)	0.635	0.139	0.000	1.887
Married (yes = 1, 0 = no)	1.658	0.346	0.000	5.251
Children (yes = 1, 0 = no)	−0.524	0.282	0.063	0.592
Constant	1.970	0.880	0.025	7.173

Note: Chi-squared = 104.729, df = 5. B = regression coefficient, S.E. = standard error of regression coefficient, Sig. = statistical significance.

A Reanalysis of the *Bell Curve* Data Using fsQCA

The success of any fuzzy-set analysis depends on the careful construction and calibration of the fuzzy sets. The core of both crisp-set and fuzzy-set analysis is the evaluation of set-theoretic relationships, for example, the assessment of whether membership in a combination of causal conditions can be considered a consistent subset of membership in a given outcome. A fuzzy subset relationship exists when the scores in one set (e.g., the fuzzy set of individuals who combine high parental income, college education, high test scores, and so on) are consistently less than or equal to the scores in another set (e.g., the fuzzy set of individuals not in poverty). Thus, it matters a great deal how fuzzy sets are constructed and how membership scores are calibrated. Serious miscalibrations can distort or undermine the identification of set-theoretic relationships. By contrast, for the conventional variable to be useful in a net-effects analysis, it needs only to vary in a meaningful way (see chapter 4). Often, the specific metric of a conventional variable is ignored altogether by researchers because it is arbitrary or meaningless. Even when a variable has a meaningful metric, researchers often focus only on the direction and significance of its effect.

In order to calibrate fuzzy-set membership scores, researchers must use their substantive knowledge (see chapter 5). The resulting membership scores must have face validity in relationship to the set in question, especially how it is conceptualized and labeled. A fuzzy score of 0.25, for example, has a very specific meaning—that a case is halfway between "full exclusion" from a set (e.g., a membership score of 0.0 in the set of individuals with high parental income) and the crossover point (0.5, the point of maximum ambiguity in whether a case is more in or more out of this set). As explained in *Fuzzy-Set Social Science* (Ragin 2000) and chapters 4 and 5 of this book, the most important decisions in the calibration of a fuzzy set involve the definition of the three qualitative anchors that structure a fuzzy set: full inclusion in the set, the crossover point (membership = 0.5), and full exclusion from the set. The main sets used in the analysis reported in this chapter are degree of membership in the outcome—the set of individuals avoiding poverty—and degree of membership in sets reflecting five background characteristics: parental income, AFQT scores, education, marital status, and children. The calibration of these fuzzy sets is detailed in the practical appendix at the end of this chapter.

At this point it is important to note that representing a single interval-scale variable with two fuzzy sets is often fruitful. For example, the variable parental income can be transformed separately into the set of individuals with high parental income and the set of individuals with low parental income. It is necessary to construct *two* fuzzy sets because of the *asymmetry* of the two target concepts. Full *non*membership in the set of individuals with high parental income (a membership score of 0.0 in high parental income) does *not* imply full *membership* in the set with low parental income (a score of 1.0), for it is possible to be fully out of the set of individuals with high parental income without being fully in the set of individuals with low parental income. The same is true for the other two interval-scale variables used as causal conditions in the logistic regression analysis (table 11.2), AFQT scores and years of education. This dual coding of key causal conditions has important theoretical benefit. For example, is it having a *high* AFQT score that is linked to superior life chances, or is it *not* having a *low* AFQT score that matters? This issue is especially important because Herrnstein and Murray (1994) argue that having a high AFQT score (which they interpret as having high cognitive ability) is the key to success in modern society.

Note also that the language and logic of "variables" does not translate directly into set theory. A case cannot have membership in a variable, for example, a high degree of membership in AFQT or a high degree of membership in parents' income. Instead a case has membership in a set, for example, strong membership in the set of people with high AFQT scores or strong membership in the set of people with high parental income. The translation of variables to sets requires careful definition and labeling of the target sets, which in turn provides the primary basis for calibrating membership. Thus, when translating such variables as parental income to fuzzy sets, it is useful to consider the different target sets that can be created from a single source variable, especially in light of the theoretical and substantive issues that inspire and guide the research.

Altogether, the fuzzy-set analysis reported in this chapter uses eight causal conditions. Two are crisp sets: married versus not married and one or more children versus no children. The remaining six are fuzzy sets: degree of membership in the set of cases with high parental income, degree of membership in the set of cases with low parental income, degree of membership in the set of cases with high AFQT scores, degree of membership in the set of cases with low AFQT scores, degree of membership in the set of cases with college education, and degree of membership in the set of cases with high school education.

After calibrating the fuzzy sets, the next task is to calculate the degree of membership of each case in each of the 2^k logically possible combinations of eight causal conditions, and then to assess the distribution of cases across these combinations. With eight causal conditions, there are 256 logically possible combinations of conditions.[1] Table 11.3 lists the 42 of these 256 combinations that have at least four cases with greater than 0.5 membership.[2] Recall that a case can have, at most, only one configuration membership score that is greater than 0.5. Thus, the 256 combinations of conditions can be evaluated with respect to case frequency by examining the number of empirical instances of each combination. If a configuration has no cases with greater than 0.5 membership, then there are no cases that are more in than out of the set defined by the combination of conditions (and no cases in the corresponding sector of the multidimensional vector space defined by the causal conditions).

Table 11.3 reveals that the data used in this analysis (and, by implication, in the logistic regression analyses reported in tables 11.1

---

1. Of course, many of these 256 combinations are not empirically possible. For example, a case cannot have high membership in both high income parents and low income parents. The number of empirically possible combinations is 108. This number still dwarfs the number of high-frequency combinations (see table 11.3).

2. An additional nineteen rows (not shown in table 11.3) have one, two, or three cases each. The remaining rows have no cases with greater than 0.5 membership.

and 11.2) are remarkably limited in their diversity. Altogether, only 42 of the 256 sectors contained within the eight-dimensional vector space have at least four empirical instances (i.e., at least four cases with greater then 0.5 membership in the corner), and most of the frequencies reported in the table are quite small. The two most populated sectors capture 25 percent of the cases; the seven most populated capture half of the cases; and the fourteen most populated capture nearly 70 percent of the cases. The number of well-populated sectors (fourteen) is small even relative to the number of sectors that exist in a five-dimensional vector space ($2^5 = 32$). This is the number of sectors that would have been obtained if the three interval-level variables (years of education, parental income, and AFQT scores) used in the logistic regression analysis had been transformed into one fuzzy set each instead of two.

In fuzzy-set analyses of this type (large N), it is important to establish a strength-of-evidence threshold for combinations of conditions, using the information on the distribution of strong instances across sectors. Specifically, causal combinations with only a few strong instances (i.e., a few cases with greater than 0.5 membership in the combination) should be filtered out and not subject to further empirical analysis. In addition to the fact that it would be unwise to base a conclusion about a combination of individual-level attributes on a small number of instances, the existence of cases in low-frequency sectors may be due to measurement or assignment error. The fuzzy-set analysis that follows uses a frequency threshold of at least ten strong instances. This value was selected because it captures more than 80 percent of the cases assigned to combinations. Using this rule, the twenty-three most common combinations of conditions are retained in this analysis. The low-frequency rows (including those shown in the bottom part of table 11.3 with frequencies ranging from four to nine) are filtered out of the analysis. Because these rows do not meet the strength-of-evidence threshold, they are treated as "remainder" combinations in the analysis that follows.

The next task is to assess the consistency of the evidence for each of the combinations of conditions (the twenty-three high-frequency

Table 11.3: Distribution of cases across vector space corners (the 42 combinations with at least 4 cases each)

Married	Children	High parental income	Low parental income	High AFQT score	Low AFQT score	High school educated	College educated	Count	Cumulative proportion
0	0	0	1	0	1	1	0	118	0.152
0	0	0	0	0	1	1	0	78	0.253
0	0	0	0	0	0	1	0	53	0.321
1	1	0	0	0	1	1	0	41	0.375
1	1	0	0	0	0	1	0	39	0.425
1	1	0	1	0	1	1	0	34	0.469
0	0	0	1	0	0	1	1	30	0.508
0	0	0	0	0	0	1	0	23	0.537
0	1	1	0	0	1	1	0	22	0.566
0	0	0	1	0	1	1	0	20	0.592
0	1	1	0	0	1	1	0	20	0.618
0	0	0	1	0	0	1	0	19	0.642
1	1	0	1	0	1	0	0	19	0.667
0	0	0	1	0	0	1	1	18	0.690
0	0	1	0	0	0	1	1	12	0.705
0	0	0	0	0	1	1	0	12	0.721
0	0	0	0	0	0	0	1	11	0.735
1	1	1	0	0	0	1	0	11	0.749
1	1	1	0	0	0	1	0	11	0.764
1	1	1	0	0	1	1	0	11	0.778

								Row count	Consistency
1	1	1	0	1	0	0	0	10	0.791
0	1	1	0	1	0	0	1	10	0.804
1	1	0	0	0	0	1	1	10	0.817
0	1	0	0	1	0	0	1	9	0.828
1	1	0	0	0	1	0	1	9	0.840
1	1	0	0	0	1	1	1	9	0.851
0	1	0	0	0	0	0	1	7	0.860
0	1	1	0	0	0	0	1	7	0.870
1	0	1	0	0	0	0	0	6	0.877
0	1	1	0	1	0	1	0	6	0.885
0	1	0	0	0	1	0	1	6	0.893
0	0	1	0	0	1	0	1	6	0.901
0	1	1	1	0	0	1	1	6	0.908
1	1	0	0	0	1	0	0	5	0.915
1	0	0	0	1	0	1	1	5	0.921
0	1	0	0	0	0	0	0	4	0.926
1	1	1	0	0	1	0	0	4	0.932
1	1	0	0	0	0	1	0	4	0.937
0	1	0	0	1	0	1	0	4	0.942
1	1	0	0	0	0	0	1	4	0.947
1	1	1	0	0	0	1	1	4	0.952
0	0	1	0	1	0	1	1	4	0.957
All remaining combinations of conditions; row counts < 4									1.000

rows from table 11.3) with the subset relation. Specifically, it is necessary to determine whether degree of membership in each combination of conditions is a subset of degree of membership in the outcome. As explained in chapter 1, the subset relation is used to assess causal sufficiency. With fuzzy sets, the subset relation is demonstrated by showing that degree of membership in a combination of conditions (which can range from 0.0 to 1.0) is consistently less than or equal to degree of membership in the outcome. These assessments use all cases in each assessment, including cases with less than 0.5 membership in a given combination. Such cases may be inconsistent, and their inconsistency counts against the set-theoretic relation in question. For example, a case with a membership of 0.40 in a causal combination and a membership of 0.20 in the outcome would lower the consistency score for that combination, even though this case is more out than in both the combination and the outcome.

As shown in chapter 3, a simple descriptive measure of the degree to which the evidence regarding a combination of conditions is consistent with the subset relation with respect to the outcome is:

$$\Sigma[\min(\mathbf{X}_i, \mathbf{Y}_i)]/\Sigma(\mathbf{X}_i)$$

where min indicates selection of the lower of the two scores, $\mathbf{X}_i$ indicates degree of membership in a combination of conditions, and $\mathbf{Y}_i$ indicates degree of membership in the outcome. When all $\mathbf{X}_i$ values are consistent (i.e., their membership scores in the combination are uniformly less than or equal to their corresponding $\mathbf{Y}_i$ values), the calculation yields a score of 1.0. If many of the $\mathbf{X}_i$ values exceed their $\mathbf{Y}_i$ values by a substantial margin, however, the resulting score is substantially less than 1.0. Generally, scores on this measure that are lower than 0.75 indicate substantial departure from the set-theoretic relation $\mathbf{X}_i \leq \mathbf{Y}_i$.

Table 11.4 reports the results of the set-theoretic consistency assessments for the twenty-three combinations in table 11.3 that meet the strength-of-evidence threshold (a frequency of at least ten cases that are more in than out of each combination). The consistency scores for the combinations range from 0.340 to 0.986, indicating a substantial spread in the degree to which the subset relation is satisfied. In the truth table analysis that follows, the seven combinations with consistency scores of at least 0.80 are treated as subsets of the outcome; the remaining sixteen fail to satisfy this criterion. Once this distinction is made, table 11.4 can be analyzed as a truth table (see chapter 7). The binary outcome, which is based on the fuzzy set–theoretic consistency scores in the adjacent column, is listed in the last column of table 11.4.

Using fsQCA (Ragin, Drass, and Davey 2007), it is possible to derive two truth table solutions, one maximizing parsimony and the other maximizing complexity (see chapter 9). The most parsimonious solution permits the incorporation of *any* counterfactual combination that contributes to the derivation of a logically simpler solution. This solution of the truth table yields three relatively simple combinations linked to poverty avoidance:

$$married \cdot \sim children +$$
$$high\_income \cdot \sim low\_AFQT +$$
$$college \cdot \sim low\_AFQT$$

where (here and in subsequent fsQCA results) college is the fuzzy set for college educated, high_school is the fuzzy set for high school educated, low_income is the fuzzy set for low parental income, high_income is the fuzzy set for high parental income, low_AFQT is the fuzzy set for low AFQT score, high_AFQT is the fuzzy set for high AFQT score, children is the crisp set for at least one child, married is the crisp set for married, ~ indicates negation or "not," · signals combined conditions (set intersection), and + signals alternate combinations of conditions (set union). The parsimonious solution reveals that the three combinations of conditions linked to poverty avoidance are (1) being married combined with not having children, (2) having high income parents combined with not having a low AFQT score, and (3) having a college degree combined with not having a low AFQT score.

While parsimonious, this solution incorporates many counterfactual combinations (i.e., remainders), and many of these, in turn, are "difficult" from the perspective of existing theoretical and substantive knowledge (see chapters 8 and 9). For example, the combination of not being high school educated but being married and not having children is included in the first combination listed above. Too few empirical instances of this combination are present to allow its assessment, but

Table 11.4: Assessments of set-theoretic consistency (for the 23 configurations passing frequency threshold of at least 10 cases)

Married	Children	High parental income	Low parental income	High AFQT score	Low AFQT score	High school	College	Count	Consistency	Outcome
0	0	1	0	0	0	1	1	12	0.986	1
1	1	0	0	0	0	1	1	10	0.893	1
0	0	0	1	0	0	1	1	12	0.892	1
1	1	1	0	0	0	1	0	11	0.884	1
1	0	0	1	0	1	1	0	10	0.876	1
0	0	0	0	0	0	1	1	23	0.864	1
0	0	1	0	0	0	1	0	19	0.830	1
1	1	1	0	0	1	1	0	11	0.792	0
0	0	0	1	0	0	1	0	53	0.788	0
0	0	0	0	0	1	1	1	10	0.767	0
1	1	0	0	0	0	1	0	39	0.754	0
1	1	0	1	0	1	1	0	41	0.706	0
1	1	0	0	0	1	1	0	34	0.657	0
1	1	1	1	0	0	1	0	19	0.641	0
0	0	0	0	0	1	1	0	78	0.636	0
0	0	0	1	0	1	1	0	20	0.620	0
0	1	0	0	0	0	1	0	30	0.617	0
0	0	0	0	0	0	0	0	11	0.578	0
0	0	0	0	0	1	1	0	11	0.498	0
0	1	0	1	0	1	1	0	118	0.482	0
0	0	0	0	0	1	1	0	22	0.402	0
0	1	0	1	0	1	1	0	20	0.376	0
0	0	0	1	0	1	0	0	18	0.340	0

the parsimonious solution assumes that individuals with this combination are able to avoid poverty, despite their failure to complete high school. With 256 logically possible combinations of conditions, many combinations are without cases or with very few cases, as table 11.3 indicates. The parsimonious solution just presented incorporates many such combinations, without regard for their empirical plausibility—that is, without regard for existing substantive knowledge.

If, instead, the researcher evaluates the plausibility of the counterfactual combinations, a less parsimonious ("intermediate") solution can be derived.[3] This intermediate solution is obtained by first deriving the most complex solution (not shown here) and then using only "easy" counterfactuals to produce an intermediate solution, as explained in chapter 9.[4] The intermediate solution is a subset of the most parsimonious solution and a superset of the most complex solution.

The intermediate solution indicates that five combinations of conditions are linked to poverty avoidance:

$$married \cdot \sim children \cdot high\_school +$$
$$married \cdot high\_income \cdot \sim low\_AFQT \cdot high\_school +$$
$$\sim children \cdot high\_income \cdot \sim low\_AFQT \cdot high\_school +$$
$$\sim children \cdot \sim low\_AFQT \cdot college +$$
$$married \cdot \sim low\_income \cdot \sim low\_AFQT \cdot college$$

These five combinations linked to poverty avoidance are similar in that they all include education (college or high_school) and some aspect of household composition (married or ~children or both). Four include not having low AFQT scores (~low_AFQT) as an ingredient, and four include conditions related to parental income (either high

---

3. The software package fsQCA will produce all three solutions (complex, parsimonious, and intermediate) when the Standard Analysis button is clicked at the bottom of the truth table spreadsheet. The user is then prompted for the input that is the basis for the derivation of the intermediate solution.

4. The substantive knowledge that is incorporated into the production of the intermediate solution in the present analysis is quite simple. For example, it is assumed that having a high school education (as opposed to not having completed high school) is linked to staying out of poverty, that having parents who are not low income is linked to staying out of poverty, that being married is linked to staying out of poverty, and so on.

parental income or not-low parental income). These results are important because they confirm that the causal conditions linked to poverty avoidance are combinatorial in nature and that it is possible to discern the relevant combinations when cases are viewed as configurations.

Recall from chapter 9 that the terms included in the parsimonious solution *must* be included in *any* representation of the results, for these are the decisive causal ingredients that distinguish combinations of conditions that are consistent subsets of the outcome from those that are not (that is, among the combinations that pass the frequency threshold). Thus, these ingredients should be considered the "core" causal conditions. The ingredients that are added in the intermediate solution are those that are also present in the cases that consistently display the outcome but that require difficult counterfactuals to remove. Thus, these conditions are "complementary" or "contributing" conditions in the sense that they make sense as important contributing factors and can be removed from the solution only if the researcher is willing to make assumptions that are at odds with existing substantive and theoretical knowledge. This researcher might have to assume, for example, that a high school dropout with a given set of characteristics (e.g., married without children) would be able to avoid poverty. Table 11.5 summarizes the five solutions in a way that differentiates core versus complementary causal conditions. This table also reports the consistency, raw coverage, and unique coverage calculations for each of the five recipes. (These calculations are explained in chapter 3.)

The results also can be summarized with the aid of a table that sorts the different recipes for poverty avoidance according to the respondent's family status. Table 11.6 shows that different recipes are clearly evident for black males in different family status categories. Those who are married and without children have the easiest time avoiding poverty. All that is required is a high school education. At the other extreme, there are no recipes for poverty avoidance for black males who are unmarried with children. For black males who are unmarried and without children, the recipe is to combine not-low AFQT scores with either college education or high school education combined with

Table 11.5: Configurations for avoiding poverty for black males

	Solution				
	1	2	3	4	5
Family Status					
Married	●	•			•
Children	⊖		⊖	⊖	
Education					
High school	•	•	•		
College				●	●
Test Scores					
High AFQT					
Low AFQT		⊖	⊖	⊖	⊖
Parental Income					
High income		●	●		
Low income					⊖
Consistency	0.92	0.94	0.91	0.92	0.95
Raw coverage	0.13	0.10	0.14	0.16	0.11
Unique coverage	0.07	0.02	0.04	0.06	0.03

Note: ● = core causal condition (present); ⊖ = core causal condition (absent); • = contributing causal condition (present); ⊖ = contributing causal condition (absent).

Table 11.6: Results of fuzzy-set analysis sorted according to family status

Family status	Recipe for poverty avoidance
Married, no children	high_school
Unmarried, no children	~low_AFQT·(college + high_school·high_income)
Married, children	~low_AFQT·(college·~low_income + high_school·high_income)
Unmarried, children	{∅}

high-income parents. For black males who are married with children, the recipe is similar, but slightly more complex: they combine not-low AFQT scores with either college education and not-low-income parents or high school education and high-income parents. In short, the table shows that domestic situation has a very powerful impact on the resources that are required for avoiding poverty.

In addition to revealing the combinatorial complexities of staying out of poverty for black males, the results also challenge the interpretation of AFQT scores offered by Herrnstein and Murray (1994). Recall that the core of their argument is that the nature of work has changed and that the labor market now places a premium on high cognitive ability. The image they conjure is one of a society that has many positions for the cognitively gifted but fewer slots for those who are more modest in their cognitive endowments. The results presented here are unequivocal: what really matters when it comes to avoiding poverty is to *not* have *low* test scores. In other words, following Herrnstein and Murray's argument, one would expect high cognitive skills to be a common ingredient in these solutions; instead, it is clear that the cognitive bar is much lower. The key is to *not* have low cognitive ability, which indicates in turn that modest cognitive ability remains adequate in today's world. Of course, this interpretation assumes that one accept the questionable claim that AFQT scores indicate cognitive ability. According to many of the critics of the *Bell Curve* thesis, AFQT scores indicate the acquisition of cultural capital. In this light, the findings reported here indicate that one ingredient in the effort to avoid poverty is the possession of at least modest cultural capital.

Discussion

The results presented here are preliminary findings drawn from a larger fuzzy-set analysis of the *Bell Curve* data. The primary goal of this illustrative research is to provide a contrast between a net-effects analysis and a configurational analysis of the same data.

The contrast between the two approaches is clear. The findings of the net-effects analysis are expressed in terms of separate variables.

They provide the final tally in the competition to explain variation in the outcome, avoiding poverty. Education and marital status win this competition, but AFQT is not eliminated, for it retains a modest net effect, despite stiff competition (compare table 11.1 and table 11.2). The logistic regression results are silent on the issue of causal combinations; the analysis of causal combinations would require the examination of complex interaction models. Examining a saturated interaction model, for example, would require the estimation of thirty-two coefficients in a single equation. Even if such a model could be estimated (extreme collinearity makes this task infeasible), the model would be virtually impossible to interpret, once estimated.

Note also that the assumptions of additivity and linearity in the logistic regression analysis allow the estimation of outcome probabilities for all thirty-two sectors of the vector space defined by the five independent variables, regardless of whether these sectors are populated with cases. Thus, the net-effects approach addresses the problem of limited diversity in an indirect and covert manner by assuming that the effect of a given variable is the same regardless of the values of the other variables and that a linear relationship can be extrapolated beyond an observed range of values. To derive the estimated probability of avoiding poverty for any point in the vector space defined by the independent variables, it is necessary simply to insert the coordinates of that point into the equation and calculate the predicted value. The issue of limited diversity is thus sidestepped altogether.

By contrast, this issue must be confronted head-on in a configurational analysis. Naturally occurring data are profoundly limited in their diversity, as illustrated in table 11.3. This fact is apparent whenever researchers examine the distribution of cases across logically possible combinations of conditions, especially when the number of conditions is more than a few. As the analysis reported here illustrates, the problem of limited diversity is *not* remedied by having a large number of cases.

When cases are viewed configurationally, it is possible to identify the different combinations of conditions linked to an outcome. The results of the configurational analyses reported in this chapter show that there are several recipes for staying out of poverty for black males in the United States. The recipes all include educational qualifications of some sort (high school or college) and a favorable household composition (either marriage or being childless or both). Not having low AFQT scores is also a condition in four of the five causal recipes, as is having either high or not-low parental income, in these same four recipes. Herrnstein and Murray (1994) dramatize the implications of their research by claiming that if one could choose at birth between having a high AFQT score and having a high parental SES (or high parental income), the better choice would be to select having a high AFQT score. The fuzzy-set results underscore the fact that the choice is really about combinations of conditions—about recipes—not about individual variables. In short, choosing to not have a low AFQT score, by itself, does not offer protection from poverty. The configurational analysis presented in this chapter shows clearly that it is combined with other resources when it is linked to staying out of poverty.

Practical Appendix: Calibrations Used in the Fuzzy-Set Analysis

As previously noted, the calibration of fuzzy sets is central to fuzzy-set analysis. Miscalibrations distort the results of set-theoretic assessments. The main principles guiding calibration are that (1) the target set must be carefully defined and labeled and (2) the fuzzy set scores must reflect external standards based on both substantive knowledge and the existing research literature. While some might consider the influence of calibration decisions "undue" and portray this aspect of fuzzy-set analysis as a liability, in fact it is a strength. Because calibration is important, researchers must pay careful attention to the definition and construction of their fuzzy sets, and they are forced to concede that substantive knowledge is, in essence, a prerequisite for analysis. The fuzzy sets in the analysis presented in this chapter are degree of membership in the outcome, the set of individuals avoiding poverty, and degree of membership in sets reflecting various background characteristics and conditions. These are discussed in more detail below.

Avoiding poverty. To construct the fuzzy set of individuals avoiding poverty, this analysis uses the official poverty threshold adjusted for household size as provided by the NLSY, the same measure used by both Herrnstein and Murray (1994) and Fischer et al. (1996). In their analyses, both Herrnstein and Murray and Fischer et al. use the poverty status variable as a binary dependent variable in logistic regression analyses. However, their dichotomous measure places families with incomes just barely above the poverty level in the same category as those families with incomes far above the poverty threshold, such as comfortably upper-middle-class families. The fuzzy set procedure avoids this problem and is based on the ratio of household income to the poverty level for that household. Using the direct method for calibrating fuzzy sets (described in chapter 5), the threshold for full membership in the set of households not in poverty (fuzzy score = 0.95) is a ratio of 3.0 (household income is three times the poverty level for that household), the crossover point (fuzzy score = 0.5) is a ratio of 2.0 (household income is double the poverty level), and the threshold for full exclusion from the set of households not in poverty (fuzzy score = 0.05) is a ratio of 1.0 (household income is the same as the poverty level).

High school and college education. To measure educational attainment, the NLSY uses "Highest Grade Completed" (Center for Human Resource Research 1999, 138). This variable translates years of education directly into degrees (i.e., completing twelve years of education indicates a high school degree, while completing sixteen years completed indicates a college degree). Respondents with twelve or more years of school are fully in the set with a high school education (a fuzzy score of 1.0). On the other hand, those with only a primary school education (i.e., six years of school or less) are treated as fully out of the set of respondents with a high school education (a fuzzy score of 0.0). The fuzzy set thus embraces the six years of secondary school: 11 years = 0.75; 10 years = 0.60; 9 years = 0.45; 8 years = 0.30; and 7 years = 0.15. The fuzzy set of college-educated respondents was constructed by defining respondents with sixteen or more years of education as having full membership in the set with a college education (1.0), while those with twelve years of education or less were coded as fully out of the set (0.0). The in-between years were coded as follows: 13 years = 0.20; 14 years = 0.40; and 15 years = 0.60.

Parental income. The measure of parental income is based on the average of the reported 1978 and 1979 total net family income in 1990 dollars. It is the same measure used by Fischer et al. (1996) and was generously provided by Richard Arum. These data were used to create two fuzzy sets: the set of respondents with low parental income and the set of respondents with high parental income.

The fuzzy set of respondents with low parental income is similar in construction to the fuzzy set of households in poverty. First, the ratio of parents' household income to the poverty level was calculated using NLSY data on the official poverty threshold in 1979, adjusted for household size. Using the direct method of calibration described in chapter 5, it was determined that the threshold for full membership in the set with low parental income (0.95) is a ratio of 1.0 (parents' income is the same as the poverty level). Respondents with ratios less than 1.0 received fuzzy scores greater than 0.95. Conversely, the threshold for full exclusion (0.05) from the set with low parental income is a ratio of 3.0 (parents' household income was three times the poverty level). Respondents with ratios greater than 3.0 received fuzzy scores less than 0.05. The crossover point was determined to be two times the household-adjusted poverty level.

Multiples of the poverty ratio (household income divided by poverty level adjusted for household composition) were also used to construct the fuzzy set of respondents with high parental income. The threshold for exclusion from the set with high-income parents (0.05) is a ratio of three times the adjusted poverty level. The crossover point (0.50) was set at 5.5 times the adjusted poverty level, and the threshold for full membership was set at eight times the adjusted poverty level. The threshold for full membership corresponds roughly to three times the median family income, while the crossover point corresponds to roughly two times the median family income. Again, the direct method of fuzzy set calibration was used to calibrate degree of membership in this set.

Test scores. The AFQT scores used by Herrnstein and Murray (1994) are based on the *Armed Services Vocational Aptitude Battery,* which was introduced by the U.S. Department of Defense in 1976 to determine eligibility for enlistment. To construct the fuzzy-set measures of those with high AFQT scores and low AFQT scores, the analysis relies on categories used by the Department of Defense to place enlistees. Thus, the calibration of these fuzzy sets is grounded in practical decisions made by the military.

The military divides the AFQT scale into five categories based on percentiles. These five categories have substantive importance in that they determine eligibility for and assignment into different qualification groups. Persons in categories I (93rd to 99th percentile) and II (65th to 92nd percentile) are considered to be above average in trainability; those in category III (31st to 64th percentile) are about average; those in category IV (10th to 30th percentile) are designated as below average in trainability; and those in category V (1st to 9th percentile) are markedly below average. To determine eligibility for enlistment, the Department of Defense uses both aptitude and education as criteria. Regarding aptitude, the current legislated minimum standard is the 10th percentile, meaning that those who score in category V (1st to 9th percentile) are not eligible for military service. Furthermore, those scoring in category IV (10th to 30th percentile) are not eligible for enlistment unless they also have at least a high school education. Legislation further requires that no more than 20 percent of the enlistees be drawn from category IV, which further indicates that respondents in this category are substantially different from those in categories I to III.[5]

To construct the fuzzy set of respondents with low AFQT scores, respondents' AFQT percentile scores are used. The threshold for full membership (0.95) in the set of respondents with low AFQT scores was placed at the 10th percentile, in line with its usage by the military; respondents who scored lower than the 10th percentile received fuzzy

---

5. Of course, these standards are allowed to erode as the demand for military recruits increases.

membership scores greater than 0.95. The crossover point (0.5) was set at the 20th percentile, and the threshold for nonmembership was set at the 30th percentile, again reflecting the practical application of AFQT scores by the military. Respondents who scored better than the 30th percentile received fuzzy scores less than 0.05 in the set of respondents with low AFQT score.

The threshold for full membership (0.95) in the set of respondents with high AFQT scores was placed at the 93rd percentile, in line with the military's designation of the lower boundary of the highest category; the crossover point (0.5) was set at the 80th percentile; and the threshold for full nonmembership (0.05) in the set of respondents with high AFQT scores was placed at the 65th percentile, the bottom of the military's second highest AFQT category.

Household composition. Household composition has two main components: whether or not the respondent is married and whether or not there are children present in the household. All four combinations of married/not married and children/no children are present with substantial frequency in the NLSY data set. Respondents' marital status is coded as a crisp set, with a value of one assigned to those who were married in 1990. In general, married individuals are much less likely to be in poverty. While Fischer et al. (1996) use the actual number of respondents' children in 1990, having children is coded here as a crisp set. The rationale is that being a parent imposes certain status and lifestyle constraints. As any parent will readily attest, the change from having no children to becoming a parent is much more momentous, from a lifestyle and standard of living point of view, than having a second or third child. In general, households with children are more likely to be in poverty than households without children. The most favorable household composition, with respect to staying out of poverty, is the married/no children combination. The least favorable is the not-married/children combination.

REFERENCES

Achen, Christopher. 2005a. "Let's Put Garbage-Can Regressions and Garbage-Can Probits Where They Belong." *Conflict Management and Peace Science* 22: 327–39.

———. 2005b. "Two Cheers for Charles Ragin.." *Studies in Comparative International Development* 40: 27–32.

Allison, Paul D. 1977. "Testing for Interaction in Multiple Regression." *American Journal of Sociology* 82: 144–53.

Amenta, Edwin, and Jane Duss Poulsen. 1996. "Social Politics in Context: The Institutional Politics Theory and Social Spending at the End of the New Deal." *Social Forces* 75: 33–60.

Becker, Howard S. 1958. "Problems of Inference and Proof in Participant Observation." *American Sociological Review* 23: 652–60.

Berg-Schlosser, Dirk. 2002. "Macro-Quantitative vs. Macro-Qualitative Methods in the Social Sciences—Testing Empirical Theories of Democracy." COMPASSS Working Paper 2002-2. www.COMPASSS.org/wp.htm.

Bollen, Kenneth. 1989. *Structural Equations with Latent Variables.* New York: Wiley Interscience.

Boswell, Terry, and Cliff Brown. 1999. "The Scope of General Theory. Methods for Linking Deductive and Inductive Comparative History." *Sociological Methods and Research* 28: 154–85.

Brady, Henry E. 2003. "Models of Causal Inference: Going beyond the Neyman-Rubin-Holland Theory." Paper presented at the Annual Meeting of Midwest Political Science Association, Chicago, April 4.

Brady, Henry, and David Collier, eds. 2004. *Rethinking Social Inquiry: Diverse Tools, Shared Standards.* Lanham, MD: Rowman and Littlefield.

Braumoeller, Bear. 2003. "Causal Complexity and the Study of Politics." *Political Analysis* 11: 208–33.

Braumoeller, Bear, and Gary Goertz. 2000. "The Methodology of Necessary Conditions." *American Journal of Political Science* 44: 844–58.

Brueggemann, John, and Terry Boswell. 1998. "Realizing Solidarity: Sources of Interracial Unionism during the Great Depression." *Work and Occupations* 25: 436–82.

Byrne, David. 2002. *Interpreting Quantitative Data*. London: Sage.

Center for Human Resource Research. 1999. *NLSY79 User's Guide*. Columbus, OH: The Ohio State University.

Cicourel, Aaron V. 1964. *Method and Measurement in Sociology*. New York: Free Press.

Clément, Caty. 2004. "Un modèle commun d'effondrement de l'Etat? Une AQQC du Liban, de la Somalie et de l'ex-Yougoslavie." *Revue Internationale De Politique Comparée (RIPC)* 11: 35–50.

Cronqvist, Lasse. 2004. "Presentation of TOSMANA: Adding Multi-Value Variables and Visual Aids to QCA." COMPASSS Working Paper 2004-16. www.COMPASSS.org/wp.htm.

De Meur, Gisèle, and Benoît Rihoux. 2002. *L'Analyse Quali-Quantitative Comparée: Approche, Techniques et applications en sciences humaines*. Louvain-la-Neuve: Bruylant-Academia.

Dion, Douglas. 1998. "Evidence and Inference in the Comparative Case Study." *Comparative Politics* 30: 127–45.

Duncan, Otis Dudley. 1984. *Notes on Social Measurement*. New York: Russell Sage Foundation.

Eckstein, Harry. 1975. "Case Study and Theory in Political Science." In *Handbook of Political Science, Vol. 7: Strategies of Inquiry*, ed. F. I. Greenstein and N. W. Polsby. Reading, MA: Addison-Wesley.

Elster, Jon. 1978. *Logic & Society: Contradictions and Possible Worlds*. New York: John Wiley & Sons.

Fearon, James D. 1991. "Counterfactuals and Hypothesis Testing in Political Science." *World Politics* 43: 169–95.

———. 1996. "Causes and Counterfactuals in Social Science: Exploring an Analogy between Cellular Automata and Historical Processes." In *Counterfactual Thought Experiments in World Politics*, ed. P. E. Tetlock and A. Belkin. Princeton, NJ: Princeton University Press.

Fischer, Claude S., Michael Hout, Martin Sanchez Jankowsk, Samuel Lucas, Ann Swidler, and Kim Voss. 1996. *Inequality By Design: Cracking the Bell Curve Myth*. Princeton, NJ: Princeton University Press.

George, Alexander. 1979. "Case Studies and Theory Development: The Method of Structured, Focussed Comparison." In *Diplomacy: New Approaches in History, Theory and Policy*, ed. Paul G. Lauren. New York: Free Press.

George, Alexander, and Andrew Bennett. 2005. *Case Studies and Theory Development*. Cambridge, MA: MIT Press.

Glaser, Barney, and Anslem Strauss. 1967. *The Discovery of Grounded Theory: Strategies for Qualitative Research.* New York: Weidenfeld and Nicholson.

Goertz, Gary. 2002. "The Substantive Importance of Necessary Condition Hypotheses." In *Necessary Conditions: Theory, Methodology, and Applications,* ed. Gary Goertz and Harvey Starr. New York: Rowman and Littlefield.

———. 2003. "Assessing the Importance of Necessary or Sufficient Conditions in Fuzzy-Set Social Science." COMPASSS working paper WP2003-7. www.COMPASSS.org/wp.htm.

———. 2006. *Social Science Concepts: A User's Guide.* Princeton, NJ: Princeton University Press.

Goertz, Gary, and Harvey Starr, eds. 2002. *Necessary Conditions: Theory, Methodology, and Applications.* New York: Rowman and Littlefield.

Hawthorn, Geoffrey. 1991. *Plausible Worlds: Possibility and Understanding in History and the Social Sciences.* New York: Cambridge University Press.

Herrnstein, Richard, and Charles Murray. 1994. *The Bell Curve: Intelligence and Class Structure in American Life.* New York: Free Press.

Hicks, Alexander, Joya Misra, and Tang Nah Ng. 1995. "The Programmatic Emergence of the Social Security State." *American Sociological Review* 60: 329–49.

Holland, Paul W. 1986. "Statistics and Causal Inference." *Journal of the American Statistical Association* 81: 945–60.

Katz, Jack 1982. *Poor People's Lawyers in Transition.* New Brunswick, NJ: Rutgers University Press.

King, Gary, Robert O. Keohane, and Sidney Verba. 1994. *Designing Social Inquiry: Scientific Inference in Qualitative Research.* Princeton, NJ: Princeton University Press.

King, Robert L., and Arch G. Woodside. 2000. "Qualitative Comparative Analysis of Travel and Tourism Purchase-Consumption Systems." *Tourism Analysis* 5: 105–11.

Kitchener, Martin, Malcolm Beynon, and Charlene Harrington. 2002. "Qualitative Comparative Analysis and Public Services Research: Lessons from an Early Application." *Public Management Review* 4: 485–504.

Kittel, Bernhard, Herbert Obinger, and Uwe Wagschal. 2000. "Wohlfahrtsstaaten im internationalen Vergleich. Politisch-institutionelle Faktoren der Entstehung und Entwicklungsdynamik." In *Der "gezügelte" Wohlfahrtsstaat: Sozialpolitik in Australien, Japan, Schweiz, Kanada Neuseeland and den Vereinigten Staaten,* ed. Herbert Obinger and Uwe Wagschal. Frankfurt: Campus Verlag.

Kosko, Bart. 1993. *Fuzzy Thinking: The New Science of Fuzzy Logic*. New York: Hyperion.

Laitin, David. 1992. *Language Repertoires and State Construction in Africa*. New York: Cambridge University Press.

Lakoff, George. 1973. "Hedges: A Study in Meaning Criteria and the Logic of Fuzzy Concepts." *Journal of Philosophical Logic* 2: 458–508.

Lieberson, Stanley. 1985. *Making It Count: The Improvement of Social Research and Theory*. Berkeley: University of California Press.

———. 1992. "Small N's and Big Conclusions: An Examination of the Reasoning in Comparative Studies Based on a Small Number of Cases." In *What Is a Case?* ed. Charles Ragin and Howard Becker, 105–18. New York: Cambridge University Press.

———. 1998. "Causal Analysis and Comparative Research: What Can We Learn from Studies Based on a Small Number of Cases?" In *Rational Choice Theory and Large-Scale Data Analysis*, ed. Hans Peter Blossfeld and Gerald Prein. Boulder, CO: Westview.

Lindesmith, Alfred. 1947. *Opiate Addiction*. Bloomington, IN: Principia Press.

Mackie, John L. 1965. "Causes and Conditionals." *American Philosophical Quarterly* 2: 245–65.

Mahoney, James, and Gary Goertz. 2004. "The Possibility Principle: Choosing Negative Cases in Comparative Research." *American Political Science Review* 98: 653–69.

Merton, Robert K. 1973. *The Sociology of Science: Theoretical and Empirical Investigations*. Chicago: University of Chicago Press.

Mill, John Stuart. 1967 [1843]. *A System of Logic: Ratiocinative and Inductive*. Toronto: University of Toronto Press.

Moore, Barrington, Jr. 1966. *The Social Origins of Dictatorship and Democracy: Lord and Peasant in the Making of the Modern World*. Boston: Beacon.

Nieuwbeerta, Paul. 1995. *The Democratic Class Struggle in Twenty Countries, 1945–1990*. Amsterdam: Thesis Publishers.

Nieuwbeerta, Paul, and Nan Dirk de Graaf. 1999. "Traditional Class Voting in Twenty Postwar Societies." In *The End of Class Politics? Class Voting in Comparative Context*, ed. Geoffrey Evans. Oxford: Oxford University Press.

Nieuwbeerta, Paul, and Wout Ultee. 1999. "Class Voting in Western Industrialized Countries, 1945–1990: Systematizing and Testing Explanations." *European Journal of Political Research* 35: 123–60.

Nieuwbeerta, Paul, Nan Dirk de Graaf, and Wout Ultee. 2000. "Effects of Class Mobility on Class Voting in Post-War Western Industrialized Countries." *European Sociological Review* 16: 327–48.

Nunnally, Jum, and Ira Bernstein. 1994. *Psychometric Theory*. New York: McGraw Hill.

Pawson, Ray. 1989. *A Measure for Measures: A Manifesto for Empirical Sociology*. New York: Routledge.

Ragin, Charles C. 1987. *The Comparative Method: Moving beyond Qualitative and Quantitative Strategies*. Berkeley: University of California Press.

———. 1994. *Constructing Social Research: The Unity and Diversity of Method*. Thousand Oaks, CA: Pine Forge.

———. 1997. "Turning the Tables: How Case-Oriented Methods Challenge Variable-Oriented Methods." *Comparative Social Research* 16: 27–42.

———. 2000. *Fuzzy-Set Social Science*. Chicago: University of Chicago Press.

———. 2003a. "Making Comparative Analysis Count." COMPASSS working paper WP2003-10. www.COMPASSS.org/wp.htm.

———. 2003b. "Recent Advances in Fuzzy-Set Methods and Their Application to Policy Questions." COMPASSS working paper WP2003-9. www.COMPASSS.org/wp.htm.

———. 2004a. "From Fuzzy Sets to Crisp Truth Tables." COMPASSS working paper WP2004-28. www.COMPASSS.org/wp.htm.

———. 2004b. "La spécificité de la recherche configurationnelle." *Revue Internationale de Politique Comparée (RIPC)* 11: 138–44.

———. 2006a. "The Limitations of Net Effects Thinking." In *Innovative Comparative Methods for Policy Analysis: Beyond the Quantitative-Qualitative Divide*, ed. Benoît Rihoux and Heike Grimm. New York: Springer.

———. 2006b. "Set Relations in Social Research: Evaluating Their Consistency and Coverage." *Political Analysis* 14 (3): 291–310.

———. 2007. *User's Guide to Fuzzy-Set/Qualitative Comparative Analysis, Version 2.0*. www.fsqca.com.

Ragin, Charles C., Kriss A. Drass, and Sean Davey. 2007. *Fuzzy-Set/Qualitative Comparative Analysis 2.0*. www.fsqca.com.

Ragin, Charles C., and Benoît Rihoux. 2004. "Qualitative Comparative Analysis: State of the Art and Prospects." *Qualitative Methods* 2: 3–13.

Ragin, Charles C., and John Sonnett. 2004. "Between Complexity and Parsimony: Limited Diversity, Counterfactual Cases and Comparative Analysis." In *Vergleichen in der Politikwissenschaft*, ed. Sabine Kropp and Michael Minkenberg. Wiesbaden: VS Verlag fur Sozialwissenschaften.

Rihoux, Benoît, and Charles Ragin, eds. 2008. *Configurational Comparative Methods. Qualitative Comparative Analysis (QCA) and Related Techniques*. Thousand Oaks, CA: Sage.

Rokkan, Stein. 1975. "Dimensions of State Formation and Nation Building: A Possible Paradigm for Research on Variations Within Europe." In *The*

Formation of Nation States in Western Europe, ed. Charles Tilly. Princeton, NJ: Princeton University Press.

Skocpol, Theda. 1979. *States and Social Revolutions—A Comparative Analysis of France, Russia, and China.* Cambridge, U.K.: Cambridge University Press.

Smithson, Michael. 1987. *Fuzzy Set Analysis for the Behavioral and Social Sciences.* New York: Springer-Verlag.

Smithson, Michael, and Jay Verkuilen. 2006. *Fuzzy Set Theory.* Thousand Oaks, CA: Sage.

Sobel, Michael E. 1995. "Causal Inference in the Social and Behavioral Sciences." In *Handbook of Statistical Modeling for the Social and Behavioral Sciences,* ed. Gerhard Arminger, Clifford C. Clogg, and Michael E. Sobel. New York: Plenum Press.

Sonnett, John. 2004. "Musical Boundaries: Intersections of Form and Content." *Poetics* 32: 247–64.

Stokke, Olav Schram. 2004. "Boolean Analysis, Mechanisms, and the Study of Regime Effectiveness." In *Regime Consequences: Methodological Challenges and Research Strategies,* ed. Arild Underdal and Oran R. Young. Dordrecht: Kluwer Academic.

Tetlock, Philip E., and Aaron Belkin, eds. 1996a. *Counterfactual Thought Experiments in World Politics: Logical, Methodological, and Psychological Perspectives.* Princeton, NJ: Princeton University Press.

———. 1996b. "Counterfactual Thought Experiments in World Politics: Logical, Methodological, and Psychological Perspectives." In *Counterfactual Thought Experiments in World Politics: Logical, Methodological, and Psychological Perspectives,* ed. Philip E. Tetlock and Aaron Belkin. Princeton, NJ: Princeton University Press.

Underdal, Arild, and Oran R. Young, editors. 2004. *Regime Consequences: Methodological Challenges and Research Strategies.* Dordrecht: Kluwer Academic.

Vanderborght, Yannick, and Sakura Yamasaki. 2004. "Des cas logiques contradictoires? Un piège de l'AQQC résolu à travers l'étude de la faisabilité politique de l'Allocation Universelle." *Revue Internationale de Politique Comparée* 11: 51–66.

Vaughan, Diane. 1986. *Uncoupling: Turning Points in Intimate Relationships.* New York: Oxford University Press.

Walker, Henry, and Bernard Cohen. 1985. "Scope Statements: Imperatives for Evaluating Theory." *American Sociological Review* 50: 288–301.

Weber, Max. 1949 [1905]. "Objective Possibility and Adequate Causation in Historical Explanation." In *The Methodology of the Social Sciences,* ed. Edward A. Shils and Henry A. Finch. Glencoe, NY: Free Press.

Winship, Christopher, and Stephen L. Morgan. 1999. "The Estimation of Causal Effects from Observational Data." *Annual Review of Sociology* 25: 659–706.

Winship, Christopher, and Michael Sobel. 2004. "Causal Inference in Sociological Studies." In *Handbook of Data Analysis,* ed. Melissa Hardy and Alan Bryman. London: Sage.

Zadeh, Lotfi. 1965. "Fuzzy Sets." *Information and Control* 8: 338–53.

———. 1972. "A Fuzzy-Set-Theoretic Interpretation of Linguistic Hedges." *Journal of Cybernetics* 2 (3): 4–34.

———. 2002. "From Computing with Numbers to Computing with Words." *Applied Mathematics and Computer Science* 12 (3): 307–32.

INDEX

Achen, C., 172, 180
Allison, P., 113
Armed Forces Qualifying Test, 179–81, 187–88, 191–93, 195–99, 201–8, 211–12
Arum, R., 210

Becker, H., 78
Belkin, A., 151, 162
Bell Curve data, 10, 63–64, 179, 188–90, 206
Bennett, A., 54
Berg-Schlosser, D., 7n3
Bernstein, I., 75, 76
Bollen, K., 76
Boolean algebra, 36, 126, 154–55, 161
Boswell, T., 112
Brady, H., 1, 73, 152
Braumoeller, B., 45, 60, 153n3, 158
Brown, C., 112

calibration, 30, 64, 71–74, 77–78, 83–97, 99–100, 102–5, 133, 142, 194–95, 208–12; advantages over uncalibrated measures, 71–72, 75n3; and context, 72–74; direct method, 84–85, 87–94, 96–97, 99–100, 209–10; direct versus indirect method, 97; in economics, 72n1; indirect method, 84–85, 94–97; in the natural sciences, 72; in the physical sciences, 72–73; in qualitative research, 79;

and set-theoretic principles, 84, 97, 103; and substantive knowledge, 32, 47, 74, 78, 82–84, 86, 91, 93–94, 103, 194, 208; and variation, 33, 74, 83; versus measurement, 6, 8, 77–78
case-oriented research, 5, 17, 23, 38n4, 80–82, 86, 109–10, 112, 128, 149–50, 158, 161, 166–67, 169, 171–73, 181, 182, 190; and calibration, 80; and counterfactual analysis, 161
causal combinations, 9, 20, 23–25, 39–41, 44, 54, 63, 65, 109, 112, 121, 124–25, 149–50, 153–55, 158, 172, 183, 186–88, 190, 207–8; and case knowledge, 121; consistency of, 46–54, 134–35, 185; contradictory, 139; distribution of cases across, 128, 130–33; as empirical possibilities, 196n1; inconsistency, 50, 137; and macrovariables, 142; and membership, 39–41, 49–50, 64–65, 114–15, 128–33, 196, 200; as subset of an outcome, 41, 111, 117, 129–30, 135, 188, 200; and vector space, 129, 135. *See also* configurational thinking
causal complexity, 6, 9, 23–25, 54, 84, 124–27, 177–78
causal conditions: absence, 125–26, 131; number of, 24, 124–25, 128, 187–88; and the truth table approach, 23–25, 125. *See also* causal combinations

necessary conditions, 20, 44–45, 47, 53, 98, 111, 154, 171n3, 200; and consistency, 53, 58–59; and coverage, 45, 59–62; and plots, 47, 53, 59–60, 123; trivial versus nontrivial, 60

net effects, 1, 6, 9, 22, 112–14, 157, 176–82, 186, 207; additivity, 9–10, 178, 186, 207; defined, 113, 178; and model specification, 179–80, 192–93; and theory, 177–78

Ng, T., 150

Nieuwbeerta, P., 34, 127

Nunnally, J., 75, 76

outcome: and asymmetry, 138; consistency of, 25, 128, 134–35, 197–200; crisp sets, 38; negation, 137–38, 138n6; selecting on, 4, 111, 149; subset of, 41, 115, 117, 129–30, 134–35, 187–88, 200–1

parsimony, 120, 148–50, 161, 163–67, 172, 187

Pawson, R., 72, 74

poverty, 55–57, 64, 72n1, 174, 175, 179–87, 191–94, 201–12

protest, 110–20, 124–26

Qualitative Comparative Analysis (QCA), 23, 71, 151, 155–58, 163–64, 167, 171n3, 172–73, 182–87

quantitative and qualitative research: bridging, 1, 4–6, 71, 82, 103, 182; practical differences, 4–5, 80–81

remainders, 131, 133, 135n4, 155, 158, 163, 165, 186; and consistency, 135n4; as "don't care," 139–40, 156; as "false," 136, 139, 155, 173; simplifying assumptions, 136–37, 139–40, 156, 159, 168, 171–73

Rihoux, B., 17, 23n4, 24, 25, 111, 141

Rokkan, S., 79

scope conditions, 73, 178

set coincidence, 59n3

set-theoretic relationships, 2–3, 6–9, 13–14; asymmetry of, 3, 7, 15–17, 42, 102, 110; and calibration, 208; contrast with quantitative methods, 4–9, 15–16, 20–23, 40, 53, 65, 74, 101–3, 138; and explicit connections, 17–20; and fuzzy sets, 29, 194–95, 208; and membership, 200; similarities with quantitative methods, 45, 59n3, 63, 65; and social theory, 2–3, 38, 45, 53–54, 83, 103–4, 138, 149. See also consistency

Skocpol, T., 18

small-N research, 4, 167, 172, 182

Smithson, M., 46, 47, 52, 59n3, 71, 82, 134

Sobel, M., 152

social context, 55, 58–59, 73–74, 81, 109, 126, 181

social inequalities: as overlapping, 180, 182

social policy, 72n1, 103, 181–82; and theory, 182

social science: role of theory and knowledge, 10, 163, 173; and theory, 177, 179

solutions: complex, 164–66, 171–75; intermediate, 144, 164–67, 169, 171–75, 203–4; parsimonious, 136, 140, 156, 164–68, 171–75, 201, 203–4; as subset relations, 165–66, 170–72

Sonnett, J., 137n5, 147, 158

Starr, H., 20, 45

Stokke, O., 167, 171n3

Strauss, A., 78

strength-of-evidence threshold, 197, 200

structural equation modeling, 76

sufficient conditions, 20, 25, 53–54, 58–59, 98, 125, 171n3, 200; and

consistency, 48–49, 53, 63; and coverage, 63; and plots, 41, 47, 49
Swidler, A., 192

Tetlock, P., 151, 162
truth table, 24–25, 124–30, 183; analysis, 135–38; construction of, 25–28, 125, 128, 130, 138, 142; and crisp sets, 26, 125, 129, 185; degree of membership, 129–30; distribution of cases, 128, 130–31, 133, 183; and explicit connections, 24–25, 125; and fuzzy sets, 23n4, 126–30, 142–44, 185; and generalization, 126; and remainders, 131, 135n4, 158, 163, 184; simplification, 25, 125; and vector space, 128–30

Ultee, W., 127

variable-oriented research, 4–9, 22, 65, 80–81, 86, 176, 178
variation, 102; at ends of distribution, 78; explained, 9, 65, 74, 113, 148, 178–79, 186; observed, 75–77, 194; relevance of, 33, 74, 77–79, 83–84
Vaughan, D., 17
vector space, 128–31, 135, 143, 188; and macrovariables, 142–43
Verba, S., 1, 4, 5, 6, 111
Verkuilen, J., 46, 47, 52, 59, 82, 134
Voss, K., 192

Walker, H., 73
Weber, M., 151
welfare states, 50, 148–49, 152–57
Winship, C., 152, 152n2, 153, 158

Zadeh, L., 3, 29, 98